PETER KROPOT

Fields, Factories and Workshops Tomorrow

Edited, introduced and with additional material by
COLIN WARD

FREEDOM PRESS
London
1985

First published 1974

This edition, with additional
material published by

FREEDOM PRESS
in Angel Alley
84b Whitechapel High Street
London E1 7AX

1985

© Colin Ward & Freedom Press 1974, 1985

PUBLISHER'S NOTE

Our thanks to George Allen & Unwin Ltd, publishers of the
1974 edition, for permission to use their typography; to our
comrade Colin Ward for agreeing to a Freedom Press reprint
and for writing a new Introduction; last but not least to Hans
Deichmann for his practical support that has made this cheap
(by today's standards) edition possible.

Cover by Rufus Segar

Printed in Gt Britain by Aldgate Press, London E1

Contents

Publishing History

First edition, xii+35pp. (London, Hutchinson; Boston, Houghton, Mifflin & Co., 1899). Second impression, ix+259pp. (London, Swan Sonnenschein; New York, Putnam's, 1901). Third impression (London, Swann Sonnenschein; New York, Putnam's, 1901). Fourth impression (London, Swan Sonnenschein; New York, Putnam's, 1904). Fifth impression (London, Swann Sonnenschein; New York, Putnam's, 1907). Sixth impression (London, Swann Sonnenschein; New York, Putnam's, 1909).

New, revised and enlarged edition, 477pp. (London, Nelson; New York, Putnam's, 1913). Reprinted (1919).

Reproduction of first edition (New York, Greenwood Press, 1968).

Reproduction of second edition (New York, Benjamin Blom, 1968).

Fields, Factories and Workshops is one of those great prophetic works of the nineteenth century whose hour is yet to come. It began life as a series of articles published in 1888–90. These were collected as a book in 1899, when the reviewer of *The Times* noted that the author 'has the genuine scientific temper, and nobody can say that he does not extend his observations widely enough, for he seems to have been everywhere and to have read everything'. Reprinted several times in cheap editions during the next decade, it appeared again in a revised and enlarged edition just before the First World War. When that edition was reprinted at the end of the war, the publishers remarked: 'It pleads for a new economy in the energies used in supplying the needs of human life, since these needs are increasing and the energies are not inexhaustible.'[1]

These words echo our contemporary preoccupations, as Kropotkin's book has done for generations of perceptive readers. Bertrand Russell observed nearly sixty years ago: 'Socialists and anarchists in the main are products of industrial life, and few among them have any practical knowledge on the subject of food production. *The Conquest of Bread* and *Fields, Factories and Workshops* are very full of detailed information, and, even making great allowances for an optimistic bias, I do not think it can be denied that they demonstrate possibilities in which few of us would otherwise have believed.'[2] When Herbert Read compiled his volume of selections from Kropotkin's books in 1941, he found that this book's 'deductions and proposals remain as valid as on the day when they were written',[3] and when Paul Goodman, in 1948, celebrated the book's fiftieth anniversary, he noted:

'The ways that Kropotkin suggested, how men can at once begin to live better, are still the ways; the evils he attacked are mostly still the evils; the popular misconceptions of the relations of machinery and social planning. Recently studying the modern facts and the modern authors, I wrote a little book (*Communitas*) on a related subject; there is not one important proposition in my book that is not in *Fields, Factories and Workshops*, often in the same words.'[4]

But perhaps the most persuasive advocacy of this book comes from Lewis Mumford, who, in *The City in History*, wrote of it and its author:

'Almost half a century in advance of contemporary economic and technical opinion, he had grasped the fact that the flexibility and adaptability of electric communication and electric power, along with the possibilities of intensive biodynamic farming, had laid the foundations for a more decentralised urban development in small units, responsive to direct human contact, and enjoying both urban and rural advantages. . . .

'Kropotkin realised that the new means of rapid transit and communication, coupled with the transmission of electric power in a network, rather than a one-dimensional line, made the small community on a par in essential technical facilities with the over-congested city. By the same token, rural occupations once isolated and below the economic and cultural level of the city could have the advantage of scientific intelligence, group organisation, and animated activities, originally a big city monopoly; and with this the hard and fast division between urban and rural, between industrial worker and farm worker, would break down too. Kropotkin understood these implications before the invention of the motor car, the radio, the motion picture, the television system and the world-wide telephone – though each of these inventions further confirmed his penetrating diagnosis by equalising advantages between the central metropolis and the once peripheral and utterly dependent small communities. With the small unit as a base, he saw the opportunity for a more responsible and responsive local life, with greater scope for the human agents who were neglected and frustrated by mass organisations.'[5]

The reader may very well wonder why such an important book – a work which influenced not only Tolstoy, Gandhi and Mao Tse-tung, but also the author of the wartime Penguin guide, *Your Small-holding* – has been out of print in Britain for half a century, and why, in this edition, it has been cut to about half of its original length. The answer is that Kropotkin's conclusions were so much at variance with the consensus of opinion in his day (and in ours) that he had to burden his book with a mass of statistical and anecdotal evidence, as well as twenty-four appendixes. The effect of this, since the facts and figures he cites are three-quarters of a century old, is to disguise for the reader the significance of the book for a new generation. Consequently, while the revival of interest in the classics of anarchism during the late 1960s brought new editions of most of Kropotkin's works, with new introductions underlining their contemporary significance,[6] *Fields, Factories and Workshops* became available only in two expensive American facsimile reproductions, one of the first edition (1899)[7] and the other of the second edition (1913)[8], with no attempt to bring the argument up to date.

The intention of the present edition is to do just this. Kropotkin's arguments are retained intact, but his supporting material has been heavily pruned, while editorial appendixes at the end of each chapter attempt to indicate the significance of his ideas today. His two chapters on 'The Decentralisation of Industries', his three chapters on 'The Possibilities of Agriculture', and his two chapters on 'Small Industries and Industrial Villages' have been condensed into one chapter on each of these themes. His chapter on 'Brain Work and Manual Work' and his concluding chapter are retained virtually complete.

The combination of topics in his book is unusual, and is explained by the framework of Kropotkin's thought. He was an anarchist, an advocate of society without government. He wanted the revolutionary overthrow of capitalism and the state, and he envisaged production, distribution and social organisation in the hands of a federated network of autonomous communes. *The Conquest of Bread* is his manual for a revolutionary society, *Mutual Aid* is his treatise on social organisation. *Fields, Factories and Workshops* has several important functions in his system of ideas: firstly, to combat the view that there is any *technical* reason for the scale of industrial and agricultural organisation in modern society to grow larger and larger – which is a standard objection to anarchist and decentralist ideas; secondly – as a matter of revolutionary strategy – to cope with the problem posed by dependence on imported food which implies that a nation in revolt can be starved into submission; thirdly, to advocate the kind of dispersed production for local consumption which is appropriate to the kind of society he wanted; finally, to deny that the dehumanisation of labour is the price we must pay for a modern industrial society. His book is really a thesis (to adopt a phrase of Professor Stephen Marglin) on *the economic consequences of the humanisation of work.*[9]

The author of this remarkable book was born of aristocratic Russian parents in 1842, served as a boy in the Tsar's Corps of Pages, and as a young man travelled widely in Central Asia and the Far East, gaining a reputation as a geographer. He became involved in populist agitation, was imprisoned for two years, and made a sensational escape from a prison hospital in St Petersburg. In Western Europe, he found his home in the anarchist movement and, after imprisonment for three years in France, settled in England where he was one of the founders of the anarchist journal *Freedom* in 1886, and where he earned his living as a writer on scientific, social and political subjects. Apart from two journeys to the United States and Canada, and brief visits to Europe, he remained in Britain until 1917 when he returned to Russia. There he died in 1921.

Kropotkin's fragmentary writings on the Russian revolution, written in his last years, are of great interest (his letters to Lenin and his 'Message to the Workers of the West' are printed in several recent collections).[10] And his memoirs rank with Herzen's *My Past and Thoughts* and Tolstoy's *Childhood, Boyhood and Youth* among the great Russian autobiographical writings of the nineteenth century and have been reissued several times in the last decade, the best edition being the one lavishly annotated and edited by Nicolas Walter. One of the fullest biographies of Kropotkin is *The Anarchist Prince*, by George Woodcock and Ivan Avakumović.[11]

Kropotkin was the most widely read of all the anarchist propagandists. His books and pamphlets were translated into the major languages of the East as well as those of Europe. They appealed to guerilla fighters like Makhno in the Ukraine and Zapata in Mexico, as well as to reformers like Ebenezer Howard and Patrick Geddes. His 'inventive and pragmatic outlook' made him for George Orwell 'one of the most persuasive of anarchist writers'.[12] Within the anarchist movement, Kropotkin's influence, paradoxically, was not wholly salutary. His very eminence, both in the movement and in society at large, led to his becoming a kind of oracle whose opinions were always right. The issue came to a head in 1914 with his support of the Allied cause in the First World War, in opposition to the anti-nationalist and anti-militarist tradition of the anarchists. His most perceptive critic was another great anarchist, Errico Malatesta, whose reminiscence 'Peter Kropotkin: Recollections and Criticisms of an Old Friend'[13] is quoted in my notes on Chapter Two.

Fields, Factories and Workshops, however, was not written for an exclusively anarchist audience, nor as specifically anarchist propaganda. Its aim was to spread more widely the ideas which he had already ventilated in the 1880s in the journals *Le Révolté* and *La Révolte* and in some of the articles collected together in his books *Paroles d'un Révolté* (1885) and *The Conquest of Bread* (1892). Kropotkin's theories and generalisations were, in fact, the fruit of a lifetime of observation and accumulation of data, and this book, like most of his others, began life as a series of magazine articles.

Today we are more interested in his conclusions than with the evidence he gathered to support them. The conclusion of Chapter 1 (Chapters 1 and 2 in the original) is that there is a trend for manufacturing industry to decentralise throughout the world; that production for a local market is a rational and desirable tendency. The conclusion of Chapter 2 (Chapters 3, 4 and 5 in the original) is that intensive farming could meet the basic food needs of a country like Great Britain. The conclusion of Chapter 3 (Chapters 6 and 7 in the original) is that the dispersal of industry on a small scale and in combination with agriculture, is also rational and desirable. The conclusion of Chapter 4 (Chapter 8 in the original) is that we need an education which combines manual and intellectual work. (In this book, Kropotkin's footnotes are omitted where they simply refer to sources, but are incorporated into the text where they enhance it.)

Kropotkin's deductions are as controversial and revolutionary today as they were when he formulated them. The *dominant* trend in our society contradict them in almost all respects. They are arguments in fact for revolutionary changes in the direction of industry and agriculture. They are pointers to a different kind of future. At one time this view of our future might have been regarded as a dream, confined to Kropotkin's anarchist disciples, or to enthusiasts for a simpler life-style. Today, as a result of the growing realisation of the elementary fact that the world's resources of energy and raw materials are finite, that food is our most precious commodity, and that most people's working lives are futile and stultifying, the lessons of this book are both topical and hopeful. It is an argument for a plausible future.

In preparing this edition I have been indebted to all the people whose findings are cited, but especially to Robin Best, Murray Bookchin, Ralph Borsodi, Leonard Elmhirst, Roger Franklin, the late Paul Goodman, George McRobie, Lewis Mumford, Sir Frederic Osborn, Keith Paton and Gerald Wibberley. For practical information on intensive horticulture I owe much to my cousin Anthony Ward and to my friend Vernon Richards who, like Nicolas Walter, has given me the benefit of years of reflection on Kropotkin's significance. None of these are responsible for the use made here of their wisdom.

Colin Ward

viii

EDITOR'S INTRODUCTION (1985 EDITION)

No enterprise could be more foolhardy than that of bringing an old book by a long-dead author up to date. Because the updating becomes dated much more rapidly than the original text. I need to reassure the reader that this is not the case with this version of Kropotkin's *Fields, Factories and Workshops*. But more does need saying.

His book of 1899 was made of articles he had published in 1888-1890 in a British context, and I happened to have the opportunity to present his text to a modern audience in the early 1970s, pruning his supporting material but pointing to the contemporary relevance of his arguments. He made four points, for reasons discussed in the Introduction. The first was that there is a trend for manufacturing industry to decentralise throughout the world, and that production for a local market is a rational and desirable tendency. The second was that this implies that each region of the globe must feed itself, and that intensive farming could meet the basic needs of a country like Britain. The third was that the dispersal of industry on a small scale and in combination with agriculture is also rational and desirable, and the fourth is that we need an education which combines manual and intellectual work.

Let us take these points one by one from the standpoint of the 1980s. The world decentralisation of industry continues at an advancing pace, as everyone living in old industrial regions knows to their cost. Jane Jacobs, in the most recent study of the process, comments on the inability of the economic advisers of all governments to comprehend the process. The results of their plans to save old industries or to develop new ones "range from outright disasters, as in Poland, Iran, Uruguay, Argentina, Brazil, Mexico, Turkey and most of Africa, to the mere disappointments, as in Ireland, Canada, southern Italy, Yugoslavia, Cuba and India . . ." China thrashes about trying first one strategy then another, "each petering out in confusion and recrimination"; the Soviet Union is "eerily beginning to resemble a colonial country, for it depends increasingly upon exporting natural resources to more highly developed countries and on importing sophisticated manufactured goods". Britain has continued in the grip of unrelenting decline, and in the United States industry steadily wanes, with the sinister corollary that "military production has become increasingly indispensable to keep skilled people at work and to prevent whole regions of the country that rely heavily upon military work from collapsing economically" [1]

[1]

What Kropotkin calls, on page 32, "the consecutive development of nations", Jane Jacobs in her *Cities and the Wealth of Nations* calls "import-replacing", and it is a continuous process. She points out that the import-replacing economies (contrary to Kropotkin's anticipation) "even become competitive producers of the items they formerly imported". The decline of the motor industry in both Britain and the United States is the most obvious example of this. Kropotkin, who wrote at a time when the motor car was a rich man's plaything, could not have imagined the economic idiocy of the modern car industry. A little of this is spelt out on pages 42-43, but one point needs further stressing. Anthony Wedgewood Benn, as Minister for Trade and Industry in the Labour government of the 1960s in Britain, engineered a shotgun wedding through the Industrial Reorganisation Corporation of those sections of the British car industry not American-owned. British Leyland was formed to compete effectively for overseas markets with European giants – the state-owned Renault company, FIAT and Volkswagen (Hitler's original People's Car). Britain became, and remains, a net importer of cars. The economics of large-scale production failed to deliver the goods, and by 1985 British Leyland, bailed out by the taxpayer by a government whose ideology is that of the free play of market forces, is desperately seeking to do a deal with the Japanese because it believes that its productive capacity is not enough to compete effectively. Meanwhile Japanese manufacturers are worried about competition from the expanding economies of other countries on the Pacific Rim.

When Kropotkin's book was published it was his second point that was thought to be unrealistically optimistic. The notion that a country like Britain could be agriculturally self-sufficient was laughable during the long period of agricultural depression that ended with the Second World War. The comments made in my appendix to Kropotkin's chapter remain true. The only further observation that need be made is that we, like the rest of Europe, have reached the stage of embarrassing over-production in a world where, thanks to mass communications, we are acutely aware of starvation in huge areas of Africa.

I draw attention to my appendix to the fact that this huge expansion has been achieved in precisely opposite ways to those anticipated by Kropotkin. He expected labour-intensive small-scale production. We have had capital-intensive large-scale production, aided by subsidies which have made rich farmers richer and have ignored or eliminated small producers. The characteristic literature

[2]

of farming in the post-war years, as noted on p 119, was concerned with answering the question Can Britian Feed Itself? The typical books about British agriculture of the 1980s have been concerned with the social, political and environmental consequences of subsidised over-production.[2] These authors criticise agricultural policy from every point of view, including that of the Thatcher government's own free market ideology. The critics closest to Kropotkin's standpoint are Charles Pye-Smith and Richard North, who in *Working the Land*, argue that "For forty years now agricultural expansion has gone hand in hand with rural decline. The survival of the British country-side and its village communities will depend on more than a reversal of present labour trends on the farm. However a healthy agriculture means a healthy countryside — and a healthy agriculture is one based on people and their skills, not on machines and robots"

They point out that "efficiency on farms is still measured by how few people can be employed. (Labour is almost the only thing that has not been subsidised)", and what they want to see is more useful work for more people in the country, "intensively cultivating the land, substituting good husbandry for heavy inputs of fertilizers and pesticides, diversifying into food processing and other related jobs".[3]

This leads us to Kropotkin's fourth chapter, on Small Industries and Industrial Villages, where he claims firstly that contrary to the general impression, the greater part of industrial production is in small workshops rather than huge factories, and secondly that it is to the advantage of both for industry to be combined with agriculture. Beyond the comments made in my appendix to Kropotkin's chapter, there are several points to be made here. The re-emergence of mass unemployment in the economies of the west has brought a new interest in small enterprises precisely because they generate employ-ment at a far lower *per capital* cost than large-scale industry, where huge investment provides jobs at enormous cost since the object of large scale capital investment is to do without labour. In the United States a House of Representatives Inquiry in 1979 showed that in the previous eight years the biggest thousand firms in the country had generated only 0.8% of new jobs, most having arisen in small business or having been self-generating.

The collapse of the traditional large-scale heavy industries in Britain was, as Kropotkin foresaw in his first chapter, inevitable. Everyone today laments the way Britain's great cities are falling apart and attributes their plight and their problems to this industrial collapse and to the loss of the economic base which gave rise to the mushroom growth of the cities in the 19th century. We tend to

[3]

forget that when Birmingham, Manchester, Newcastle, Liverpool or Glasgow were in their industrial heyday, when the docks were full of ships and the factories loaded with orders, these cities were bywords for deprivation and squalor. Their overcrowding, their squalor and their incredible mortality rates were at their worst when the city's economy was booming.

The process of dispersal of industry and population has been accelerating all through the century, and the newest 'silicon valleys' or 'sunrise corridors' of computer technology are simply the latest phase in this continuous trend. It was Ebenezer Howard, Kropotkin's contemporary, who declared in 1904: "I venture to suggest that while the age in which we live is the age of the great closely-compacted, overcrowded city, there are already signs, for those who can read them, of a coming change so great and momentous that the twentieth century will be known as the period of the great exodus, the return to the land . . ."

But this return to the land, in the form that Kropotkin envisaged: the combination of industry and agriculture, with a society composed of men and women, each of whom is able to work with his or her hands, as well as with his or her brain, and to do so in more directions than one" just has not happened, except on an individual level. Plenty of people do live in just that way, through choice or necessity in what is known as the informal economy, and I will return to this subject.

Kropotkin believed it was a matter of education, to which he devoted his final chapter. His educational views have been set in the context of the anarchist tradition in educational thinking in an excellent book by Michael Smith, *The Libertarians and Education.*[4] At the moment, with demoralised teachers and pupils, we have a moral panic about the state of education, which implies that the schools are responsible for the decline of the British manufacturing industry. The Labour Prime Minister, James Callaghan, made a speech in 1976 at Ruskin College lamenting the unwillingness of the young to take up industrial jobs (he actually assumed that they existed). His Conservative successors have similarly treated the education system as a scapegoat. It is ironical that, having discovered that the young don't like the idea of industrial work, the first thing that occurrs to the politicians is that children should be acclimatised to industry, rather than that industrial work should be changed to make it more attractive to the young.

All this posturing, since if the aim is to cure Britain's balance of payments problems, they should steer the young into the few expanding currency-earning activities like insurance or tourism. But these somehow lack the moral stance of a man in overalls clutching an oily rag and a spanner. Nevertheless, the current heart-searchings about the school system are long overdue. The schools *are* geared to academic success for a minority and academic failure for a majority. In the days of relatively full employment that majority was able to leave school thankfully and get jobs. Now that the jobs have evaporated, society, and its schools, are going to reap a harvest of resentment. They have a choice. Either they will develop an approach combining brain work and manual work in an education for resource-fullness and independence, or they will pursue what has already become known as 'the new vocationalism' of schooling for the dole. And this leads me to some further reflections on re-reading Kropotkin's text.

Of the various spectres haunting Europe the most terrifying is that of nuclear war, but the most pervasive is that of mass unemployment. It is more than a spectre. In most countries of the world it is the ordinary condition that people live in all their lives. Ivan Illich remarks that "unemployment, a term first introduced in 1898 to designate people without a fixed income, is now recognised as the condition in which most of the world's people live anyway".

In the rich countries we have been bludgeoned into indifference by forecasts of the millions of permanently unemployed adults expected by the year 2000. Somehow we feel that it won't happen to us, or that its effect will be mitigated by the welfare machinery which is intended to ensure that nobody actually starves.

But what is to happen when, as long-term, large-scale unemployment grows, the privileged, employed section of the population shrugs off the responsibility for providing an income for those who cannot get a job and are never likely to have one? There have been glimpses of such a future in the taxpayers' revolt signalled by Proposition 13 in California in 1978 and on the return of a crudely fundamentalist Conservative government in Britain in the following years, as well as in the increasingly vicious harrassment of 'social parasites' in the Soviet Union and its satellites. The Governor of California was elected as President of the United States with an overwhelming popular vote, and re-elected for a second term. Mrs Thatcher's welfare-bashing government in Britain was similarly endorsed.

The town planner Graeme Shankland, attempting to grapple with the unemployment problems of British cities, saw a prospect of "increasing impoverished, depressed and demoralised millions,

[5]

barely sustained by supplementary benefits and on pensions paid for by a diminishing, powerful and resentful elite work-force", [5] just as Andre Gorz in his *Farewell to the Working Class* envisages a society where the *majority* will be "marginalised by an unholy alliance of unionised elite workers with managers and capitalists".[6]

We have already moved a long way from the expansive 1950s when our prophets were urging us to sever, at last, the connection between work and purchasing power. In those days Robert Theobald was demanding a "guaranteed annual income" to be paid to every American as a constitutional right, and John Kenneth Galbraith was arguing for what he called Cyclically Graduated Compensation – a dole which went up when the economy took a down-turn, so that people could go on spending, as Keynes before him urged, and consequently keep other people employed, and which went down when full employment was approached. But have you noticed that nobody talks about full employment any more?

"One day", Galbraith forecast, "we shall remove the economic penalties and also the social stigma associated with involuntary unemployment. This will make the economy much easier to manage." But, he added in 1960, "we haven't done this yet".[7] Nor have we by the 1980s. Two decades of radicalism and reaction have gone by, and some of the same people who in the 1960s were urging us that the work ethic was obsolete in the days of automation and cybernetics, are by the 1980s protesting as governments cut back on their token job creation schemes, when faced by the era of micro-processors.

All these ingenious calculations of how short a working day, or working week, or working lifetime could be in a rationally organised society were made in the days of relatively full employment. They began to lose their attractiveness as unemployment grew. The prophesies are still being made, all the same. In a paper commissioned by the British Cabinet Office, Professor Tom Stonier of Bradford University declares that by early in the next century only 10% of the present labour force will be required to provide a technologically advanced society with all its material wants or needs.[8]

None of the prophesies are plausible enough to banish the spectre that is haunting the world of work. Still less comforting are the short-term forecasts of politicians and economists. We don't really believe that British or American manufacturing industries are going to recover lost markets. We don't really believe that robots or micro-processors are going to create more than a small proportion of the jobs that they eliminate. Nor do we believe that big business has any answers for us. Even our faith that the tertiary or service economy

[6]

is bound to expand to replace the jobs lost in the productive sector, has been shattered by the democratisation by Jonathan Gershuny of the Science Policy Research Unit at Sussex University that employment in service industries in western societies is already declining.[9]

Dr Gershuny, however, does provide a ray of hope that could lead us to look at the future of work in a quite different way. He sees the decline of the service economy as accompanied by the emergence of a *self*-service economy in the same way that the automatic washing machine in the home can be said to supercede the laundry industry. His American equivalent is Scott Burns, author of *The Household Economy*, with his claim that "America is going to be transformed by nothing more or less that the inevitable maturation and decline of the market economy. The instrument for this positive change will be the household − the family − revitalised as a powerful and relatively autonomous productive unit". [10]

The only way to banish the spectre of unemployment is to break free from our enslavement to the idea of employment. The pre-industrial economy was, after all, a domestic economy, and the old American phrase for an employee, a 'hired man' carries with it the notion that he was something less than a free citizen, as does the old socialist definition of the working class as those with nothing to sell but their labour power. The very word 'employment' has only been used in its modern sense since the 1840s just as 'unemployment' in the sense in which we use it, is even more recent.

We do need of course to remind ourselves that wage labour and even factory production existed before the industrial revolution. Adam Smith in the mid-18th century told readers of *The Wealth of Nations* that in every part of Europe twenty workmen serve under a master for one that is independent, and he gave us the classic account of the division of labour. A century after him, Marx concluded that the condition he called alienation resulted from the worker's loss of *ownership* of his skills, tools, products, time and space. Any account of the industrial revolution in this country tells how workers were driven by starvation to accept the disciplines of employment. For me, the classical description was that of J L and Barbara Hammond in their book *The Town Labourer*. The home worker in domestic industry, they observed, "worked long hours, but they were his own hours; his wife and children worked, but they worked beside him, and there was no alien power over their lives; his house was stifling, but he could slip into his garden; he had spells of unemployment, but he could use them for cultivating cabbages. The forces that ruled his fate were in a sense outside his daily life; they did not overshadow and envelop his home, his family, his movements and habits, his hours for work and his hours for food . . ."

They declare that, "No economist of the day, in estimating the gains and the losses of factory employment, ever allowed for the strain and violence that a man suffered in his feelings when he passed from a life in which he could smoke or eat, or dig or sleep as he pleased, to one in which someone turned the key on him, and for fourteen hours he had not even the right to whistle. It was like entering the airless and laughterless life of a prison. Unless we keep this moral sacrifice in mind, we shall not understand why the hand-loom weavers refused to go into the power-loom factories, where they would have earned much higher wages: a refusal that is an important fact in the history of the cotton industry.'[11]

The three main kinds of informal economy are illustrated in a homely example by Professor Pahl, taking the options available to someone who wants to get a broken window repaired. He might:

Firstly, hire a glazier through the formal economy, paying him the full cost including his share of the overheads of the building firm and value-added tax.

Secondly, find someone nearby who is known to be able to mend windows and pay cash for the job, possibly thereby entering the Black Economy because he would not know whether such a person was declaring all his or her income, paying all his or her tax, or working in time already paid for by another employer.

Thirdly, he might ask a neighbour to do it within the communal economy, either in exchange for specific goods or services now or in the future, or as part of a broader ongoing relationship.

Or, fourthly, he might do the job himself in his own time with his own tools, within the household economy.

Now, with some honourable exceptions, public discussion of the informal economy has concentrated on the Black Economy aspect: tax evasion, fiddles and so on. Efforts are made to calculate what proportion of the Gross Domestic Product is in this aspect of the economy. They differ enormously, just because it is so unquantifiable, but they aren't at all helpful, because the greater part of activities and transactions outside the measurable economy have no tax-evasion aspect.

There are just two points I would like to make about the Black Economy, since the government announced that another five hundred dedicated civil servants would be investigating it for the Inland Revenue. The first point relates to 'moonlighting': people employed in the regular economy with tax deducted under the PAYE arrange-

[8]

ments, who have another job in the evenings or at weekends, which may have tax deducted at source, but is unlikely to, or on which they may make a tax return, but are unlikely to. Most of the people I have spoken to in this situation have in fact a tone of outraged moral probity, pointing out that, like anyone else, rich or poor, they pay one third of their regular income in tax, and that if they choose to spend their evenings on the serving side of the bar for cash, instead of on the drinking side spending it, that is their affair, and not conceivably anyone else's.

The second point is that the Black Economy is entirely the creation of fiscal policy. PAYE and purchase tax were introduced during the war to mop up consumer demand for non-existent goods when, for the very first time in their lives, wage-earners had more cash to spare. They remain in existence today with the secondary function of turning market traders, unregistered for VAT, into criminals. Before the Second World War no-one would have understood what was meant by the Black Economy, apart from bootleggers in the USA during the prohibition period, or the entire citizenship of the Soviet Union, who only stayed alive because of its existence. (The finest flowering of the Black Economy, even today, is in the Soviet Union and its satellites.)

In Britain, a reader of *Freedom* reminds us, "In 1939 a man started to pay income tax if he earned more than £380 a year, and he did so at the rate of 1s 8d (about 8½p) in the pound. Because that income was comparatively high, most paid no tax at all, so that by today's standards 1939 was an almost tax free society. Yet it was a society that provided most of the basic services even though money was spent on preparations for war. In 1976 a man would be liable for tax if he earned more than £1,500 a year, but (taking inflation into account) this figure represented less than half of the national average so that most of the people were forced to pay tax and they did so at the rate of 35p in the pound. The amount of tax had increased even more rapidly than inflation."

Let me repeat that the Black Economy is the creation of fiscal policy and is not a moral issue. Many of us, for a whole variety of reasons, do not accept the unspoken doctrine that the State is all-powerful and all-wise. If you make it a moral issue you have to cope with the fact that the governments of the world spend more than a million dollars of their tax income every ninety seconds on their armed forces and on war preparations. Was this what their citizens wanted?

The Black Economy is part, and not the most important part, of

[9]

the *Informal* economy, which I use as a blanket word to cover all the possible conceptions of alternative economies, listed above, including ordinary self-employment, which is the official designation of two million workers in Britain and millions more in the US, and including that multitude of mutual services where money doesn't change hands at all. But each of the descriptions I have listed has its own particular connotations, and they add up to an enormous range of human activities without which life on this planet would be impossible. The formal economy *depends* on the informal economy, but the reverse is also true. The household economy depends on manufactured articles produced in the regular economy. So does the hidden economy of illicit sales, the communal economy of joint use of expensive equipment, or the enormous variety of sub-contracting which is combined in the finished and measurable product of the official economy.

It *does* in fact make sense to help people on the way to employing themselves, not as a temporary, bankrupt gesture, but because, whether we like it or not, this is the only discernible pattern of the future economy. In what other possible light can you read the daily newspaper headlines? 'Productivity up and the number in work falls' reports the business editor. 'Half those being trained on youth programmes returning to dole queues' is the headline for the social services correspondent. Victor Keegan remarks "the most seductive theory of all is that what we are experiencing now is nothing lass than a movement back towards an informal economy after a brief flirtation of 200 years or so with a formal one".

We are talking about the movement of work back into the domestic economy. There are certainly class divisions in the assumptions we make about this. People selling high technology often fantasise about this when persuading business executives that there was no need for that tedious commuter journey to work, since their personal computer outlet, word processor and videophone would enable them to do all their work from the comfort of home. Since one of the privileges of that station of life is to do most of your work from the company car by radiotelephone anyway, we don't have to worry about them.

What about ordinary productive work at home? Home-working has always been a by-word for exploitation, low pay and sweated labour. This is why the trade unions are hostile to it. But it is by no means a declining industry and it is possible to reduce its least desirable aspects. One example of the improvement of the situation of home-workers in the Nottingham lace industry (not a century ago, but in the 1970s) was given by Peggy Edwards and Eric Flounders in Frank Field's book *Are Low Wages Inevitable?*[12] The most suggestive illustration of one of the preconditions for effectively moving industrial production back into the home comes from the many studies of the informal economy in Italy. Sebastiano Brusco claimed that it was only the existance of a vast informal sector of small workshops that saved the Italian economy from ruin in the 1970s. He points to the phenomenon of whole villages of small workshops with power tools sub-contracting for the industrial giants of the motor industry, and when hit by recession, turning to other kinds of industrial components.[13]

A BBC film took us to another Italian industrial village where 80% of the women's tights made in Italy are produced. It illustrated two aspects of the informal economy there: the woman who, using a hand machine, earns a pittance from the contractor who brings her the unfinished goods for assembly and collects them finished, in the classic sweatshop situation, and as a completely contrasted example, the woman who, with her mother, makes a good living assembling tights in her home, using a sophisticated machine which cost them £5,000 and is now paid for. Brusco claimed that what we were seeing was the decentralisation of manufacturing industry in a way which for him, as for Kropotkin, foreshadowed the pattern of a post-industrial society. Even Kropotkin's combination of industry and agriculture can be found, and is in fact traditional, in Italy. Philip Mattera reports that "there are even people who have been moonlighting in agriculture. Studies of employees of the few large factories of the South, especially the huge Italsider plant at Taranto, have found that many are using their free time to resume their prior occupation as small farmers."

The key difference between Brusco's two examples of the tight makers was that one was trapped in the sweated labour situation and the other was freed from it by increased productivity, in just the same way as do-it-yourself users of power tools have increased theirs. It is, of course, a matter of access to a very modest amount of credit. This is the lesson of the informal economy in the exploding cities of the Third World too. Kenneth King, studying the multitude of small-scale producers in Nairobi, reminds us that the enterprising artisans do not use the improvised equipment from choice: "Many would be anxious to obtain and use lathes if power were available, but the most popular brands now cost £3,000-£5,000. Although Western observers may admire the cheapness and ingenuity of the various Heath Robinson machines, their inventors regard them very differently. They know precisely what sort of Czechoslovakian centre-lathe they would buy first, what it would cost and why they cannot afford it." He contrasts the millions of pounds worth of credit advanced for the high technology plastics industry with the extraordinary difficulties experienced in raising any kind of credit in the artisan sector. "It is not principally the technical dimension which constitutes the obstacle, but rather the lack of a basic credit infrastructure, security of tenure in the urban areas and a technoloy policy that would support the very small-scale entrepreneur."

In the rich world, where we have fallen so far under the spell of capitalist ideology, and of Marxist ideology too, which can only see petty trades as some kind of primitive left-over from some less advanced stage in industrial evolution, the informal economy is similarly neglected, apart from token aid to the people who start small businesses in the expectation that they will become big business. Yet while we have begun to look at its implications and its potential simply out of despair at the irresponsible decline of employment, we tend to forget that it also represents an aspiration for millions of employed people. Ask anyone employed by someone else what he or she would do if a legacy or a gambling win suddenly provided working capital. In four cases out of five the answer would not be to live a life of idleness on a sun drenched island. It would be to set up o one's own, individually or collectively, to be one's own boss, to start a little business, a shop, a workshop, a smallholding or a country pub. It may be just a matter of dreams, but even a survey conducted by the Consumer's Association and published in its journal *Which*, indicated that the happiest and most satisfied workers were the self-employed.

What poor people in the world's poor cities do out of necessity, the poor *and* the securely employed of the rich world aspire to. The obstacle in both cases is the same: lack of access to capital or credit, lack of security, since in all countries social security is geared to the employed, controllable worker, not to the self-employed, and the absence of a social welfare infrastructure which would automatically favour the small, local provider.

I often wonder how we reached the situation when honourable words like 'enterprise', 'initiative' and 'self-help' are automatically associated with the political right and the defence of capitalism, while it is assumed that the political left stands for a big brother state with a responsibility to provide a pauper's income for all and an inflation-proof income for its own functionaries.

Ninety years ago people's mental image of a socialist was a radical self-employed cobbler, sitting in his shop with a copy of William Morris's *Useful Work versus Useless Toil* on the workbench, his hammer in his hand and his lips full of brass tacks. His mind was full of notions of liberating his fellow workers from industrial serfdom in a dark satanic mill. No doubt the current mental picture is of a university lecturer with a copy of *The Inevitable Crisis of Capitalism* in one hand and a banner labelled 'Fight the Cuts' in the other, while his mind is full of strategies for unseating the sitting Labour candidate in the local pocket borough.

Whatever did happen to all those aspirations for the liberation of work? Clive Jenkins at least wrote a book called *The Collapse of Work* about the way the micro revolution was going to destroy jobs at a terrifying rate, and urging us to outgrow the work ethic.[14] But he got it all wrong. In the first place, who actually wants a cradle-to-grave contract with some Mitsubushi type employer just for the privilege of being put out to grass at 55 instead of 65, which is essentially what he is advocating. In the second place, he has got the language wrong. He is talking, perfectly correctly, about the collapse of *employment*. There will never be a shortage of *work* in the sense of coping with useful tasks.

Pierre-Joseph Proudhon, the paradoxical anarchist, would have taken it for granted. His vision of industrial organisation was that of a federation of self-employed craftsmen. We certainly get echoes of the Proudhonist view in Robert Frost's observation, "Men work together, I told him from the heart, whether they work together or apart".

Prophesies seldom come true in the way that their originators anticipate. But the idea that Kropotkin's decentralist and anarchist vision will come through the collapse of employment and the growth of the informal economy is less absurd than the faith of his socialist contemporaries that the humanisation of work would come through the conquest of the power of the State by the proletariat. The French socialist Andre Gorz argues that the political left has become frozen into authoritarian collectivist attutudes belonging to the past: "As long as the protagonists of socialism continue to make centralised planning . . . the lynchpin of their programme, and the adherence of everyone to the 'democratically formulated' objectives of their plan the core of their political doctrine, socialism will remain an unattractive proposition in industrial societies. Classical socialist doctrine finds it difficult to come to terms with political and social pluralism, understood not simply as a plurality of parties and trade unions but as the co-existence of various ways of working, producing and living, various distinct cultural areas and levels of social existence. . . . Yet this kind of pluralism precisely conforms to the lived experience and aspirations of the post-industrial proletariat, as well as the major part of the traditional working class."[15]

How on earth, he asks, has the socialist movement got itself into the position of dismissing as petit-bourgeois individualism all those freedoms which people actually value: everything that belongs to the private dreams that people really cherish? This is an important question, and as I stress in my original introduction, Kropotkin's contribution to all our private dreams in *Fields, Factories and Workshops* is that it is a thesis on the economic consequences of the humanisation of work.

1 Peter Kropotkin, *Fields, Factories and Workshops*, Publishers' Note to reprint of second edition (London, Edinburgh and New York, Nelson, n.d. [1919])

2 Bertrand Russell, *Roads to Freedom: Socialism, Anarchism and Syndicalism* (London, Allen & Unwin, 1918, 1966)

3 Herbert Read (ed.), *Kropotkin: Selections from his Writings* (London, Freedom Press, 1942)

4 Paul Goodman, 'Fifty Years Have Passed', *Resistance* (New York, March/April 1948)

5 Lewis Mumford, *The City in History* (London, Secker & Warburg, 1961; Harmondsworth, Penguin, 1963)

6 Peter Kropotkin, *Ethics* (New York, Tudor Publishing, 1947; New York, Benjamin Blom, 1968)
Peter Kropotkin, *The Conquest of Bread*, edited by Paul Avrich (London, Allen Lane, 1972)
Peter Kropotkin, *The Great French Revolution*, foreword by George Woodcock and Ivan Avakumović (New York, Schocken Books, 1971; London, Orbach & Chambers, 1971)
Peter Kropotkin, *Memoirs of a Revolutionist*, edited by Nicolas Walter (New York, Dover Publications, 1971)
Peter Kropotkin, *Mutual Aid: A Factor of Evolution*, edited by Ashley Montagu (Boston, Extending Horizons, 1955); edited by Paul Avrich (London, Allen Lane, 1972)
Peter Kropotkin, *In Russian and French Prisons*, edited by Paul Avrich (New York, Schocken Books, 1971)
Peter Kropotkin, *The State: Its Historic Role*, a new translation by Vernon Richards (London, Freedom Press, 1969)
Peter Kropotkin, *Kropotkin's Revolutionary Pamphlets*, edited by Roger Baldwin (New York, Dover Publications, 1970)
Peter Kropotkin, *Selected Writings on Anarchism and Revolution*, edited by Martin A. Miller (Cambridge, Mass., and London, M.I.T. Press, 1970)
Peter Kropotkin, *Words of a Rebel*, translated and edited by Nicolas Walter (forthcoming)

7 Peter Kropotkin, *Fields, Factories and Workshops* (New York, Greenwood Press, 1968)

8 Peter Kropotkin, *Fields, Factories and Workshops* (New York, Benjamin Blom, 1968)

9 Stephen Marglin (Professor of Economics, Harvard University), Lethaby Lecture delivered at the Royal College of Art (9 and 10 May 1973) on 'The Economic Consequences of the Humanisation of Work'

[15]

10 In Paul Avrich (ed.), *The Anarchists in the Russian Revolution* (London, Thames & Hudson, 1973); and in Baldwin ('Message') and Miller ('Letters'), *op. cit.*

11 George Woodcock and Ivan Avakumović, *The Anarchist Prince* (London, Boardman, 1950; New York, Schocken Books, 1971)

12 George Orwell, 'The Writer's Dilemma', *The Observer* (28 August 1948)

13 Errico Malatesta, 'Peter Kropotkin: Recollections and Criticisms of an Old Friend' (1931); reprinted in Vernon Richards (ed.), *Errico Malatesta: Life and Ideas* (London, Freedom Press, 1965)

EDITOR'S NOTES (1985 EDITION)

1 Jane Jacobs: *Cities and the Wealth of Nations* (Viking 1985)

2 See for example Marion Shoard: *The Theft of the Countryside* (Temple Smith 1980), Richard Body: *Agriculture: The Triumph and the Shame* (Temple Smith 1982), Richard Body: *Farming in the Clouds* (Temple Smith 1984), J K Bowers and Paul Cheshire: *Agriculture, the Countryside and Land Use* (Methuen 1983)

3 Charlie Pye-Smith and Richard North: *Working the Land* (Temple Smith 1984)

4 Michael Smith: *The Libertarians and Education* (Allen & Unwin 1984)

5 Graeme Shankland: *Our Secret Economy* (Anglo-German Foundation 1980)

6 Andre Gorz: *Farewell to the Working Class* (Pluto Press 1983)

7 J K Galbraith: *The Liberal Hour* (Hamish Hamilton 1960)

8 Tom Stonier: *Materials Production Labour Requirements in Post-Industrial Society* (Central Policy Review Staff 1978)

9 Jonathan Gershuny: *After Industrial Society: The Emerging Self-Service Economy* (Macmillan 1978)

10 Scott Burns: *The Household Economy* (Boston: Beacon Press 1976)

11 J L and Barbara Hammond: *The Town Labourer* (Bell 1917)

12 Frank Field (ed): *Are Low Wages Inevitable?* (Spokesman 1976)

13 See Philip Mattera: *Off the Books: The Rise of the Underground Economy* (Pluto Press 1985)

14 Clive Jenkins and Barrie Sherman: *The Collapse of Work* (Eyre Methuen 1979)

15 Andre Gorz: *op cit*

[16]

Author's Preface to the First Edition

Under the name of profits, rent, interest upon capital, surplus value, and the like, economists have eagerly discussed the benefits which the owners of land or capital, or some privileged nations, can derive, either from the under-paid work of the wage-labourer, or from the inferior position of one class of the community towards another class, or from the inferior economical development of one nation towards another nation. These profits being shared in a very unequal proportion between the different individuals, classes and nations engaged in production, considerable pains were taken to study the present apportionment of the benefits, and its economical and moral consequences, as well as the changes in the present economical organisation of society which might bring about a more equitable distribution of a rapidly accumulating wealth. It is upon questions relating to the right to that increment of wealth that the hottest battles are now fought between economists of different schools.

In the meantime the great question – 'What have we to produce, and how?' necessarily remained in the background. Political economy, as it gradually emerges from its semi-scientific stage, tends more and more to become a science devoted to the study of the needs of men and of the means of satisfying them with the least possible waste of energy – that is, a sort of physiology of society. But few economists, as yet, have recognised that this is the proper domain of economics, and have attempted to treat their science from this point of view. The main subject of social economy – that is, the *economy of energy required for the satisfaction of human needs* – is consequently the last subject which one expects to find treated in a concrete form in economical treatises.

The following pages are a contribution to a portion of this vast subject. They contain a discussion of the advantages which civilised societies could derive from a combination of industrial

B

pursuits with intensive agriculture, and of brain work with manual work.

The importance of such a combination has not escaped the attention of a number of students of social science. It was eagerly discussed some fifty years ago under the names of 'harmonised labour', 'integral education', and so on. It was pointed out at that time that the greatest sum total of well-being can be obtained when a variety of agricultural, industrial and intellectual pursuits are combined in each community; and that man shows his best when he is in a position to apply his usually-varied capacities to several pursuits in the farm, the workshop, the factory, the study or the studio, instead of being riveted for life to one of these pursuits only.

Half a century ago a harmonious union between agricultural and industrial pursuits, as also between brain work and manual work, could only be a remote desideratum. The conditions under which the factory system asserted itself, as well as the obsolete forms of agriculture which prevailed at that time, prevented such a union from being feasible. Synthetic production was impossible. However, the wonderful simplification of the technical processes in both industry and agriculture, partly due to an ever-increasing division of labour – in analogy with what we see in biology – has rendered the synthesis possible; and a distinct tendency towards a synthesis of human activities becomes now apparent in modern economical evolution. This tendency is analysed in the subsequent chapters – a special weight being laid upon the present possibilities of agriculture, which are illustrated by a number of examples borrowed from different countries, and upon the small industries to which a new impetus is being given by the new methods of transmission of motive power.

The substance of these essays was published in 1888–90 in the *Nineteenth Century*, and of one of them in the *Forum*. However, the tendencies indicated therein have been confirmed during the last ten years by such a mass of evidence that a very considerable amount of new matter had to be introduced, while the chapters on agriculture and the small trades had to be written anew.

Bromley, Kent, 1898   *P. Kropotkin*

[18]

Author's Preface to the Second Edition

Fourteen years have passed since the first edition of this book was published, and in revising it for this new edition I found at my disposal an immense mass of new materials, statistical and descriptive, and a great number of new works dealing with the different subjects that are treated in this book. I have thus had an excellent opportunity to verify how far the previsions that I had formulated when I first wrote this book have been confirmed by the subsequent economical evolution of the different nations.

This verification permits me to affirm that the economical tendencies that I had ventured to foreshadow then have only become more and more definite since. Everywhere we see the same decentralisation of industries going on, new nations continually entering the ranks of those which manufacture for the world market. Each of these new-comers endeavours to develop, and succeeds in developing, on its own territory the principal industries, and thus frees itself from being exploited by other nations, more advanced in their technical evolution. All nations have made a remarkable progress in this direction, as will be seen from the new data that are given in this book.

On the other hand, one sees, with all the great industrial nations, the growing tendency and need of developing at home a more intensive agricultural productivity, either by improving the now existing methods of extensive agriculture, by means of small-holdings, 'inner colonisation', agricultural education, and co-operative work, or by introducing different new branches of intensive agriculture. This country is especially offering us at this moment a most instructive example of a movement in the said direction. And this movement will certainly result, not only in a much-needed increase of the productive forces of the nation, which will contribute to free it from the international speculators in food produce, but also in awakening in the nation a fuller appreciation of the immense value of its soil, and the desire of repairing the error that has been committed in leaving it in the hands of great land-owners and of those who find it now more advantageous to rent the land to be turned into shooting preserves.

It is especially in revising the chapters dealing with the small industries that I had to incorporate the results of a great number of new researches. In so doing I was enabled to show that the growth of an infinite variety of small enterprises by the side of the very great centralised concerns is not showing any signs of abatement. On the contrary, the distribution of electrical motive power has given them a new impulse. In those places where water power was utilised for distributing electric power in the villages, and in those cities where the machinery used for producing electric light during the night hours was utilised for supplying motive power during the day, the small industries are taking a new development.

In this domain' I am enabled to add to the present edition the interesting results of work only possible when the British Factory Inspectors had published (in 1898, in virtue of the Factories Act of 1895) their first reports, from which I could determine the hitherto unknown numerical relations between the great and the small industries in the United Kingdom.

Until then no figures whatever as regards the distribution of operatives in the large and small factories and workshops of Great Britain were available; so that when economists spoke of the 'unavoidable' death of the small industries they merely expressed hypotheses based upon a limited number of observations, which were chiefly made upon part of the textile industry and metallurgy. Only after Mr Whitelegge had published the first figures from which reliable conclusions could be drawn was it possible to see how little such wide-reaching conclusions were confirmed by realities. In this country, as everywhere, the small industries continue to exist, and new ones continue to appear as a necessary growth, in many important branches of national production, by the side of the very great factories and huge centralised works.

As to the need, generally felt at this moment, of an education which would combine a wide scientific instruction with a sound knowledge of manual work – a question which I treat in the last chapter – it can be said that this cause has already been won in this country during the last twenty years. The *principle* is generally recognised by this time, although most nations, impoverished as they are by their armaments, are much too slow in applying the principle in life.

P. Kropotkin

Brighton, October 1912

Chapter 1

The Decentralisation of Industries

Who does not remember the remarkable chapter by which Adam Smith opens his inquiry into the nature and causes of the wealth of nations? Even those of our contemporary economists who seldom revert to the works of the father of political economy, and often forget the ideas which inspired them, know that chapter almost by heart, so often has it been copied and recopied since. It has become an article of faith; and the economical history of the century which has elapsed since Adam Smith wrote has been, so to speak, an actual commentary upon it.

'Division of labour' was its watchword. And the division and subdivision – the permanent subdivision – of functions has been pushed so far as to divide humanity into castes which are almost as firmly established as those of old India. We have, first, the broad division into producers and consumers: little-consuming producers on the one hand, little-producing consumers on the other hand. Then, amidst the former, a series of further subdivisions: the manual worker and the intellectual worker, sharply separated from one another to the detriment of both; the agricultural labourers and the ʼworkers in the manufacture; and, amidst the mass of the latter, numberless subdivisions again – so minute, indeed, that the modern ideal of a workman seems to be a man or a woman, or even a girl or a boy, without the knowledge of any handicraft, without any conception whatever of the industry he or she is employed in, who is only capable of making all day long and for a whole life the same infinitesimal part of something: who from the age of 13 to that of 60 pushes the coal cart at a given spot of the mine or makes the spring of a penknife, or 'the eighteenth part of a pin'. Mere servants to some machine of a given description; mere flesh-and-bone parts of some immense machinery; having no idea how and why the machinery performs its rhythmical movements.

Skilled artisanship is being swept away as a survival of a past condemned to disappear. The artist who formerly found aesthetic enjoyment in the work of his hands is substituted by the human slave of an iron slave. Nay, even the agricultural labourer, who formerly used to find a relief from the hardships of his life in the home of his ancestors – the future home of his children – in his love of the field and in a keen intercourse with nature, even he has been doomed to disappear for the sake of division of labour. He is an anachronism, we are told; he must be substituted, in a Bonanza farm, by an occasional servant hired for the summer, and discharged as the autumn comes: a tramp who will never again see the field he has harvested once in his life. 'An affair of a few years', the economists say, 'to reform agriculture in accordance with the true principles of division of labour and modern industrial organisation.'

Dazzled with the results obtained by a century of marvellous inventions, especially in England, our economists and political men went still farther in their dreams of division of labour. They proclaimed the necessity of dividing the whole of humanity into national workshops having each of them its own speciality. We were taught, for instance, that Hungary and Russia are predestined by nature to grow corn in order to feed the manufacturing countries; that Britain had to provide the world-market with cottons, iron goods, and coal; Belgium with woollen cloth; and so on. Nay, within each nation, each region had to have its own speciality. So it has been for some time since; so it ought to remain. Fortunes have been made in this way, and will continue to be made in the same way. It being proclaimed that the wealth of nations is measured by the amount of profits made by the few, and that the largest profits are made by means of a specialisation of labour, the question was not conceived to exist as to whether human beings *would* always submit to such a specialisation; whether nations could

[24]

be specialised like isolated workmen. The theory was good for today – why should we care for tomorrow? Tomorrow might bring its own theory!

And so it did. The narrow conception of life which consisted in thinking that *profits* are the only leading motive of human society, and the stubborn view which supposes that what has existed yesterday would last for ever, proved in disaccordance with the tendencies of human life; and life took another direction. Nobody will deny the high pitch of production which may be attained by specialisation. But, precisely in proportion as the work required from the individual in modern production becomes simpler and easier to be learned, and, therefore, also more monotonous and wearisome – the requirements of the individual for varying his work, for exercising all his capacities, become more and more prominent. Humanity perceives that there is no advantage for the community in riveting a human being for all his life to a given spot, in a workshop or a mine; no gain in depriving him of such work as would bring him into free intercourse with nature, make of him a conscious part of the grand whole, a partner in the highest enjoyments of science and art, of free work and creation.

Nations, too, refuse to be specialised. Each nation is a compound aggregate of tastes and inclinations, of wants and resources, of capacities and inventive powers. The territory occupied by each nation is in its turn a most varied texture of soils and climates, of hills and valleys, of slopes leading to a still greater variety of territories and races. Variety is the distinctive feature, both of the territory and its inhabitants; and that variety implies a variety of occupations. Agriculture calls manufactures into existence, and manufactures support agriculture. Both are inseparable; and the combination, the integration of both brings about the grandest results. In proportion as technical knowledge becomes everybody's virtual domain, in proportion as it becomes international, and can be concealed no longer, each nation acquires the possibility of applying the whole variety of her energies to the whole variety of industrial and agricultural pursuits. Knowledge ignores artificial political boundaries. So also do the industries; and the present tendency

[25]

of humanity is to have the greatest possible variety of industries gathered in each country, in each separate region, side by side with agriculture. The needs of human agglomerations correspond thus to the needs of the individual; and while a *temporary* division of functions remains the surest guarantee of success in each separate undertaking, the *permanent* division is doomed to disappear, and to be substituted by a variety of pursuits – intellectual, industrial, and agricultural – corresponding to the different capacities of the individual, as well as to the variety of capacities within every human aggregate.

When we thus revert from the scholastics of our text-books, and examine human life as a whole, we soon discover that, while all the benefits of a temporary division of labour must be maintained, it is high time to claim those of the *integration of labour*. Political economy has hitherto insisted chiefly upon *division*. We proclaim *integration*; and we maintain that the ideal of society – that is, the state towards which society is already marching – is a society of integrated, combined labour. A society where each individual is a producer of both manual and intellectual work; where each able-bodied human being is a worker, and where each worker works both in the field and the industrial workshop; where every aggregation of individuals, large enough to dispose of a certain variety of natural resources – it may be a nation, or rather a region – produces and itself consumes most of its own agricultural and manufactured produce.

Of course, as long as society remains organised so as to permit the owners of the land and capital to appropriate for themselves, under the protection of the state and historical rights, the yearly surplus of human production, no such change can be thoroughly accomplished. But the present industrial system, based upon a permanent specialisation of functions, already bears in itself the germs of its proper ruin. The industrial crises, which grow more acute and protracted, and are rendered still worse and still more acute by the armaments and wars implied by the present system, are rendering its maintenance more and more difficult. Moreover, the workers plainly manifest their intention to support no longer patiently the

[26]

misery occasioned by each crisis. And each crisis accelerates the day when the present institutions of individual property and production will be shaken to their foundations with such internal struggles as will depend upon the more or less good sense of the now privileged classes.

But we maintain also that any socialist attempt at remodelling the present relations between Capital and Labour will be a failure, if it does not take into account the above tendencies towards integration. These tendencies have not yet received, in our opinion, due attention from the different socialist schools – but they must. A reorganised society will have to abandon the fallacy of nations specialised for the production of either agricultural or manufacstured produce. It will have to rely on itself for the production of food and many, if not most, of the raw materials; it must find the best means of combining agriculture with manufacture – the work in the field with a decentralised industry; and it will have to provide for 'integrated education', which education alone, by teaching both science and handicraft from earliest childhood, can give to society the men and women it really needs.

Each nation – her own agriculturist and manufacturer; each individual working in the field and in some industrial art; each individual combining scientific knowledge with the knowledge of a handicraft – such is, we affirm, the present tendency of civilised nations.

The prodigious growth of industries in Great Britain, and the simultaneous development of the international traffic which now permits the transport of raw materials and articles of food on a gigantic scale, have created the impression that a few nations of West Europe were destined to become *the* manufacturers of the world. They need only – it was argued – to supply the market with manufactured goods, and they will draw from all over the surface of the earth the food they cannot grow themselves, as well as the raw materials they need for their manufactures. The steadily increasing speed of trans-oceanic communications and the steadily increasing facilities of shipping have contributed to enforce the above impression. If we take the enthusiastic pictures of international traffic, drawn in such a masterly way by Neumann Spallart – the statistician and almost the poet of the world-trade – we are inclined indeed to fall into ecstasy before the results achieved. 'Why shall we grow corn, rear oxen and sheep, and cultivate orchards, go through the painful work of the labourer and the farmer, and anxiously watch the sky in fear of a bad crop, when we can get, with much less pain, mountains of corn from India, America, Hungary, or Russia, meat from New Zealand, vegetables from the Azores, apples from Canada, grapes from Malaga, and so on?' exclaim the West Europeans. 'Already now,' they say, 'our food consists, even in modest households, of produce gathered from all over the globe. Our cloth is made out of fibres grown and wool sheared in all parts of the world. The prairies of America and Australia; the mountains and steppes of Asia; the frozen wildernesses of the Arctic regions; the deserts of Africa and the depths of the oceans; the tropics and the lands of the midnight sun are our tributaries. All races of men contribute their share in supplying us with our staple food and luxuries, with plain clothing and fancy dress, while we are sending them in exchange the produce of our higher intelligence, our technical knowledge, our powerful industrial and commercial organising capacities! Is it not a grand sight, this busy and intricate exchange of produce all over the earth which has suddenly grown up within a few years?'

Grand it may be, but is it not a mere nightmare? Is it necessary? At what cost has it been obtained, and how long will it last?

Let us turn a hundred years back. France lay bleeding at the end of the Napoleonic wars. Her young industry, which had begun to grow by the end of the eighteenth century, was crushed down. Germany, Italy were powerless in the industrial field. The armies of the great Republic had struck a mortal blow to serfdom on the Continent; but with the return of reaction efforts were made to revive the decaying institution, and serfdom meant no industry worth speaking of. The terrible wars between France and England, which wars are often explained by merely political causes, had a much deeper meaning – an economical meaning. They were wars for the supremacy

[28]

on the world market, wars against French industry and commerce, supported by a strong navy which France had begun to build – and Britain won the battle. She became supreme on the seas. Bordeaux was no more a rival to London; as to the French industries, they seemed to be killed in the bud. And, aided by the powerful impulse given to natural sciences and technology by a great era of inventions, finding no serious competitors in Europe, Britain began to develop her manufactures. To produce on a large scale in immense quantities became the watchword. The necessary human forces were at hand in the peasantry, partly driven by force from the land, partly attracted to the cities by high wages. The necessary machinery was created, and the British production of manufactured goods went on at a gigantic pace. In the course of less than seventy years – from 1810 to 1878 – the output of coal grew from 10 to 133,000,000 tons; the imports of raw materials rose from 30 to 380,000,000 tons; and the exports of manufactured goods from 46 to 200,000,000 pounds. The tonnage of the commercial fleet was nearly trebled. Fifteen thousand miles of railways were built.

It is useless to repeat now at what a cost the above results were achieved. The terrible revelations of the parliamentary commissions of 1840–2 as to the atrocious condition of the manufacturing classes, the tales of 'cleared estates', and kidnapped children are still fresh in the memory. They will remain standing monuments for showing by what means the great industry was implanted in this country. But the accumulation of wealth in the hands of the privileged classes was going on at a speed never dreamed of before. The incredible riches which now astonish the foreigner in the private houses of England were accumulated during that period; the exceedingly expensive standard of life which makes a person considered rich on the Continent appear as only of modest means in Britain was introduced during that time. The taxed property alone doubled during the last thirty years of the above period, while during the same years (1810–78) no less than £1,112,000,000 – nearly £2,000,000,000 by this time – was invested by English capitalists either in foreign industries or in foreign loans.

[29]

But the monopoly of industrial production could not remain with England for ever. Neither industrial knowledge nor enterprise could be kept for ever as a privilege of these islands. Necessarily, fatally, they began to cross the Channel and spread over the Continent. The Great Revolution had created in France a numerous class of peasant proprietors, who enjoyed nearly half a century of a comparative well-being, or, at least, of a guaranteed labour. The ranks of homeless town workers increased slowly. But the middle-class revolution of 1789-93 had already made a distinction between the peasant householders and the village *prolétaires*, and, by favouring the former to the detriment of the latter, it compelled the labourers who had no household nor land to abandon their villages, and thus to form the first nucleus of working classes given up to the mercy of manufacturers. Moreover, the peasant-proprietors themselves, after having enjoyed a period of undeniable prosperity, began in their turn to feel the pressure of bad times, and their children were compelled to look for employment in manufactures. Wars and revolution had checked the growth of industry; but it began to grow again during the second half of our century; it developed, it improved; and now, notwithstanding the loss of Alsace, France is no longer the tributary to England for manufactured produce which she was sixty years ago. Today her exports of manufactured goods are valued at nearly one-half of those of Great Britain, and two-thirds of them are textiles; while her imports of the same consist chiefly of the finer sorts of cotton and woollen yarn – partly re-exported as stuffs – and a small quantity of woollen goods. For her own consumption France shows a decided tendency towards becoming entirely a self-supporting country, and for the sale of her manufactured goods she is tending to rely, not on her colonies, but especially on her own wealthy home market.

Germany follows the same lines. During the last fifty years, and especially since the last war, her industry has undergone a thorough reorganisation. Her population having rapidly increased from 40 to 60,000,000, this increment went entirely to increase the urban population – without taking hands from agriculture – and in the cities it went to increase the population

[30]

engaged in industry. Her industrial machinery has been thoroughly improved, and her new-born manufacturers are supplied now with a machinery which mostly represents the last word of technical progress. She has plenty of workmen and technologists endowed with a superior technical and scientific education; and in an army of learned chemists, physicists and engineers her industry has a most powerful and intelligent aid, both for directly improving it and for spreading in the country serious scientific and technical knowledge. As a whole, Germany offers now the spectacle of a nation in a period of *Aufschwung*, of a sudden development, with all the forces of a new start in every domain of life. Fifty years ago she was a customer to England. Now she is already a competitor in the European and Asiatic markets, and at the present speedy rate of growth of her industries, her competition will soon be felt even more acutely than it is already felt.

At the same time the wave of industrial production, after having had its origin in the north-west of Europe, spreads towards the east and south-east, always covering a wider circle. And, in proportion as it advances east, and penetrates into younger countries, it implants there all the improvements due to a century of mechanical and chemical inventions; it borrows from science all the help that science can give to industry; and it finds populations eager to grasp the last results of modern knowledge. The new manufactures of Germany begin where Manchester arrived after a century of experiments and gropings; and Russia begins where Manchester and Saxony have now reached. Russia, in her turn, tries to emancipate herself from her dependency upon Western Europe, and rapidly begins to manufacture all those goods she formerly used to import, either from Britain or from Germany.

Protective duties may, perhaps, sometimes help the birth of new industries: always at the expense of some other growing industries, and always checking the improvement of those which already exist; but the decentralisation of manufactures goes on with or without protective duties – I should even say, notwithstanding the protective duties. Austria, Hungary and Italy follow the same lines – they develop their home industries

[31]

– and even Spain and Servia are going to join the family of manufacturing nations. Nay, even India, even Brazil and Mexico, supported by English, French, and German capital and knowledge, begin to start home industries on their respective soils. Finally, a terrible competitor to all European manufacturing countries has grown up of late in the United States. In proportion as technical education spreads more and more widely, manufactures grow in the States; and they do grow at such a speed – an American speed – that in a very few years the now neutral markets will be invaded by American goods.

The monopoly of the first comers on the industrial field has ceased to exist. And it will exist no more, whatever may be the spasmodic efforts made to return to a state of things already belonging to the domain of history. New ways, new issues must be looked for: the past *has* lived, and it will live no more.

The chief reason for the successes of Germany in the industrial field is the same as it is for the United States. Both countries have only lately entered the industrial phase of their development, and they have entered it with all the energy of youth. Both countries enjoy a widely-spread scientifically-technical – or, at least, concrete scientific – education. In both countries manufactories are built according to the newest and best models which have been worked out elsewhere; and both countries are in a period of awakening in all branches of activity – literature and science, industry and commerce. They enter now on the same phase in which Great Britain was in the first half of the nineteenth century, when British workers took such a large part in the invention of the wonderful modern machinery.

We have simply before us a fact of *the consecutive development of nations.* And instead of decrying or opposing it, it would be much better to see whether the two pioneers of the great industry – Britain and France – cannot take a new initiative and do something new again; whether an issue for the creative genius of these two nations must not be sought for in a new direction – namely, the utilisation of both the land and the industrial powers of man for securing well-being to the whole nation instead of to the few.

[32]

Volumes have been written about the crisis of 1886-7, a crisis which, to use the words of the Parliamentary Commission, lasted since 1875, with but 'a short period of prosperity enjoyed by certain branches of trade in the years 1880 to 1883', and a crisis, I shall add, which extended over all the chief manufacturing countries of the world. All possible causes of the crisis have been examined; but whatever the cacophony of conclusions arrived at, all unanimously agreed upon one, namely, that of the Parliamentary Commission, which could be summed up as follows: 'The manufacturing countries do not find such customers as would enable them to realise high profits.' Profits being the basis of capitalist industry, low profits explain all ulterior consequences.

Low profits induce the employers to reduce the wages, or the number of workers, or the number of days of employment during the week, or eventually compel them to resort to the manufacture of lower kinds of goods, which, as a rule, are paid worse than the higher sorts. As Adam Smith said, low profits ultimately mean a reduction of wages, and low wages mean a reduced consumption by the worker. Low profits mean also a somewhat reduced consumption by the employer; and both together mean lower profits and reduced consumption with that immense class of middlemen which has grown up in manfacturing countries, and that, again, means a further reduction of profits for the employers.

A country which manufactures to a great extent for export, and therefore lives to a considerable amount on the profits derived from her foreign trade, stands very much in the same position as Switzerland, which lives to a great extent on the profits derived from the foreigners who visit her lakes and glaciers. A good 'season' means an influx of from £1,000,000 to £2,000,000 of money imported by the tourists, and a bad 'season' has the effects of a bad crop in an agricultural country: a general impoverishment follows. So it is also with a country which manufactures for export. If the 'season' is bad, and the exported goods cannot be sold abroad for twice their value at home, the country which lives chiefly on these bargains suffers. Low profits for the inn-keepers of the Alps mean narrowed circumstances in large parts of Switzerland; and low profits for the Lancashire and Scotch manufacturers, and the wholesale exporters, mean narrowed circumstances in Great Britain. The cause is the same in both cases.

For many decades past we had not seen such a cheapness of wheat and manufactured goods as we saw in 1883–4, and yet in 1886 the country was suffering from a terrible crisis. People said, of course, that the cause of the crisis was over-production. But over-production is a word utterly devoid of sense if it does not mean that those who are in need of all kinds of produce have not the means for buying them with their low wages. Nobody would dare to affirm that there is too much furniture in the crippled cottages, too many bedsteads and bedclothes in the workmen's dwellings, too many lamps burning in the huts, and too much cloth on the shoulders, not only of those who used to sleep (in 1886) in Trafalgar Square between two newspapers, but even in those households where a silk hat makes a part of the Sunday dress. And nobody will dare to affirm that there is too much food in the homes of those agricultural labourers who earn twelve shillings a week, or of those women who earn from fivepence to sixpence a day in the clothing trade and other small industries which swarm in the outskirts of all great cities. Over-production means merely and simply a want of purchasing powers amidst the workers. And the same want of purchasing powers of the workers was felt everywhere on the Continent during the years 1885–7.

After the bad years were over, a sudden revival of international trade took place; and, as the British exports rose in fours years (1886–90) by nearly 24 per cent, it began to be said that there was no reason for being alarmed by foreign competition; that the decline of exports in 1885–7 was only temporary, and general in Europe; and that England, now as of old, fully maintained her dominant position in the international trade. It is certainly true that if we consider exclusively the money value of the exports for the years 1876–95, we see no permanent decline, we notice only fluctuations. British exports, like commerce altogether, seem to show a certain periodicity.

This periodicity being a fact, Mr Giffen could make light in

[34]

1886 of 'German competition' by showing that exports from the United Kingdom had not decreased. It can even be said that, per head of population, they had remained unchanged until 1904, undergoing only the usual ups and downs. However, when we come to consider the *quantities* exported, and compare them with the *money values* of the experts, even Mr Giffen had to acknowledge that the prices of 1883 were so low in comparison with those of 1873 that in order to reach the same money value the United Kingdom would have had to export 4 pieces of cotton instead of 3, and 8 or 10 tons of metallic goods instead of 6.

We thus see that while the total value of the exports from the United Kingdom, in proportion to its growing population, remains, broadly speaking, unaltered for the last thirty years, the high prices which could be got for the exports thirty years ago, and with them the high profits, are gone. And no amount of arithmetical calculations will persuade the British manufacturers that such is not the case. They know perfectly well that the home markets grow continually overstocked; that the best foreign markets are escaping; and that in the neutral markets Britain is being undersold. This is the unavoidable consequence of the development of manufactures all over the world.

Great hopes were laid, some time ago, in Australia as a market for British goods; but Australia will soon do what Canada already does. She will manufacture. And the colonial exhibitions, by showing to the 'colonists' what they are able to do, and how they must do, are only accelerating the day when each colony *farà da sé* in her turn. Canada and India already impose protective duties on British goods. As to the much-spoken-of markets on the Congo, and Mr Stanley's calculations and promises of a trade amounting to £26,000,000 a year if the Lancashire people supply the Africans with loin-cloths, such promises belong to the same category of fancies as the famous nightcaps of the Chinese which were to enrich England after the first Chinese war. The Chinese prefer their own home-made nightcaps; and as to the Congo people, four countries at least are already competing for supplying them

[35]

with their poor dress: Britain, Germany, the United States and, last but not least, India.

There was a time when this country had almost the monopoly in the cotton industries; but already in 1880 she possessed only 55 per cent of all the spindles at work in Europe, the United States and India and a little more than one-half of the looms. In 1893 the proportion was further reduced to 49 per cent of the spindles, and now the United Kingdom has only 41 per cent of all the spindles. It was thus losing ground while the others were winning. And the fact is quite natural: it might have been foreseen. There is no reason why Britain should always be the great cotton manufactory of the world, when raw cotton has to be imported into this country as elsewhere. It was quite natural that France, Germany, Italy, Russia, India, Japan, the United States, and even Mexico and Brazil, should begin to spin their own yarns and to weave their own cotton stuffs. But the appearance of the cotton industry in a country, or, in fact, of any textile industry, unavoidably becomes the starting-point for the growth of a series of other industries; chemical and mechanical works, metallurgy and mining feel at once the impetus given by a new want. The whole of the home industries, as also technical education altogether, *must* improve in order to satisfy that want as soon as it has been felt.

What has happened with regard to cottons is going on also with regard to other industries. Great Britain, which stood in 1880 at the head of the list of countries producing pig-iron, came in 1904 the third in the same list, which was headed by the United States and Germany; while Russia, which occupied the seventh place in 1880, comes now fourth, after Great Britain. Britain and Belgium have no longer the monopoly of the woollen trade. Immense factories at Verviers are silent; the Belgian weavers are misery-stricken, while Germany yearly increases her production of woollens, and exports nine times more woollens than Belgium. Austria has her own woollens and exports them; Riga, Lodz and Moscow supply Russia with fine woollen cloths; and the growth of the woollen industry in each of the last-named countries calls into existence hundreds of connected trades.

[36]

For many years France has had the monopoly of the silk trade. Silkworms being reared in Southern France, it was quite natural that Lyons should grow into a centre for the manufacture of silks. Spinning, domestic weaving, and dyeing works developed to a great extent. But eventually the industry took such an extension that home supplies of raw silk became insufficient, and raw silk was imported from Italy, Spain and Southern Austria, Asia Minor, the Caucasus and Japan, to the amount of from £9,000,000 to £11,000,000 in 1875 and 1876, while France had only £800,000 worth of her own silk. Thousands of peasant boys and girls were attracted by high wages to Lyons and the neighbouring district; the industry was prosperous.

However, by-and-by new centres of silk trade grew up at Basel and in the peasant houses round Zürich. French emigrants imported the trade into Switzerland, and it developed there, especially after the civil war of 1871. Then the Caucasus administration invited French workmen and women from Lyons and Marseilles to teach the Georgians and the Russians the best means of rearing the silkworm, as well as the whole of the silk trade; and Stavropol became a new centre for silk-weaving. Austria and the United States did the same; and what are now the results?

During the years 1872–81 Switzerland more than doubled the produce of her silk industry; Italy and Germany increased it by one-third; and the Lyons region, which formerly manufactured to the value of 454 million francs a year, showed in 1887 a return of only 378 millions. And it is reckoned by French specialists that at present no less than one-third of the silk stuffs used in France are imported from Zürich, Crefeld and Barmen. Nay, even Italy, which has now 191,000 pesons engaged in the industry, sends her silks to France and competes with Lyons.

Like examples could be produced by the score. Greenock no longer supplies Russia with sugar, because Russia has plenty of her own at the same price as it sells at in England. The watch trade is no more a speciality of Switzerland: watches are now made everywhere. India extracts from her 90 collieries two-thirds of her annual consumption of coal. The chemical trade which grew up on the banks of the Clyde and Tyne, owing to the special advantages offered for the import of Spanish pyrites and the agglomeration of such a variety of industries along the two estuaries, is now in decay. Spain, with the help of English capital, is beginning to utilise her own pyrites for herself; and Germany has become a great centre for the manufacture of sulphuric acid and soda – nay, she already complains about over-production.

But enough! I have before me so many figures, all telling the same tale, that examples could be multiplied at will. It is time to conclude, and, for every unprejudiced mind, the conclusion is self-evident. Industries of all kinds decentralise and are scattered all over the globe; and everywhere a variety, an integrated variety, of trades grows, instead of specialisation. Such are the prominent features of the times we live in. Each nation becomes in its turn a manufacturing nation; and the time is not far off when each nation of Europe, as well as the United States, and even the most backward nations of Asia and America, will themselves manufacture nearly everything they are in need of. Wars and several accidental causes may check for some time the scattering of industries: they will not stop it; it is unavoidable. For each new-comer the first steps only are difficult. But, as soon as any industry has taken firm root, it calls into existence hundreds of other trades; and as soon as the first steps have been made, and the first obstacles have been overcome, the industrial growth goes on at an accelerated rate.

The fact is so well felt, if not understood, that the race for colonies has become the distinctive feature of the last twenty years. Each nation will have her own colonies. But colonies will not help. There is not a second India in the world, and the old conditions will be repeated no more. Nay, some of the British colonies already threaten to become serious competitors with their mother country; others, like Australia, will not fail to follow the same lines. As to the yet neutral markets, China will never be a serious customer to Europe: she can produce much cheaper at home; and when she begins to feel

[38]

a need for goods of European patterns, she will reproduce them herself. Woe to Europe, if on the day that the steam engine invades China she is still relying on foreign customers! As to the African half-savages, their misery is no foundation for the well-being of a civilised nation.

Progress must be looked for in another direction. *It is in producing for home use.* The customers for the Lancashire cottons and the Sheffield cutlery, the Lyons silks and the Hunparian flour-mills, are not in India, nor in Africa. The true consumers of the produce of our factories must be our own populations. And they *can* be that, once we organise our economical life so that they might issue from their present destitution. No use to send floating shops to New Guinea with British or German millinery, when there are plenty of would-be customers for British millinery in these very islands, and for German goods in Germany. Instead of worrying our brains by schemes for getting customers abroad, it would be better to try to answer the following questions: Why the British worker, whose industrial capacities are so highly praised in political speeches; why the Scotch crofter and the Irish peasant, whose obstinate labours in creating new productive soil out of peat bogs are occasionally so much spoken of, are no customers to the Lancashire weavers, the Sheffield cutlers and the Northumbrian and Welsh pitmen? Why the Lyons weavers not only do not wear silks, but sometimes have no food in their attics? Why the Russian peasants sell their corn, and for four, six, and sometimes eight months every year are compelled to mix bark and auroch grass to a handful of flour for baking their bread? Why famines are so common amidst the growers of wheat and rice in India?

Under the present conditions of division into capitalists and labourers, into property-holders and masses living on uncertain wages, the spreading of industries over new fields is accompanied by the very same horrible facts of pitiless oppression, massacre of children, pauperism, and insecurity of life. The Russian Fabrics Inspectors' Reports, the Reports of the Plauen Handelskammer, the Italian inquests, and the reports about the growing industries of India and Japan are full of the same

[39]

revelations as the Reports of the Parliamentary Commissions of 1840 to 1842, or the modern revelations with regard to the 'sweating system' at Whitechapel and Glasgow, London pauperism, and York unemployment. The Capital and Labour problem is thus universalised; but, at the same time, it is also simplified. To return to a state of affairs where corn is grown, and manufactured goods are fabricated, *for the use of those very people who grow and produce them* – such will be, no doubt, the problem to be solved during the next coming years of European history. Each region will become its own producer and its own consumer of manufactured goods. But that unavoidably implies that, at the same time, it will be its own producer and consumer of agricultural produce; and that is precisely what I am going to discuss next.

EDITOR'S APPENDIX

Kropotkin's arguments, though they will surely evoke a response from the student of Britain's chronic balance-of-payments crisis, deliberately contradict the conventional wisdom of economics as enunciated both in his day and ours. The principle of comparative costs implies that any country will concentrate its production on those goods in which it has the greatest relative advantage over other countries and will obtain other goods by exchange, and that consequently a capital-abundant country like Switzerland will produce capital goods like machinery, a labour-abundant country like Japan will produce goods with a high labour content like textiles, and a land-abundant country like Australia will produce goods like wool, requiring large areas of land. That this is all for the best is explained by the argument that this international division of labour results in a country getting otherwise unobtainable goods, getting more of them, and getting them more cheaply, and that in consequence total production will increase cumulatively.

Kropotkin rejected this approach, declaring that *integration* rather than *division* of labour is the characteristic of the future economy. He was addressing himself primarily to a British audience which assumed that Britain was the workshop of the world, and that for ever more the world would depend on textiles from Lancashire, coal from Newcastle, and ships from the Clyde. In an age when the word 'textiles' brings to mind Hong Kong, 'fuel' means various sheikdoms in the Middle East, and 'shipping' reminds us that the European country producing the biggest tonnage is Spain, we may be more ready to question traditional assumptions.

In 1938 the United Kingdom and Germany were the world's leading exporters, each with about 22 per cent by value of manufactured goods exported. Today the United Kingdom share is about 10 per cent. J. M. Livingstone emphasises that this is not simply the effect of the Second World War on the economy: 'In every year, except 1935, Britain had a deficit on current account, and this had to be met by accepting increasing indebtedness and the gradual liquidation of overseas assets. The war accelerated the process, but there is no doubt that the British economy would eventually have found itself in much the same position as it did in the early 1940s. The war merely brought the crisis forward by a decade or two.'[1]

[41]

The United Kingdom is in fact in a very vulnerable position. It has less than 2 per cent of the world's population, and this is likely to fall to about 1 per cent by the end of the century, but it takes up about 15 per cent of raw material imports. Dr Livingstone remarks that 'Britain, lacking virtually all the major raw materials save coal, lives by trade. Her only hope of making a living is an industrial economy based on the import of food and raw materials and the export of manufactured goods. In the past this has proved an exceedingly successful approach, affording the British people a standard of living in the top 10 per cent of all mankind.'[2] But he goes on to note that:

'One of the more ominous developments of the 1960s for British overseas trade has been the change in the content of imports from the traditional food and raw-material items, to semi-finished products and even fully manufactured goods. In part, of course, this may represent a lowering of tariff duties as the world moves towards freer trade. But it also suggests that the British economy is not competitive in that very sector on whose exports her livelihood depends.'[3]

At the same time, the long-term crisis was masked by the movement in the terms of trade for export prices to rise, while import prices fell, to the detriment of those countries whose economy was dominated by the export of raw materials: one of the reasons for the trend of the rich nations to get richer while the poor ones get poorer.

The response of the British economy to this situation has contradicted Kropotkin. Both capitalists and governments have put their faith in the giant corporations and multi-national companies. (By 1968 there were more companies than countries with incomes greater than the Gross National Product of the Irish Republic.) The Labour government in Britain set up the Industrial Reorganisation Corporation to promote mergers precisely because, as Graham Turner put it, its members 'believed that it was meaningless to speak of the permanent independence of British industry and that the best hope was to fatten up British companies so that they might wield effective influence in the international mergers of the future'.[4] The British government's decision to enter the European Common Market was determined by its faith in those well-known 'economies of scale' and by the thought that a potential 'domestic' market of 250 million is a more appetising proposition than one of 50 million. 'It is possible, for example, to foresee in an industry like car production that Europe might be dominated by three or four huge firms planning production not by the hundred thousand, but by the million.'⁵ The trouble is, of course, that every car manufacturer in Europe is licking his lips over the same prospect, while Britain is already a net importer of cars.

The ghost of Kropotkin would point to the existence of a thriving Australian car industry (an American subsidiary, admittedly) or to the Indian car industry (based on obsolescent British machine tools and die castings, but bringing the inestimable advantage of locally available spares), to illustrate his prediction of production for a *local* market. He might, with more relevance, point to the fact that the output of the car industry depends upon artificial stimulation of demand and on artificial obsolescence. Doubling the useful life of a vehicle would ruin the industry because it would cancel out the assumed advantages of widening the potential market. Henry Ford nearly bankrupted his firm by his insistence on continuing production of his Model T which 'any hick up a dirt road could keep running'.

The motor industry, Britain's largest earner of foreign exchange through the export of manufactured goods, is the archetypical example of an industry depending on huge markets for the economies of scale. It is also a pre-eminent example of the kind of industry which is difficult to imagine surviving into the twenty-first century:

Its demands on non-renewable resources are fantastic; vast quantities of energy and of water are absorbed in its manufacture; provision for it, in roads, in fossil fuels and human lives, is exorbitant; it is a major polluter. Sir Herbert Manzoni, the late City Engineer of Birmingham (in which capacity he carved up that city to keep the traffic flowing), remarked that 'it is probably the most wasteful and uneconomic contrivance which has yet appeared among our personal possessions. The average passenger-load of motor cars in our streets is certainly less than two persons, and in terms of transportable load some 400 cubic feet of vehicle weighing over 1 ton is used to convey 4 cubic feet of humanity weighing about 2 hundredweight, the ratio being about 10 to 1 in weight and 100 to 1 in bulk. The economic implication of this situation is ridiculous and I cannot believe it to be permanent.'⁶ Kropotkin, who defined economics as 'a science devoted to the study of the needs of men and of the means of satisfying them with the least possible waste of energy', would have been dumbfounded by the profligate waste of resources in our mass-market industries. His only question (and ours) would be: 'How long can it last?'

Some contemporary observers see Kropotkin's world-wide distribution of industry coming true simply through capital's search for cheap labour:

'As wages rise in the rich countries, pushing up the manufacturer's costs, the industries on which these countries built their technological structure – textiles, agriculture, iron- and steel-making, and ship-building among them – are gradually being transferred to the poorer countries where manufacturers can pay their staff lower wages. The mass-production industries, such as cars, plastics and washing machines, will be the next to go. Moreover, the search for fuels and materials is spreading into the hitherto unexplored or unexploited parts of the world. As the rich nations deplete or exhaust their reserves, the developing countries that possess them in plenty will command a better bargaining position as supplies of raw materials. This of itself will enforce a new relationship between the two.'[7]

The last point (made by the industrial editor of *New Scientist*) is underlined by a remark of E. F. Schumacher:

'It is not realistic to treat the world as a unit. Fuel resources are very unevenly distributed, and any shortage of supplies, no matter how slight, would immediately divide the world into "haves" and "have nots" along entirely novel lines. The specially favoured areas, such as the Middle East and North Africa, would attract envious attention on a scale scarcely imaginable today, while some high consumption areas, such as Western Europe and Japan, would move into the unenviable position of residuary legatees.'[8]

Or (he might have added) would intensify their policies of economic imperialism. Dr Schumacher is well known as the originator of the concept of 'intermediate' or 'appropriate' technology, a notion which evaded the governments, advisers, aiders and traders of most of the non-industrial countries for a quarter of a century after the Second World War. The rulers of the poor and newly independent countries were bent on developing high-technology, capital-intensive industries, playing into the hands of the exporters of capital goods, while the actual needs of the people were for simple, labour-intensive industries. (This is, of course, the message Gandhi gave to India, where it was totally ignored by his heirs except for those associated with the Bhoodan movement of Vinoba Bhave and Jayaprakash Narayan, and the most important message that Mao gave to China or that Julius Nyerere has attempted to bring to Tanzania.)

[44]

Dr Schumacher identified the economic needs of the poor countries thus:

'*First*, that workplaces have to be created in the areas where the people are living now, and not primarily in metropolitan areas into which they tend to migrate.

'*Second*, that these workplaces must be, on average, cheap enough to be created in large numbers without this calling for an unattainable level of capital formation and imports.

'*Third*, that the production methods employed must be relatively simple, so that the demands for high skills are minimised, not only in the production process itself but also in matters of organisation, raw-material supply, financing, marketing, and so forth.

'*Fourth*, that production should be mainly from local materials and mainly for local use.'[9]

He observed that these four requirements can be met only if there is a 'regional' approach to development, and if there is a conscious effort to develop and apply an 'intermediate' technology. When he started the Intermediate Technology Development Group, the kind of request that the Group received from Third World countries was: 'Some twenty years ago there existed a bit of equipment which one could purchase for £20 to do a particular job. Now it costs £2,000 and is fully automated and we cannot afford to buy it. Can you help us?' And he comments: 'These are the requirements of the poor people for whom nobody really cares. The powerful people, who are no longer poor are more interested in nuclear reactors, huge dams, steel works.'[10]

His colleague George McRobie told me of the evolution of the Group's ideology. They began by considering the needs of the poor countries. Then they realised the importance of the principles they evolved for the poor areas of the rich world. And finally they came to see that in a world faced (as it is certainly going to be) with a crisis of resources and scarcity, and a superfluity of labour, these principles are of universal application. This is the point where they join hands with the advocates of 'alternative' technology, who seek the satisfaction of human needs through the use of renewable resources: wind-power, water-power, tidal energy, solar energy, human energy, rather than through the reckless exploitation of finite mineral resources.[11]

Editor's Notes

1 J. M. Livingstone, *Britain and the World Economy* (Harmonds-worth, Penguin, 1971)

2 *Ibid.*

3 *Ibid.*

4 Graham Turner, *Business in Britain* (London, Eyre & Spottiswoode, 1969)

5 Livingstone, *op. cit.*

6 Sir Herbert Manzoni at the R.I.B.A., 21 January 1958 (*R.I.B.A. Journal*, March 1958)

7 David Hamilton, *Technology, Man and the Environment* (London, Faber, 1973)

8 E. F. Schumacher, 'The Economics of Permanence', *Resurgence*, Vol. 3, No. 1 (May/June 1970)

9 E. F. Schumacher, 'Social and Economic Problems Calling for the Development of Intermediate Technology' (Intermediate Technology Development Group, 1967)

10 E. F. Schumacher, 'Economic Development and Poverty', *Bulletin* of the I.T.D.G., No. 1 (1966)

11 For an anarchist presentation of the argument, see Lewis Herber, 'Ecology and Revolutionary Thought', *Anarchy*, No. 69 (November 1966) and 'Towards a Liberatory Technology', *Anarchy*, No. 78 (August 1967). Both are reprinted in Murray Bookchin, *Post-Scarcity Anarchism* (Berkeley, Cal., Ramparts Press, 1971; London, Wildwood House, 1974)

Chapter 2

The Possibilities of Agriculture

The industrial and commercial history of the world during the last fifty years has been a history of decentralisation of industry. It was not a mere shifting of the centre of gravity of commerce, such as Europe witnessed in the past, when the commercial hegemony migrated from Italy to Spain, to Holland, and finally to Britain: it had a much deeper meaning, as it excluded the very possibility of commercial or industrial hegemony. It has shown the growth of quite new conditions, and now conditions require new adaptations. To endeavour to revive the past would be useless: a new departure must be taken by civilised nations.

Of course, there will be plenty of voices to argue that the former supremacy of the pioneers must be maintained at any price: all pioneers are in the habit of saying so. It will be suggested that the pioneers must attain such a superiority of technical knowledge and organisation as to enable them to beat all their younger competitors; that force must be resorted to if necessary. But force is reciprocal; and if the god of war always sides with the strongest battalions, those battalions are strongest which fight for new rights against outgrown privileges. As to the honest longing for more technical education – surely let us all have as much of it as possible: it will be a boon for humanity; for humanity, of course – not for a single nation, because knowledge cannot be cultivated for home use only. Knowledge and invention, boldness of thought and enterprise, conquests of genius and improvements of social organisation have become international growths; and no kind of progress – intellectual, industrial or social – can be kept within political boundaries; it crosses the seas, it pierces the mountains; steppes are no obstacle to it. Knowledge and inventive powers are now so thoroughly international that if a simple newspaper paragraph announces tomorrow that the problem of storing force, of printing without inking, or of aerial navigation, has received a practical solution in one country of the world, we may feel sure that within a few weeks the same problem will be solved, almost in the same way, by several inventors of different nationalities. (I leave these lines on purpose as they were written for the first edition of this book.) Continually we learn that the same scientific discovery, or technical invention, has been made within a few days' distance, in countries a thousand miles apart; as if there were a kind of atmosphere which favours the germination of a given idea at a given moment. And such an atmosphere exists: steam print and the common stock of knowledge have created it.

Those who dream of monopolising technical genius are therefore fifty years behind the times. The world – the wide, wide world – is now the true domain of knowledge; and if each nation displays some special capacities in some special branch, the various capacities of different nations compensate one another, and the advantages which could be derived from them would be only temporary. The fine British workmanship in mechanical arts, the American boldness for gigantic enterprise, the French systematic mind, and the German pedagogy, are becoming international capacities. Sir William Armstrong, in his works established in Italy and Japan, has already communicated to Italians and Japanese those capacities for managing huge iron masses which have been nurtured on the Tyne; the uproarious American spirit of enterprise pervades the Old World; the French taste for harmony becomes European taste; and German pedagogy – improved, I dare say – is at home in Russia. So, instead of trying to keep life in the old channels, it would be better to see what the new conditions are, what duties they impose on our generation.

The characters of the new conditions are plain, and their consequences are easy to understand. As the manufacturing nations of West Europe are meeting with steadily growing difficulties in selling their manufactured goods abroad, and get-

[48]

ting food in exchange, they will be compelled to grow their food at home; they will be bound to rely on home customers for their manufactures, and on home producers for their food. And the sooner they do so the better.

Two great objections stand, however, in the way against the general acceptance of such conclusions. We have been taught, both by economists and politicians, that the territories of the West European states are so overcrowded with inhabitants that they cannot grow all the food and raw produce which are necessary for the maintenance of their steadily increasing populations. Therefore the necessity of exporting manufactured goods and of importing food. And we are told, moreover, that even if it were possible to grow in Western Europe all the food necessary for its inhabitants, there would be no advantage in doing so as long as the same food can be got cheaper from abroad. Such are the present teachings and the ideas which are current in society at large. And yet it is easy to prove that both are totally erroneous: plenty of food could be grown on the territories of Western Europe for much more than their present populations, and an immense benefit would be derived from doing so. These are the two points which I have now to discuss.

To begin by taking the most disadvantageous case: is it possible that the soil of Great Britain, which at present yields food for one-third only of its inhabitants, could provide all the necessary amount and variety of food for 41,000,000 human beings when it covers only 56,000,000 acres all told – forests and rocks, marshes and peat-bogs, cities, railways and fields – out of which only 33,000,000 acres are considered as cultivable? The current opinion is, that it by no means can; and that opinion is so inveterate that we even see men of science, who are generally cautious when dealing with current opinions, endorse that opinion without even taking the trouble of verifying it. It is accepted as an axiom. And yet, as soon as we try to find out any argument in its favour, we discover that it has not the slightest foundation, either in facts or in judgement based upon well-known facts.

Let us take, for instance, J. B. Lawes's estimates of crops

D

which were published every year in *The Times*. In his estimate of the year 1887 he made the remark that during the eight harvest years 1853–60 'nearly three-fourths of the aggregate amount of wheat consumed in the United Kingdom was of home growth, and little more than one-fourth was derived from foreign sources'; but five-and-twenty years later the figures were almost reversed – that is, 'during the eight years 1879–86, little more than one-third has been provided by home crops and nearly two-thirds by imports'. But neither the increase of population by 8,000,000 nor the increase of consumption of wheat by six-tenths of a bushel per head could account for the change. In the years 1853–60 the soil of Britain nourished one inhabitant on every two acres cultivated: why did it require three acres in order to nourish the same inhabitant in 1887? The answer is plain: merely and simply because agriculture had fallen into neglect.

In fact, the area under wheat had been reduced since 1853–60 by a full 1,590,000 acres, and therefore the average crop of the years 1883–6 was below the average crop of 1853–60 by more than 40,000,000 bushels; and this deficit alone represented the food of more than 7,000,000 inhabitants. At the same time the area under barley, oats, beans, and other spring crops had also been reduced by a further 560,000 acres, which, alone, at the low average of 30 bushels per acre, would have represented the cereals necessary to complete the above, for the same 7,000,000 inhabitants. It can thus be said that if the United Kingdom imported cereals for 17,000,000 inhabitants in 1887, instead of for 10,000,000 in 1860, it was simply because more than 2,000,000 acres had gone out of cultivation.

These facts are well known; but usually they are met with the remark that the character of agriculture had been altered: that instead of growing wheat, meat and milk were produced in this country. However, the figures for 1887, compared with the figures for 1860, show that the same downward movement took place under the heads of green crops and the like. The area under potatoes was reduced by 280,000 acres; under turnips by 180,000 acres; and although there was an increase under the heads of mangold, carrots, etc., still the aggregate area under all these crops was reduced by a further 330,000 acres. An increase of area was found only for permanent pasture (2,800,000 acres) and grass under rotation (1,600,000 acres); but we should look in vain for a corresponding increase of live-stock. The increase of livestock which took place during tnose twenty-seven years was not sufficient to cover even the area reclaimed from waste land.

Since the year 1887 affairs went, however, from worse to worse. If we take Great Britain alone, we see that in 1885 the area under all corn crops was 8,392,006 acres; that is very small, indeed, in comparison to the area which could have been cultivated; but even that little was further reduced to 7,400,227 acres in 1895. The area under wheat was 2,478,318 acres in 1885 (as against 3,630,300 in 1874); but it dwindled away to 1,417,641 acres in 1895, while the area under the other cereals increased by a trifle only – from 5,198,026 acres to 5,462,184 – the total loss on all cereals being nearly 1,000,000 acres in ten years! Another 5,000,000 people were thus compelled to get their food from abroad.

Did the area under green crops increase correspondingly, as it would have done if it were only the character of agriculture that had changed? Not in the least! This area was further reduced by nearly 500,000 acres (3,521,602 in 1885, 3,225,762 in 1895, and 3,006,000 in 1909–11). Or was the area under clover and grasses in rotation increased in proportion to all these reductions? Alas no! It also was reduced (4,654,173 acres in 1885, 4,729,801, in 1895, and 4,164,000 acres in 1909–11). In short, taking all the land that is under crops in rotation (17,201,490 acres in 1885, 16,166,950 acres in 1895, 14,795,570 only in 1905, and 14,682,550 in 1909–11), we see that within the last twenty-six years another 2,500,000 acres went out of cultivation, without any compensation whatever. It went to increase that already enormous area of more than 17,000,000 acres (17,460,000 in 1909–11) – *more than one-half of the cultivable area* – which goes under the head of 'permanent pasture', and hardly suffices to feed 1 cow on each 3 acres!

Need I say, after that, that quite to the contrary of what we are told about the British agriculturists becoming 'meat makers' instead of 'wheat-growers', no corresponding increase of livestock took place during the last twenty-five years. Far from devoting the land freed from cereals to 'meat-making', the country further reduced its livestock in 1885–95, and began to show a slight increase during the last few years only. True, the number of horses increased; every butcher and greengrocer runs now a horse 'to take orders at the gents' doors' (in Sweden and Switzerland, by the way, they do it by telephone). But if we take the numbers of horses used in agriculture, unbroken, and kept for breeding, we find only small oscillations between 1,408,790 in 1885 and 1,553,000 in 1909. But numbers of horses are imported, as also the oats and a considerable amount of the hay that is required for feeding them. And if the consumption of meat has really increased in this country, it is due to cheap imported meat, not to the meat that would be produced in these islands.

In short, agriculture has not changed its direction, as we are often told; it simply went down in all directions. Land is going out of culture at a perilous rate, while the latest improvements in market-gardening, fruit-growing and poultry-keeping are but a mere trifle if we compare them with what has been done in the same direction in France, Belgium and America.

It must be said that during the last few years there was a slight improvement. The area under all corn crops was slightly increasing, and it fluctuated about 7,000,000 acres, the increase being especially notable for wheat (1,906,000 acres in 1911 as against 1,625,450 in 1907), while the areas under barley and oats were slightly diminished. But with all that, the surface under corn crops is still nearly *one-and-a-half million acres* below what it was in 1885, and nearly *two-and-a-half million acres* below 1874. This represents, let us remember it, the bread-food of *ten million people*.

The cause of this general downward movement is self-evident. It is the desertion, the abandonment of the land. Each crop requiring human labour has had its area reduced; and almost one-half of the agricultural labourers have been sent away since 1861 to reinforce the ranks of the unemployed in the cities, so that far from being over-populated, the fields of Britain are *starved of human labour*, as James Caird used to say. The British nation does not work on her soil; *she is prevented from doing so*; and the would-be economists complain that the soil will not nourish its inhabitants!

I once took a knapsack and went on foot out of London, through Sussex. I had read Léonce de Lavergne's work and expected to find a soil busily cultivated; but neither round London nor still less further south did I see men in the fields. In the Weald I could walk for twenty miles without crossing anything but heath or woodlands, rented as pheasant-shooting grounds to 'London gentlemen', as the labourers said. 'Ungrateful soil' was my first thought; but then I would occasionally come to a farm at the crossing of two roads and see the same soil bearing a rich crop; and my next thought was *tel seigneur, telle terre*, as the French peasants say. Later on I saw the rich fields of the midland counties; but even there I was struck by not perceiving the same busy human labour which I was accustomed to admire on the Belgian and French fields. But I ceased to wonder when I learnt that only 1,383,000 men and women in England and Wales work in the fields, while more than 16,000,000 belong to the 'professional, domestic, indefinite, and unproductive class', as these pitiless statisticians say. One million human beings cannot productively cultivate an area of 33,000,000 acres, unless they can resort to the Bonanza farms' methods of culture.

Again, taking Harrow as the centre of my excursions, I could walk five miles towards London, or turning my back upon it, and I could see nothing east or west but meadow land on which they hardly cropped 2 tons of hay per acre – scarcely enough to keep alive one milch cow on each 2 acres. Man is conspicuous by his absence from those meadows; he rolls them with a heavy roller in the spring; he spreads some manure every two or three years; then he disappears until the time has come to make hay. And that – within ten miles from Charing Cross, close to a city with 5,000,000 inhabitants, supplied with Flemish and Jersey potatoes, French salads and Canadian apples. In the hands of the Paris gardeners, each 1,000 acres situated within the same distance from the city would be cultivated by at least 2,000 human beings, who would get vegetables to the value of from £50 to £300 per acre. But here the acres which only need human hands to become an inexhaustible source of golden crops lie idle, and they say to us, 'Heavy clay!' without even knowing that in the hands of man there are no unfertile soils; that the most fertile soils are not in the prairies of America, nor in the Russian steppes; that they are in the peat-bogs of Ireland, on the sand downs of the northern sea-coast of Franch, on the craggy mountains of the Rhine, where they have been made by man's hands.

The most striking fact is, however, that in some undoubtedly fertile parts of the country things are even in a worse condition. My heart simply aches when I saw the state in which land is kept in South Devon, and when I learned to know what 'permanent pasture' means. Field after field is covered with nothing but grass, 3 inches high, and thistles in profusion. Twenty, thirty such fields can be seen at one glance from the top of every hill; and thousands of acres are in that state, notwithstanding that the grandfathers of the present generation have devoted a formidable amount of labour to the clearing of that land from the stones, to fencing it, roughly draining it, and the like. In every direction I could see abandoned cottages and orchards going to ruin. A whole population has disappeared, and even its last vestiges must disappear if things continue to go on as they have gone. And this takes place in a part of the country endowed with a most fertile soil and possessed of a climate which is certainly more congenial than the climate of Jersey in spring and early summer – a land upon which even the poorest cottages occasionally raise potatoes as early as the first half of May. But how can that land be cultivated when there is nobody to cultivate it? 'We have fields; men go by, but never go in', an old labourer said to me; and so it is in reality.

Such were my impressions of British agriculture twenty years ago. Unfortunately, both the official statistical data and the mass of private evidence published since tend to show that but little improvement took place in the general conditions of agriculture in this country within the last twenty years. Some successful attempts in various new directions have been made in different parts of the country, and I will have the pleasure to mention them further on, the more so as they show what a quite average soil in these islands can give when it is properly treated. But over large areas, especially in the southern counties, the general conditions are even worse than they were twenty years ago.

Altogether one cannot read the mass of review and newspaper articles, and books dealing with British agriculture that have been published lately, without realising that the agricultural depression which began in the 'seventies' and the 'eighties' of the nineteenth century had causes much more deeply seated than the fall in the prices of wheat in consequence of American competition. However, it would lie beyond the scope of this book to enter here into such a discussion.

In Scotland the conditions are equally bad. The population described as 'rural' is in a steady decrease: in 1911 it was already less thân 800,000; and as regards the agricultural labourers, their number has decreased by 42,370 (from 135,970 to 93,600) in the twenty years 1881–1901. *The land goes out of culture*, while the area under 'deer forests' – that is, under hunting grounds established upon what formerly was *arable* land for the amusement of the rich – increases at an appalling rate. No need to say that at the same time the Scotch population is emigrating, and Scotland is depopulated at an appalling speed.

My chief purpose being to show here what *cart and ought to be* obtained from the land under a proper and intelligent treatment, I shall only indicate one of the disadvantages of the systems of husbandry in vogue in this country. Both landlords and farmers gradually came of late to pursue other aims than that of obtaining from the land the greatest amount of produce than can be obtained; and when this problem of a maximum productivity of the land arose before the European nations, and therefore a complete modification of the methods of husbandry was rendered imperative, such a modification was *not* accomplished in this country. While in France, Belgium, Germany and Denmark the agriculturists did their best to meet the effects of American competition by rendering their culture more intensive in all directions, in this country the already antiquated method of reducing the area under corn crops and laying land for grass continues to prevail, although it ought to be evident that mere *grazing* will pay no more, and that some effort in the right direction would increase the returns of the corn crops, as also those of the roots and plants cultivated for industrial purposes. The land continues to go out of culture, while the problem of the day is to render culture more and more intensive.

Many causes have combined to produce that undesirable result. The concentration of land-ownership in the hands of big land-owners; the high profits obtained previously; the development of a class of both landlords and farmers who rely chiefly upon other incomes than those they draw from the land, and for whom farming has thus become a sort of pleasant by-occupation or sport; the rapid development of game reserves for sportsmen, both British and foreign; the absence of men of initiative who would have shown to the nation the necessity of a new departure; the absence of a desire to win the necessary knowledge, and the absence of institutions which could widely spread practical agricultural knowledge and introduce improved seeds and seedlings, as the Experimental Farms of the United States and Canada are doing; the dislike of that spirit of agricultural co-operation to which the Danish farmers owe their succeses, and so on – all these stand in the way of the unavoidable change in the methods of farming, and produce the results of which the British writers on agriculture are complaining.

It may be said, of course, that this opinion strangely contrasts with the well-known superiority of British agriculture. Do we not know, indeed, that British crops average 28 to 30 bushels of wheat per acre, while in France they reach only from 17 to 20 bushels? Does it not stand in all almanacs that Britain gets every year £200,000,000 sterling worth of animal produce – milk, cheese, meat and wool – from her fields? All that is true, and there is no doubt that in many respects British agriculture is superior to that of many other nations. As regards obtaining the greatest amount of produce with the least amount of labour, Britain undoubtedly took the lead until she was superseded by America in the Bonanza farms (now disappeared or rapidly disappearing). Again, as regards the fine breeds of cattle, the splendid state of the meadows and the results obtained in separate farms, there is much to be learned from Britain. But a closer acquaintance with British agriculture as a whole discloses many features of inferiority.

However splendid, a meadow remains a meadow, much inferior in productivity to a cornfield; and the fine breeds of cattle appear to be poor creatures as long as each ox requires 3 acres of land to be fed upon. As regards the crops, certainly one may indulge in some admiration at the average 28 or 30 bushels grown in this country; but when we learn that only 1,600,000 to 1,900,000 acres out of the cultivable 33,000,000 bear such crops, we are quite disappointed. Anyone could obtain like results if he were to put all his manure into one-twentieth part of the area which he possesses. Again, the 28 to 30 bushels no longer appear to us so satisfactory when we learn that without any manuring, merely by means of a good culture, they have obtained at Rothamstead an average of 14 bushels per acre from the same plot of land for forty consecutive years.

If we intend to have a correct appreciation of British agriculture, we must not base it upon what is obtained on a few selected and well-manured plots; we must inquire what is done with the territory, taken as a whole. Now, out of each 1,000 acres of the aggregate territory of England, Wales and Scotland, 435 acres are left under wood, coppice, heath, buildings, and so on. We need not find fault with that division, because it depends very much upon natural causes. In France and Belgium one-third of the territory is in like manner also treated as uncultivable, although portions of it are continually reclaimed and brought under culture. But, leaving aside the 'uncultivable' portion, let us see what is done with the 565 acres out of 1,000 of the 'cultivable' part (32,145,930 acres in Great

Britain in 1910). First of all, it is divided into two parts, and one of them, the largest – 308 acres out of 1,000 – is left under 'permanent pasture', that is, in most cases it is entirely uncultivated. Very little hay is obtained from it, and some cattle are grazed upon it. More than one-half of the cultivable area is thus left without cultivation, and only 257 acres out of each 1,000 acres are under culture. Out of these last, 124 acres are under corn crops, 21 acres under potatoes, 53 acres under green crops, and 73 acres under clover fields and grasses under rotation. And finally, out of the 124 acres given to corn crops, the best 33, and some years only 25 acres (one-fortieth part of the territory, one-twenty-third of the cultivable area), are picked out and sown with wheat. They are well cultivated, well manured, and upon them an average of from 28 to 30 bushels to the acre is obtained; and upon these 25 or 30 acres out of 1,000 the world superiority of British agriculture is based.

The net result of all that is, that on nearly 33,000,000 acres of cultivable land the food is grown for one-third part only of the population (more than two-thirds of the food it consumes is imported), and we may say accordingly that, although nearly two-thirds of the territory is cultivable, British agriculture provides home-grown food for each 125 or 135 inhabitants only per square mile (out of 466). In other words, nearly 3 acres of the *cultivable area* are required to grow the food for each person. Let us then see what is done with the land in France and Belgium.

Now, if we simply compare the average 30 bushels per acre of wheat in Great Britain with the average 19 to 20 bushels grown in France within the last ten years, the comparison is all in favour of these islands; but such averages are of little value because the two systems of agriculture are totally different in the two countries. The Frenchman also has his picked and heavily manured '25 to 30 acres' in the north of France and in Ile-de-France, and from these picked areas he obtains average crops ranging from 30 to 33 bushels. However, he sows with wheat, not only the best picked out areas, but also such fields on the Central Plateau and in Southern France as hardly yield

10, 8 and even 6 bushels to the acre, without irrigation; and these low crops reduce the average for the whole country.

The Frenchman cultivates much that is left here under permanent pasture – and this is what is described as his 'inferiority' in agriculture. In fact, although the proportion between what we have named the 'cultivable area' and the total territory is very much the same in France as it is in Great Britain (624 acres out of each 1,000 acres of the territory), the area under wheat crops is nearly *six times* as great, in proportion, as what it is in Great Britain (182 acres instead of 25 or 30, out of each 1,000 acres): the corn crops altogether cover nearly two-fifths of the cultivable area (375 acres out of 1,000), and large areas are given besides to green crops, industrial crops, vine, fruit and vegetables.

Taking everything into consideration, although the Frenchman keeps less cattle, and especially grazes less sheep than the Briton, he nevertheless obtains from his soil nearly all the food that he and his cattle consume. He imports, in an average year, but one-tenth only of what the nation consumes, and he exports to this country considerable quantities of food produce (£10,000,000 worth), not only from the south, but also, and especially, from the shores of the Channel (Brittany butter and vegetables; fruit and vegetables from the suburbs of Paris, and so on).

The net result is that, although one-third part of the territory is also treated as 'uncultivable', the soil of France yields the food for 170 inhabitants per square mile (out of 188), that is, for 40 persons more, per square mile, than this country.

The comparison with Belgium is even more striking – the more so as the two systems of culture are similar in both countries. To begin with, in Belgium we also find an average crop of over 30 bushels of wheat to the acre; but the area given to wheat is five times as big as in Great Britain, in comparison to the cultivable area, and the cereals cover two-fifths of the land available for culture.

All taken, they grow in Belgium more than 76,000,000 bushels of cereals – that is, fifteen and seven-tenths bushels per acre of the cultivable area – while the corresponding figure for

[59]

Great Britain is only eight and a half bushels; and they keep almost twice as many cattle upon each cultivable acre as is kept in Great Britain.

However, it must not be believed that the soil of Belgium is more fertile than the soil of this country. On the contrary, to use the words of Laveleye, 'only one-half, or less, of the territory offers natural conditions which are favourable for agriculture'; the other half consists of a gravelly soil, or sands, 'the natural sterility of which could be overpowered only by heavy manuring'. Man, not nature, has given to the Belgium soil its present productivity. With this soil and labour, Belgium succeeds in supplying nearly all the food of a population which is denser than that of England and Wales, and numbers 589 inhabitants to the square mile.

If Belgium produces in cereals the food of more than two-thirds of its very dense population, this is already a quite respectable figure; but it must also be said that it exports every year considerable quantities of products of the soil. There is thus no possibility of contesting the fact, that if the soil of Great Britain were cultivated only as the unfertile soil of Belgium is cultivated – notwithstanding all the social obstacles which stand in the way of an intensive culture, in Belgium as elsewhere – a much greater part of the population of these islands would obtain its food from the soil of its own land than is the case nowadays.

Another example of what could be achieved by means of an effort of the nation seconded by its educated classes is given by Denmark. After the war of 1864, which ended in the loss of one of their provinces, the Danes made an effort widely to spread education amongst their peasants, and to develop at the same time an intensive culture of the soil. The result of these efforts is now quite evident.

Everyone knows that it is now Danish butter which rules the prices in the London market, and that this butter is of a high quality, which can only be attained in co-operative creameries with cold storage and certain uniform methods in producing butter. But it is not generally known that the Siberian butter, which is now imported in immense quantities into this country, is also a creation of the Danish co-operators. When they began to export their butter in large quantities, they used to import butter for their own use from the southern parts of the West Siberian provinces of Tobolsk and Tomsk, which are covered with prairies very similar to those of Winnipeg in Canada. At the outset, this butter was of a most inferior quality, as is was made by every peasant household separately. The Danes began therefore to teach co-operation to the Russian peasants, and they were rapidly understood by the intelligent population of this fertile region. The co-operative creameries began to spread with an astounding rapidity, without us knowing for some time wherefrom came this interesting movement. At the present time a steamer loaded with Siberian butter leaves every week one of the Baltic ports and brings to London many thousands of casks of Siberian butter. If I am not wrong, Finland has also joined lately in the same export.

Without going as far as China, I might quote similar examples from elsewhere, especially from Lombardy. But the above will be enough to caution the reader against hasty conclusions as to the impossibility of feeding 46,000,000 people from 78,000,000 acres. They also will enable me to draw the following conclusions: (1) If the soil of the United Kingdom were cultivated only as it *was* forty-five years ago, 24,000,000 people, instead of 17,000,000, could live on home-grown food; and this culture, while giving occupation to an additional 750,000 men, would give nearly 3,000,000 wealthy home customers to the British manufactures. (2) If the cultivable area of the United Kingdom were cultivated as the soil is cultivated *on the average* in Belgium, the United Kingdom would have food for at least 37,000,000 inhabitants; and it might export agricultural produce without ceasing to manufacture, so as freely to supply all the needs of a wealthy population. And finally (3). If the population of this country came to be doubled, all that would be required for producing the food for 90,000,000 inhabitants would be to cultivate the soil as it is cultivated in the best farms of this country, in Lombardy, and in Flanders, and to utilise some meadows, which at present lie almost unproductive, in the same way as the neighbourhoods of the big cities

[61]

in France are utilised for market-gardening. All these are not fancy dreams, but mere realities; nothing but the modest conclusions from what we see round about us, without any allusion to the agriculture of the future.

If we want, however, to know what agriculture *can be*, and what can be grown on a given amount of soil, we must apply for information to such regions as the district of Saffelare in East Flanders, the island of Jersey, or the irrigated meadows of Lombardy. Or else we may apply to the market-gardeners in this country, or in the neighbourhoods of Paris, or in Holland, or to the 'truck farms' in America, and so on.

While science devotes its chief attention to industrial pursuits, a limited number of lovers of nature and a legion of workers whose very names will remain unknown to posterity have created of late a quite new agriculture, as superior to modern farming as modern farming is superior to the old three-field system of our ancestors. Science seldom guided them, and sometimes misguided – as was the case with Liebig's theories, developed to the extreme by his followers, who induced us to treat plants as glass recipients of chemical drugs, and who forgot that the only science capable of dealing with life and growth is physiology, not chemistry. Science seldom has guided them: they proceeded in the empirical way; but, like the cattle-growers who opened new horizons to biology, they have opened a new field of experimental research for the physiology of plants. They have created a totally new agriculture. They smile when we boast about the rotation system, having permitted us to take from the field one crop every year, or four crops each three years, because their ambition is to have 6 and 9 crops from the very same plot of land during the twelve months. They do not understand our talk about good and bad soils, because they make the soil themselves, and make it in such quantities as to be compelled yearly to sell some of it: otherwise it would raise up the level of their gardens by half an inch every year. They aim at cropping, not 5 or 6 tons of grass on the acre, as we do, but from 50 to 100 tons of various vegetables on the same space; not £5 worth of hay but £100 worth of vegetables, of the plainest description, cabbage and carrots, and

[62]

more than £200 worth under intensive horticultural treatments. This is where agriculture is going now.

We know that the dearest of all varieties of our staple food is meat; and those who are not vegetarians, either by persuasion or by necessity, consume on the average 225 pounds of meat – that is, roughly speaking, a little less than the third part of an ox – every year. And we have seen that, even in this country and Belgium, 2 to 3 acres are wanted for keeping one head of horned cattle; so that a community of, say, 1,000,000 inhabitants would have to reserve somewhere about 1,000,000 acres of land for supplying it with meat. But if we go to the farm of M. Goppart – one of the promoters of *ensilage* in France – we shall see him growing, on a drained and well-manured field, no less than an average of 120,000 pounds of corngrass to the acre, which gives 30,000 pounds of dry hay – that is, the food of 1 horned beast per acre. The produce is thus trebled.

As to bootroot, which is used also for feeding cattle, Mr Champion, at Whitby, succeeded, with the help of sewage, in growing 100,000 pounds of beet on each acre, and occasionally 150,000 and 200,000 pounds. He thus grew on each acre the food of, at least, two or three head of cattle. And such crops are not isolated facts; thus, M. Gros, of Autun, succeeds in cropping 600,000 pounds of beet and carrots, which crop would permit him to keep 4 horned cattle on each acre. In fact, crops of 100,000 pounds of beet occur in numbers in the French competitions, and the success depends entirely upon good culture and appropriate manuring. It thus appears that while under ordinary high farming we need 2,000,000 acres, or more, to keep 1,000,000 horned cattle, double that amount could be kept on one-half of that area; and if the density of population required it, the amount of cattle could be doubled again, and the area required to keep it might still be one-half, or even one-third of what it is now.

The above examples are striking enough, and yet those afforded by the market-gardening culture are still more striking. I mean the culture carried on in the neighbourhood of big cities, and more especially the *culture maraîchère* round Paris. In this culture each plant is treated according to its age. The seeds germinate and the seedlings develop their first four leaflets in especially favourable conditions of soil and temperature; then the best seedlings are picked out and transplanted into a bed of fine loam, under a frame or in the open air, where they freely develop their rootlets, and, gathered on a limited space, receive more than the usual care. Only after this preliminary training are they bedded in the open ground, where they grow till ripe. In such a culture the primitive condition of the soil is of little account, because loam is made out of the old forcing beds. The seeds are carefully tried, the seedlings receive proper attention, and there is no fear of drought, because of the variety of crops, the liberal watering with the help of a steam engine, and the stock of plants always kept ready to replace the weakest individuals. Almost each plant is treated individually.

There prevails, however, with regard to market-gardening, a misunderstanding which it would be well to remove. It is generally supposed that what chiefly attracts market-gardening to the great centres of population is the market. It must have been so; and so it may be still, but to some extent only. A great number of the Paris *maraîchers*, even of those who have their gardens within the walls of the city and whose main crop consists of vegetables in season, export the whole of their produce to England. What chiefly attracts the gardener to the great cities is stable manure; and this is not wanted so much for increasing the richness of the soil – one-tenth part of the manure used by the French gardeners would do for that purpose – but for keeping the soil at a certain temperature. Early vegetables pay best, and in order to obtain early produce not only the air but the soil as well must be warmed; and this is done by putting great quantities of properly mixed manure into the soil; its fermentation heats it. But it is evident that with the present development of industrial skill, the heating of the soil could be obtained more economically and more easily by hot-water pipes. Consequently, the French gardeners begin more and more to make use of portable pipes, or *thermosiphons*, provisionally established in the cool frames. This new improvement becomes of general use, and we have the authority of Barral's *Diction-*

[64]

naire d'Agriculture to affirm that it gives excellent results. Under this system, stable manure is used mainly for producing loam.

As to the different degrees of fertility of the soil – always the stumbling-block of those who write about agriculture – the fact is that in market-gardening the soil is always *made*, whatever it originally may have been. Consequently, it is now a usual stipulation of the renting contracts of the Paris *maraîchers* that the gardener may carry away his soil, down to a certain depth, when he quits his tenancy. He himself makes it, and when he moves to another plot he carts his soil away, together with his frames, his water-pipes, and his other belongings.

Let us take, for instance, the orchard – the *marais* – of M. Ponce, the author of a well-known work on the *culture maraîchère*. His orchard covered only two and seven-tenths acres. The outlay for the establishment, including a steam engine for watering purposes, reached £1,136. Eight persons, M. Ponce included, cultivated the orchard and carried the vegetables to the market, for which purpose 1 horse was kept; when returning from Paris they brought in manure, for which £100 was spent every year. Another £100 was spent in rent and taxes. But how to enumerate all that was gathered every year on this plot of less than 3 acres, without filling two pages or more with the most wonderful figures? One must read them in M. Ponce's work, but here are the chief items: More than 20,000 pounds of carrots; more than 20,000 pounds of onions, radishes and other vegetables sold by weight; 6,000 heads of cabbage; 3,000 of cauliflower; 5,000 baskets of tomatoes; 5,000 dozen of choice fruit; and 154,000 heads of salad; in short, a total of 250,000 pounds of vegetables. The soil was made to such an amount out of forcing beds that every year 250 cubic yards of loam had to be sold. Similar examples could be given by the dozen, and the best evidence against any possible exaggeration of the results is the very high rent paid by the gardeners, which reaches in the suburbs of London from £10 to £15 per acre, and in the suburbs of Paris attains as much as £32 per acre. No less than 2,125 acres are cultivated round Paris in that way by 5,000 persons, and thus not only the 2,000,000 Parisians

E

are supplied with vegetables, but the surplus is also sent to London.

The above results are obtained with the help of warm frames, thousands of glass bells, and so on. But even without such costly things, with only 36 yards of frames for seedlings, vegetables are grown *in the open air* to the value of £200 per acre. It is obvious, however, that in such cases the high selling prices of the crops are not due to the high prices fetched by early vegetables in winter; they are entirely due to the high crops of the plainest ones.

Let me add also that all this wonderful culture has entirely developed in the second half of the nineteenth century. Before that, it was quite primitive. But now the Paris gardener not only defies the soil – he would grow the same crops on an ashphalt pavement – he defies climate. His walls, which are built to reflect light and to protect the wall-trees from the northern winds, his wall-tree shades and glass protectors, his frames and *pépinières* have made a real garden, a rich Southern garden, out of the suburbs of Paris. He has given to Paris the 'two degrees less of latitude' after which a French scientific writer was longing; he supplies his city with mountains of grapes and fruit at any season; and in the early spring he inundates and perfumes it with flowers. But he does not only grow articles of luxury. The culture of plain vegetables on a large scale is spreading every year; and the results are so good that there are now practical *maraîchers* who venture to maintain that if all the food, animal and vegetable, necessary for 4,500,000 inhabitants of the departments of Seine and Seine-et-Oise had to be grown on their own territory (3,250 square miles), it could be grown without resorting to any other methods of culture than those already in use – methods already tested on a large scale and proved to be successful.

And yet the Paris gardener is not our ideal of an agriculturist. In the painful work of civilisation he has shown us the way to follow; but the ideal of modern civilisation is elsewhere. He toils, with but a short interruption, from 3 in the morning till late in the night. He knows no leisure; he has no time to live the life of a human being; the commonwealth does not exist

[66]

for him; his world is his garden, more than his family. He cannot be our ideal; neither he nor his system of agriculture. Our ambition is, that he should produce even *more* than he does with *less* labour, and should enjoy all the joys of human life. And this is fully possible.

As a matter of fact, if we put aside those gardeners who chiefly cultivate the so-called *primeurs* – strawberries ripened in January, and the like – if we take only those who grow their crops in the open field, and resort to frames exclusively for the earlier days of the life of the plant, and if we analyse their system, we see that its very essence is, first, to create for the plant a nutritive and porous soil, which contains both the necessary decaying organic matter and the inorganic compounds; and then to keep that soil and the surrounding atmosphere at a temperature and moisture superior to those of the open air. The whole system is summed up in these few words. If the French *maraîcher* spends prodigies of labour, intelligence and imagination in combining different kinds of manure, so as to make them ferment at a given speed, he does so for no purpose but the above: a nourishing soil, and a desired equal temperature and moisture of the air and the soil. All his empirical art is devoted to the achievement of these two aims. But both can also be achieved in another and much easier way. The soil can be *improved* by hand, but it need not be *made* by hand. Any soil, of any desired composition, can be made by machinery. We already have manufacturers of manure, engines for pulverising the phosphorites, and even the granites of the Vosges; and we shall see manufactures of loam as soon as there is a demand for them.

It is obvious that at present, when fraud and adulteration are exercised on such an immense scale in the manufacture of artificial manure, and the manufacture of manure is considered as a chemical process, while it ought to be considered as a physiological one, the gardener prefers to spend an unimaginable amount of labour rather than risk his crop by the use of a pompously labelled and unworthy drug. But that is a social obstacle which depends upon a want of knowledge and a bad social organisation, not upon physical causes.

[67]

Of course, the necessity of creating for the earlier life of the plant a warm soil and atmosphere will always remain, and sixty years ago Léonce de Lavergne foretold that the next step in culture would be to warm the soil. But heating pipes give the same results as the fermenting manures at a much smaller expense of human labour.

It is obvious that now, when the capitalist system makes us pay for everything three or four times its labour value, we often spend about £1 for each square yard of a heated conservatory. But how many middlemen are making fortunes on the wooden sashes imported from Drontheim? If we only could reckon our expenses in labour, we should discover to our amazement that, thanks to the use of machinery, the square yard of a conservatory does not cost more than half a day of human labour; and we will see presently that the Jersey and Guernsey average for cultivating 1 acre under glass is only 3 men working ten hours a day. Therefore the conservatory, which formerly was a luxury, is rapidly entering into the domain of high culture. And we may foresee the day when the glass conservatory will be considered as a necessary appendix to the field, both for the growth of those fruits and vegetables which cannot succeed in the open air, and for the preliminary training of most cultural plants during the earlier stages of their life.

Home-grown fruit is always preferable to the half-ripe produce which is imported from abroad, and the additional work required for keeping a young plant under glass is largely repaid by the incomparable superiority of the crops. As to the question of labour, when we remember the incredible amount of labour which has been spent on the Rhine, and in Switzerland for making the vineyards, their terraces and stone walls, and for carrying the soil up the stony crags, as also the amount of labour which is spent every year for the culture of those vineyards and fruit gardens, we are inclined to ask, which of the two, all taken, requires less of human labour – a vinery (I mean the cold vinery) in a London suburb, or a vineyard on the Rhine, or on Lake Leman? And when we compare the prices realised by the grower of grapes round London (not

[68]

those which are paid in the West End fruit shops, but those received by the grower for his grapes in September and October) with those current in Switzerland or on the Rhine during the same months, we are inclined to maintain that nowhere in Europe, beyond the forty-fifth degree of latitude, are grapes grown at less expense of human labour, both for capital outlay and yearly work, than in the vineries of the London and Brussels suburbs.

At any rate, let us not overrate the productivity of the exporting countries, and let us remember that the vine-growers of Southern Europe drink themselves an abominable *piquette*; that Marseilles fabricates wine for home use out of dry raisins brought from Asia; and that the Normandy peasant who sends his apples to London, drinks real cider only on great festivities. Such a state of things will not last for ever; and the day is not far when we shall be compelled to look to our own resources to provide many of the things which we now import. And we shall not be the worse for that. The resources of science, both in enlarging the circle of our production and in new discoveries, are inexhaustible. And each new branch of activity calls into existence more and more new branches, which steadily increase the power of man over the forces of nature.

If we take all into consideration; if we realise the progress made of late in the gardening culture, and the tendency towards spreading its methods to the open field; if we watch the cultural experiments which are being made now – experiments today and realities tomorrow – and ponder over the resources kept in store by science, we are bound to say that *it is utterly impossible to foresee at the present moment the limits as to the* maximum *number of human beings who could draw their means of subsistence from a given area of land*, or as to what a variety of produce they could advantageously grow in any latitude. Each day widens former limits, and opens new and wide horizons. All we can say now is, that, *even now*, 600 persons could easily live on a square mile; and that, with cultural methods already used on a large scale, 1,000 human beings – not idlers – living on 1,000 acres could easily, without any kind of overwork, obtain from that area a luxurious vegetable and animal food, as well as the flax, wool, silk and hides necessary for their clothing. As to what may be obtained under still more perfect methods – also known but not yet tested on a large scale – it is better to abstain from any forecast: so unexpected are the recent achievements of intensive culture.

We thus see that the over-population fallacy does not stand the very first attempt at submitting it to a closer examination. Those only can be horror-stricken at seeing the population of this country increase by one individual every 1,000 seconds who think of a human being as a mere claimant upon the stock of material wealth of mankind, without being at the same time a contributor to that stock. But we, who see in each new-born babe a future *worker* capable of producing much more than his own share of the common stock – we greet his appearance.

We know that a crowded population is a necessary condition for permitting man to increase the productive powers of his labour. We know that highly productive labour is impossible so long as men are scattered, few in numbers, over wide territories, and are thus unable to combine together for the higher achievements of civilisation. We know what an amount of labour must be spent to scratch the soil with a primitive plough, to spin and weave by hand; and we know also how much less labour it costs to grow the same amount of food and weave the same cloth with the help of modern machinery.

We also see that it is infinitely easier to grow 200,000 pounds of food on 1 acre than to grow them on 10 acres. It is all very well to imagine that wheat grows by itself on the Russian steppes; but those who have seen how the peasant toils in the 'fertile' black earth region will have one desire: that the increase of population may permit the use of the steam digger and gardening culture in the steppes; that it may permit those who are now the beasts of burden of humanity to raise their backs and to become at last men.

We must, however, recognise that there are a few economists fully aware of the above truths. They gladly admit that Western Europe could grow much more food than it does;

but they see no necessity nor advantage in doing so, as long as there are nations which can supply food in exchange for manufactured goods. Let us then examine how far this view is correct.

It is obvious that if we are satisfied with merely stating that it is cheaper to bring wheat from Riga than to grow it in Lincolnshire, the whole question is settled in a moment. But is it so in reality? Is it really cheaper to have food from abroad? And, supposing it is, are we not yet bound to analyse that compound result which we call price, rather than to accept it as a supreme and blind ruler of our actions?

We know, for instance, how French agriculture is burdened by taxation. And yet, if we compare the prices of articles of food in France, which herself grows most of them, with the prices in this country, which imports them, we find no difference in favour of the importing country. On the contrary, the balance is rather in favour of France, and it decidedly was so for wheat until the new protective tariff was introduced. As soon as one goes out of Paris, one finds that every *home produce* is cheaper in France than it is in England, and that the prices decrease further when we go farther east on the Continent.

There is another feature still more unfavourable for this country: namely, the enormous development of the class of middlemen who stand between the importer and the home producer on the one side and the consumer on the other. We have lately heard a good deal about the quite disproportionate part of the prices we pay which goes into the middleman's pockets. We have all heard of the East End clergyman who was compelled to become butcher in order to save his parishioners from the greedy middleman. We read in the papers that many farmers of the midland counties do not realise more than 9d for a pound of butter, while the customer pays from 1s 6d to 1s 8d; and that from 1½d to 2d for the quart of milk is all that the Cheshire farmers can get, while we pay 4d for the adulterated, and 5d for the unadulterated milk. An analysis of the Covent Garden prices and a comparison of the same with retail prices, which is being made from time to time in

[71]

the daily papers, proves that the customer pays for vegetables at the rate of 6d to 1s, and sometimes more, for each penny realised by the grower. But in a country of imported food it *must* be so: the grower who himself sells his own produce disappears from its markets, and in his place appears the middleman. If we move, however, towards the East, and go to Belgium, Germany, and Russia, we find that the cost of living is more and more reduced, so that finally we find that in Russia, which remains still agricultural, wheat costs one-half or two-thirds of its London prices, and meat is sold throughout the provinces at about 10 farthings (kopecks) the pound. And we may therefore hold that it is not yet proved at all that it is cheaper to live on imported food than to grow it ourselves.

But if we analyse *price*, and make a distinction between its different elements, the disadvantage becomes still more apparent. If we compare, for instance, the costs of growing wheat in this country and in Russia, we are told that in the United Kingdom the hundredweight of wheat cannot be grown at less than 8s 7d; while in Russia the costs of production of the same hundredweight are estimated at from 3s 6d to 4s 9d. The difference is enormous, and it would still remain very great even if we admit that there is some exaggeration in the former figure. But why this difference? Are the Russian labourers paid so much less for their work? Their money wages surely are much lower, but the difference is equalised as soon as we reckon their wages in produce. The 12s a week of the British agricultural labourer represents the same amount of wheat in Britain as the 6s a week of the Russian labourer represents in Russia. As to the supposed prodigious fertility of the soil in the Russian prairies, it is a fallacy. Crops of from 16 to 23 bushels per acre are considered good crops in Russia, while the average hardly reaches 13 bushels, even in the corn-exporting parts of the empire. Besides, the amount of labour which is necessary to grow wheat in Russia with no threshing-machines, with a plough dragged by a horse hardly worth the name, with no roads for transport, and so on, is certainly much greater than the amount of labour which is necessary to grow the same amount of wheat in Western

[72]

Europe. The false condition of British rural economy, not the infertility of the soil, is thus the chief cause of the Russian competition.

Twenty-five years have passed since I wrote these lines – the agricultural crisis provoked by the competition of cheap American wheat being at that time at its climax, and, I am sorry to say, I must leave these lines such as they were written. I do not mean, of course, that no adaptation to the new conditions created by the fall in the prices of wheat should have taken place during the last quarter of a century, in the sense of a more intensive culture and a better utilisation of the land. On the contrary, I mention in different parts of this book the progress accomplished of late in the development of separate branches of intensive culture, such as fruit-culture, market-gardening, culture under glass, French gardening, and poultry farming, and I also indicate the different steps taken to promote further improvements, such as better conditions of transport, co-operation among the farmers, and especially the development of small-holdings.

However, after having taken into account all these improvements, one cannot but see with regret that the same regressive movement in British agriculture, which began in the 1870s, continues still; and while more and more of the land that was once under the plough goes out of culture, no corresponding increase in the quantities of livestock is to be seen. And if we consult the mass of books and review articles which have been dealing lately with this subject, we see that all the writers recognise that British agriculture *must* adapt itself to the new conditions by a thorough reform of its general character; and yet the same writers recognise that only a few steps were taken till now in the proper direction, and none of them was taken with a sufficient energy. Society at large remains indifferent to the needs of British agriculture.

It must not be forgotten that the competition of American wheat has made the same havoc in the agriculture of most European countries – especially in France and Belgium; but in the last two countries the adaptations which were necessary to resist the effects of the competition have already taken place

[73]

to a great extent. Both in Belgium and in France the American imports gave a new impetus towards a more intensive utilisation of the soil, and this impetus was strongest in Belgium, where no attempt was made to protect agriculture by an increase of the import duties, as was the case in France. On the contrary, the duties upon imported wheat were abolished in Belgium precisely at the time when the American competition began to be felt – that is, between 1870 and 1880.

Much more ought to be said with regard to American competition, and therefore I must refer the reader to the remarkable series of articles dealing with the whole of the subject which Schaeffle published in 1886. These were written at the time when American competition was something new and made much havoc in English agriculture, causing a fall of from 30 to 50 per cent in the rents of land for agricultural purposes.

It appeared from these works that the fertility of the American soil had been grossly exaggerated, as the masses of wheat which America sent to Europe from its north-western farms were grown on a soil the natural fertility of which is not higher, and often lower, than the average fertility of the unmanured European soil. The Casselton farm in Dakota, with its 20 bushels per acre, was an exception; while the average crop of the chief wheat-growing states in the West was only 11 to 12 bushels. In order to find a fertile soil in America, and crops of from 30 to 40 bushels, one must go to the old Eastern states, where the soil is made by man's hands.

The same applies to the American supplies of meat. Schaeffle pointed out that the great mass of livestock which appeared in the census of cattle in the States was not reared in the prairies, but in the stables of the farms, in the same way as in Europe; as to the prairies, he found on them only one-eleventh part of the American horned cattle, one-fifth of the sheep and one-twenty-first of the pigs. 'Natural fertility' being thus out of question, we must look for social causes; and we have them, for the Western states, in the cheapness of land and a proper organisation of production; and for the Eastern states in the rapid progress of *intensive* high farming.

It is evident that the methods of culture must vary according to different conditions. In the vast prairies of North America, where land could be *bought* from 8s to 40s the acre, and where spaces of from 100 to 150 square miles in one block could be given to wheat culture, special methods of culture were applied and the results were excellent. Land was bought – not rented. In the autumn, whole studs of horses were brought, and the tilling and sowing were done with the aid of formidable ploughs and sowing machines. Then the horses were sent to graze in the mountains; the men were dismissed, and one man, occasionally two or three, remained to winter on the farm. In the spring the owners' agents began to beat the inns for hundreds of miles round, and engaged labourers and tramps, both freely supplied by Europe, for the crop. Battalions of men were marched to the wheat fields, and were camped there; the horses were brought from the mountains, and in a week or two the crop was cut, threshed, winnowed, put in sacks, by specially invented machines, and sent to the next elevator, or directly to the ships which carried it to Europe. Whereupon the men were disbanded again, the horses were sent back to the grazing grounds, or sold, and again only a couple of men remained on the farm.

The crop from each acre was small, but the machinery was so perfected that in this way 300 days of one man's labour produced from 200 to 300 quarters of wheat; in other words – the area of land being of no account – every man produced in one day his yearly bread food (eight and a half bushels of wheat); and taking into account all subsequent labour, it was calculated that the work of 300 men in one single day delivered to the consumer at Chicago the flour that is required for the yearly food of 250 persons. Twelve hours and a half of work are thus required in Chicago to supply one man with his yearly provision of wheat-flour.

Under the special conditions offered in the Far West this certainly was an appropriate method for increasing all of a sudden the wheat supplies of mankind. It answered its purpose when large territories of unoccupied land were opened to enterprise. But it could not answer for ever. Under such a system of culture the soil was soon exhausted, the crop declined, and *intensive* agriculture (which aims at high crops on a limited area) had soon to be resorted to. Such was the case in Iowa in the year 1878. Up till then, Iowa was an emporium for wheat-growing on the lines just indicated. But the soil was already exhausted, and when a disease came the wheat plants had no force to resist it. In a few weeks nearly all the wheat crop, which was expected to beat all previous records, was lost; 8 to 10 bushels per acre of bad wheat were all that could be cropped. The result was that 'mammoth farms' had to be broken up into small farms, and that the Iowa farmers (after a terrible crisis of short duration – everything is rapid in America) took to a more intensive culture. Now, they are not behind France in wheat culture, as they already grow an average of $16\frac{1}{2}$ bushels per acre on an area of more than 2,000,000 acres, and they will soon win ground. Somehow, with the aid of manure and improved methods of farming, they compete admirably with the mammoth farms of the Far West.

In fact, over and over again it was pointed out, by Schaeffle, Semler, Oetken and many other writers, that the force of 'American competition' is not in its mammoth farms, but in the countless small farms upon which wheat is grown in the same way as it is grown in Europe – that is, with manuring – but with a better organised production and facilities for sale, and without being compelled to pay to the landlord a toll of one-third part, or more, of the selling price of each quarter of wheat. However, it was only after I had myself made a tour in the prairies of Manitoba in 1897, and those of Ohio in 1901, that I could realise the full truth of the just-mentioned views. The 15,000,000 to 20,000,000 bushels of wheat, which are exported every year from Manitoba, are grown almost entirely in farms of one or two 'quarter-sections' – that is, of 160 and 320 acres. The ploughing is made in the usual way, and in an immense majority of cases the farmers buy the reaping and binding machines (the 'binders') by associating in groups of four. The threshing machine is rented by the farmer for one or two days, and the farmer carts his wheat to the elevator with his own horses, either to sell it immediately, or to keep it at the elevator if he is in no immediate need of money and hopes to get a higher price in one month or two. In short, in Manitoba one is especially struck with the fact that, even under a system of keen competition, the middle-size farm has completely beaten the old mammoth farm, and that it is not manufacturing wheat on a grand scale which pays best. It is also most interesting to note that thousands and thousands of farmers produce mountains of wheat in the Canadian province of Toronto and in the Eastern states, although the land is not prairie-land at all, and the farms are, as a rule, small.

The force of 'American competition' is thus not in the possibility of having hundreds of acres of wheat in one block. It lies in the ownership of the land, in a system of culture which is appropriate to the character of the country, in a widely developed spirit of association, and finally, in a number of institutions and customs intended to lift the agriculturist and his profession to a high level which is unknown in Europe.

Few books have exercised so pernicious an influence upon the general development of economic thought as Malthus's *Essay on the Principle of Population* exercised for three consecutive generations. It appeared at the right time, like all books which have had any influence at all, and it summed up ideas already current in the minds of the wealth-possessing minority. It was precisely when the ideas of equality and liberty, awakened by the French and American revolutions, were still permeating the minds of the poor, while the richer classes had become tired of their amateur excursions into the same domains, that Malthus came to assert, in reply to Godwin, that no equality is possible; that the poverty of the many is not due to institutions, but is a natural *law*. Population, he wrote, grows too rapidly and the new-comers find no room at the feast of nature; and that law cannot be altered by any change of institutions. He thus gave to the rich a kind of scientific argument against the ideas of equality; and we know that though all dominion is based upon force, force itself begins to totter as soon as it is no longer supported by a firm belief in its own rightfulness. As to the poorer classes – who

[77]

always feel the influence of ideas circulating at a given time amid the wealthier classes – it deprived them of the very hope of improvement; it made them sceptical as to the promises of the social reformers; and to this day the most advanced reformers entertain doubts as to the possibility of satisfying the needs of all; in case there should be a claim for their satisfaction, and a temporary welfare of the labourers resulted in a sudden increase of population.

Science, down to the present day, remains permeated with Malthus's teachings. Political economy continues to base its reasoning upon a tacit admission of the impossibility of rapidly increasing the productive powers of a nation, and of thus giving satisfaction to all wants. This postulate stands, undiscussed, in the background of whatever political economy, classical or socialist, has to say about exchange-value, wages, sale of labour force, rent, exchange and consumption. Political economy never rises above the hypothesis of a *limited and insufficient supply of the necessities of life*; it takes it for granted. And all theories connected with political economy retain the same erroneous principle. Nearly all socialists, too, admit the postulate. Nay, even in biology (so deeply inter-woven now with sociology) we have recently seen the theory of variability of species borrowing a quite unexpected support from its having been connected by Darwin and Wallace with Malthus's fundamental idea, that the natural resources must inevitably fail to supply the means of existence for the rapidly multiplying animals and plants. In short, we may say that the theory of Malthus, by shaping into a pseudo-scientific form the secret desires of the wealth-possessing classes, became the foundation of a whole system of practical philosophy, which permeates the minds of both the educated and uneducated, and reacts, as practical philosophy always does) upon the theoretical philosophy of our century.

True, the formidable growth of the productive powers of man in the industrial field, since he tamed steam and electricity, has somewhat shaken Malthus's doctrine. Industrial wealth *has* grown at a rate which no possible increase of population could attain, and it *can* grow with still greater speed. But agriculture is still considered a stronghold of the Malthusian pseudo-philosophy. The recent achievements of agriculture and horticulture are not sufficiently well known; and while our gardeners defy climate and latitude, acclimatise sub-tropical plants, raise several crops a year instead of one, and themselves make the soil they want for each special culture, the economists nevertheless continue saying that the surface of the soil is limited, and still more its productive powers; they still maintain that a population which should double each thirty years would soon be confronted by a lack of the necessities of life!

A few data to illustrate what *can* be obtained from the soil were given previously. But the deeper one goes into the subject, the more new and striking data does he discover, and the more Malthus's fears appear groundless.

To begin with an instance taken from culture in the open field – namely, that of wheat – we come upon the following interesting fact. While we are so often told that wheat-growing does not pay, and England consequently reduces from year to year the area of its wheat fields, the French peasants steadily increase the area under wheat, and the greatest increase is due to those peasant families which themselves cultivate the land they own. In the course of the nineteenth century they have nearly doubled the area under wheat, as well as the returns from each acre, so as to increase almost fourfold the amount of wheat grown in France.

At the same time, the population has only increased by 41 per cent, so that the ratio of increase of the wheat crop has been six times greater than the ratio of increase of population, although agriculture has been hampered all the time by a series of serious obstacles – taxation, military service, poverty of the peasantry, and even, up to 1884, a severe prohibition of all sorts of association among the peasants.

It must also be remarked that during the same hundred years, and even within the last fifty years, market-gardening, fruit-culture and culture for industrial purposes have immensely developed in France; so that there would be no exaggeration in

[79]

saying that the French obtain now from their soil at least six or seven times more than they obtained a hundred years ago. The 'means of existence' drawn from the soil have thus grown about fifteen times quicker than the population.

But the ratio of progress in agriculture is still better seen from the rise of the standard of requirement as regards cultivation of land. Some thirty years ago the French considered a crop very good when it yielded 22 bushels to the acre; but with the same soil the present requirement is at least 33 bushels, while in the best soils the crop is good only when it yields from 43 to 48 bushes, and occasionally the produce is as much as 55 bushes to the acre.

In fact Professor Grandeau considers it proved that by combining a series of such operations as the selection of seeds, sowing in rows, and proper manuring, the crops can be largely increased over the best present average, while the cost of production can be reduced by 50 per cent by the use of inexpensive machinery; to say nothing of costly machines, like the steam digger, or the pulverisers which make the soil required for each special culture. They are now occasionally resorted to here and there, and they surely will come into general use as soon as humanity feels the need of largely increasing its agricultural produce.

When we bear in mind the very unfavourable conditions in which agriculture stands now all over the world, we must not expect to find considerable progress in its methods realised over wide regions; we must be satisfied with noting the advance accomplished in separate, especially favoured spots, where, for one cause or another, the tribute levied upon the agriculturist has not been so heavy as to stop all possibility of progress.

An illustration of this sort may be taken from the Channel Islands, whose inhabitants have happily not known the blessings of Roman law and landlordism, as they still live under the common law of Normandy. The small island of Jersey, eight miles long and less than six miles wide, still remains a land of open-field culture; but, although it comprises only 28,707 acres, rocks included, it nourishes a population of about two inhabitants to each acre, or 1,300 inhabitants to the square mile, and there is not one writer on agriculture who, after having paid a visit to this island, did not praise the well-being of the Jersey peasants and the admirable results which they obtain in their small farms of from 5 to 20 acres – very often less than 5 acres – by means of a rational and intensive culture.

Most of my readers will probably be astonished to learn that the soil of Jersey, which consists of decomposed granite, with no organic matter in it, is not at all of astonishing fertility, and that its climate, though more sunny than the climate of these isles, offers many drawbacks on account of the small amount of sun-heat during the summer and of the cold winds in spring. But so it is in reality, and at the beginning of the nineteenth century the inhabitants of Jersey lived chiefly on imported food. The successes accomplished lately in Jersey are entirely due to the amount of labour which a dense population is putting in the land; to a system of land-tenure, land-transference and inheritance very different from those which prevail elsewhere; to freedom from state taxation; and to the fact that communal institutions have been maintained, down to quite a recent period, while a number of communal habits and customs of mutual support, derived therefrom, are alive to the present time.

It is well known that for the last thirty years the Jersey peasants and farmers have been growing early potatoes on a great scale, and that in this line they have attained most satisfactory results. Their chief aim being to have the potatoes out as early as possible, when they fetch at the Jersey Weigh-bridge as much as £17 and £20 the ton, the digging out of potatoes begins, in the best sheltered places, as early as the first days of May, or even at the end of April. Quite a system of potato-culture, beginning with the selection of tubers, the arrangements for making them germinate, the selection of properly sheltered and well-situated plots of ground, the choice of proper manure, and ending with the box in which the potatoes germinate and which has so many other useful applications – quite a system of culture has been worked out in the island for that purpose by the collective intelligence of the peasants.

F

Fifty pounds' worth of agricultural produce from each acre of the land is sufficiently good. But the more we study the modern achievements of agriculture, the more we see that the limits of productivity of the soil are not attained, even in Jersey. New horizons are continually unveiled. For the last fifty years science – especially chemistry – and mechanical skill have been widening and extending the industrial powers of man upon organic and inorganic dead matter. Prodigies have been achieved in that direction. Now comes the turn of similar achievements with living plants. Human skill in the treatment of living matter, and science – in its branch dealing with living organisms – step in with the intention of doing for the art of food-growing what mechanical and chemical skill have done in the art of fashioning and shaping metals, wood and the dead fibres of plants. Almost every year brings some new, often unexpected improvement in the art of agriculture, which for so many centuries had been dormant.

While the average potato crop in the country is 6 tons per acre, in Jersey it is nearly twice as big. But Mr Knight, whose name is well known to every horticulturist in this country, has once dug out of his fields no less than 1,284 bushels of potatoes, or 34 tons and 9 hundredweight in weight, on one single acre; and at a recent competition in Minnesota 1,120 bushels, or 30 tons, could be ascertained as having been grown on one acre.

These are undoubtedly extraordinary crops, but quite recently the French Professor Aimé Girard undertook a series of experiments in order to find out the best conditions for growing potatoes in his country. He did not care for show-crops obtained by means of extravagant manuring, but carefully studied all conditions: the best variety, the depth of tilling and planting, the distance between the plants. Then he entered into correspondence with some 350 growers in different parts of France, advised them by letters, and finally induced them to experiment. Strictly following his instructions, several of his correspondents made experiments on a small scale, and they obtained – instead of the 3 tons which they were accustomed to grow – such crops as would correspond to 20 and 36 tons to the acre. Moreover, 90 growers experimented on fields more than one-quarter of an acre in size, and more than 20 growers made their experiments on larger areas of from 3 to 28 acres. The result was that *none of them obtained less than 12 tons* to the acre, while some obtained 20 tons, and the average was, for the 110 growers, 14½ tons per acre.

However, industry requires still heavier crops. Potatoes are largely used in Germany and Belgium for distilleries; consequently, the distillery owners try to obtain the greatest possible amounts of starch from the acre. Extensive experiments have lately been made for that purpose in Germany, and the crops were: 9 tons per acre for the poor sorts, 14 tons for the better ones, and 32 and 4/10th tons for the best varieties of potatoes.

Three tons to the acre and more than 30 tons to the acre are thus the ascertained limits; and one necessarily asks oneself: Which of the two requires *less labour* in tilling, planting, cultivating and digging, and less expenditure in manure – 30 tons grown on 10 acres, or the same 30 tons grown on 1 acre or 2? If labour is of no consideration, while every penny spent in seeds and manure is of great importance, as is unhappily very often the case with the peasant – he will perforce choose the first method. But is it the most economic?

Again, in the Saffelare district and Jersey they succeed in keeping one head of horned cattle to each acre of green crops, meadows and pasture land, while elsewhere 2 or 3 acres are required for the same purpose. But better results still can be obtained by means of irrigation, either with sewage or even with pure water. In England, farmers are contented with 1½ and 2 tons of hay per acre, and in the part of Flanders just mentioned, 2½ tons of hay to the acre are considered a fair crop. But on the irrigated fields of the Vosges, the Vaucluse, etc., in France, 6 tons of dry hay become the rule, even upon ungrateful soil; and this means considerably more than the annual food of one milch cow (which can be taken at a little less than 5 tons) grown on each acre. All taken, the results of irrigation have proved so satisfactory in France that during the years 1862–82 no less than 1,355,000 acres of meadows

[83]

have been irrigated, which means that the annual meat-food of at least 1,500,000 full-grown persons, or more, has been added to the yearly income of the country; home-grown, not imported. In fact, in the valley of the Seine, the value of the land was doubled by irrigation; in the Saône valley it was increased five times, and ten times in certain *landes* of Brittany.

The example of the Campine district, in Belgium, is classical. It was a most unproductive territory – mere sand from the sea, blown into irregular mounds which were only kept together by the roots of the heath; the acre of it used to be sold, not rented, at from 5s to 7s (15 to 20 francs) per hectare. But now it is capable, thanks to the work of the Flemish peasants and to irrigation, to produce the food of one milch cow per acre – the dung of the cattle being utilised for further improvements.

The irrigated meadows round Milan are another well-known example. Nearly 22,000 acres are irrigated there with water derived from the sewers of the city, and they yield crops of from 8 to 10 tons of hay as a rule; occasionally some separate meadows will yield the fabulous amount – fabulous today, but no longer fabulous tomorrow – of 18 tons of hay per acre, that is, the food of nearly four cows to the acre, and nine times the yield of good meadows in this country. However, English readers need not go so far as Milan for ascertaining the results of irrigation by sewer water. They have several such examples in this country, in the experiments of Sir John Lawes, and especially at Craigentinny, near Edinburgh, where, to use Ronna's words, 'the growth of rye grass is so activated that it attains its full development in one year instead of in three to four years. Sown in August, it gives a first crop in autumn, and then, beginning with the next spring, a crop of 4 tons to the acre is taken every month; which represents in the fourteen months more than 56 tons (of green fodder) to the acre.'

It can thus be said that while at the present time we give two and three acres for keeping one head of horned cattle, and only in a few places one head of cattle is kept on each acre given to green crops, meadows and pasture, man has already in irrigation (which very soon repays when it is properly made) the possibility of keeping twice and even thrice as many head of cattle to the acre over parts of his territory. Moreover, the very heavy crops of roots which are now obtained (75 to 110 tons of beetroot to the acre are not infrequent) give another powerful means for increasing the number of cattle without taking the land from what is now given to the culture of cereals.

Another new departure in agriculture, which is full of promises and probably will upset many a current notion, must be mentioned in this place. I mean the almost horticultural treatment of our corn crops, which is widely practised in the Far East, and begins to claim our attention in Western Europe as well.

At the First International Exhibition, in 1851, Major Hallett, of Manor House, Brighton, had a series of very interesting exhibits which he described as 'pedigree cereals'. By picking out the best plants of his fields, and by submitting their descendants to a careful selection from year to year, he had succeeded in producing new prolific varieties of wheat and barley. Each grain of these cereals, instead of giving only 2 to 4 ears, as is the usual average in a cornfield, gave 10 to 25 ears, and the best ears, instead of carrying from 60 to 68 grains, had an average of nearly twice that number of grains.

In order to obtain such prolific varieties Major Hallett naturally could not sow his picked grains broadcast; he planted them, each separately, in rows, at distances of from 10 to 12 inches from each other. In this way he found that each grain, having full room for what is called 'tillering' (*talage* in French), would produce 10, 15, 25, and even up to 90 and 100 ears, as the case may be; and as each ear would contain from 60 to 120 grains, crops of 500 to 2,500 grains, or more, could be obtained from each separately planted grain. He even exhibited at the Exeter meeting of the British Association three plants of wheat, barley and oats, each from a single grain, which had the following number of stems: wheat, 94 stems; barley, 110 stems; oats, 87 stems, The barley plant which had 110 stems thus gave something like 5,000 to 6,000 grains from one single grain.

Two different processes were thus involved in Hallett's experiments: a process of selection, in order to create new varieties of cereals, similar to the breeding of new varieties of cattle; and a method of immensely increasing the crop from each grain and from a given area, by planting each seed separately and wide apart, so as to have room for the full development of the young plant, which is usually suffocated by its neighbours in our corn-fields.

The double character of Major Hallett's method – the breeding of *new prolific varieties*, and the method of culture by *planting the seeds wide apart* – seems, however, so far as I am entitled to judge, to have been overlooked until quite lately. The method was mostly judged upon its results; and when a farmer had experimented upon 'Hallett's Wheat', and found out that it was late in ripening in his own locality, or gave a less perfect grain than some other variety, he usually did not care more about the method. However, Major Hallett's successes or non-successes in breeding such and such varieties are quite distinct from what is to be said about the method itself of selection, or the method of planting wheat seeds wide apart. Varieties which were bred, and which I saw grown still at Manor Farm, on the windy downs of Brighton may be, or may not be, suitable to this or that locality. And now that horticulturists experienced in 'breeding' and 'crossing' have taken the matter in hand, we may feel sure that future progress will be made. But breeding is one thing; and the planting wide apart of seeds of an appropriate variety of wheat is quite another thing.

This last method was lately experimented upon by M. Grandeau, Director of the Station Agronomique de l'Est, and by M. Florimond Dessprèz at the experimental station of Capelle; and in both cases the results were most remarkable. Each seed was planted separately, 8 inches apart in a row, by means of a specially devised tool, similar to the *rayonneur* which is used for planting potatoes; and the rows, also 8 inches apart, were alternately given to the big and to the smaller seeds. One-fourth part of an acre having been planted in this way, with seeds obtained from both early and late ears, crops corresponding to 83·8 bushels per acre for the first series, and 90·4 bushels for the second series, were obtained; even the small grains gave in this experiment as much as 70·2 and 62 bushels respectively.

The crop was more than doubled by the choice of seeds and by planting them separately 8 inches apart. It corresponded in Dessprèz's experiments to *600 grains obtained on the average from each grain sown*; and one-tenth or one-eleventh part of an acre was sufficient in such case to grow the eight and a half bushels of wheat which are required on the average for the annual bread food per head of a population which would chiefly live on bread.

In fact, the eight and a half bushels required for one man's annual food were actually grown at the Tomblaine station on a surface of 2,250 square feet, or 47 feet square – that is, on very nearly one-twentieth part of an acre.

Again, we may thus say, that where we require now three acres, one acre would be sufficient for growing the same amount of food, if planting wide apart more resorted to. And there is, surely, no more objection to planting wheat than there is to sowing in rows, which is now in general use, although at the time when the system was first introduced, *in lieu* of the formerly usual mode of sowing broadcast, it certainly was met with great distrust. While the Chinese and the Japanese used for centuries to sow wheat in rows, by means of a bamboo tube adapted to the plough, European writers objected, of course, to this method under the pretext that it would require too much labour. It is the same now with planting each seed apart. Professional writers sneer at it, although all the rice that is grown in Japan is planted *and even replanted*. Everyone, however, who will think of the labour which must be spent for ploughing, harrowing, fencing, and keeping free of weeds three acres instead of one, and who will calculate the corresponding expenditure in manure, will surely admit that all advantages are in favour of the one acre as against the three acres, to say nothing of the possibilities of irrigation, or of the planting machine-tool, which will be devised as soon as there is a demand for it.

More than that, there is full reason to believe that even this method is liable to further improvement by means of *replanting*. Cereals in such cases would be treated as vegetables are treated in horticulture. Such is, at least, the idea which began to germinate since the methods of cereal culture that are resorted to in China and Japan became better known in Europe.

The future – a near future, I hope – will show what practical importance such a method of treating cereals may have. But we need not speculate about that future. We have already in the facts mentioned in this chapter, an experimental basis for quite a number of means of improving our present methods of culture and of largely increasing the crops. It is evident that in a book which is not intended to be a manual of agriculture, all I can do is to give only a few hints to set people thinking for themselves upon this subject. But the little that has been said is sufficient to show that we have no right to complain of over-population, and no need to fear it in the future. Our means of obtaining from the soil whatever we want, under *any* climate and upon *any* soil, have lately been improved at such a rate that we cannot foresee yet what is the limit of productivity of a few acres of land. The limit vanishes in proportion to our better study of the subject, and every year makes it vanish further and further from our sight.

One of the most interesting features of the present evolution of agriculture is the extension lately taken by intensive market-gardening of the same sort as has been described earlier. What formerly was limited to a few hundreds of small gardens, is now spreading with an astonishing rapidity. In this country the area given to market-gardens, after having more than doubled within the years 1879–94, when it attained 88,210 acres, has continued steadily to increased. But it is especially in France, Belgium and America that this branch of culture has lately taken a great development. At the present time no less than 1,075,000 acres are given in France to market-gardening and intensive fruit culture.

About Roscoff, which is a great centre in Brittany for the export to England of such potatoes as will keep till late in summer, and of all sorts of vegetables, a territory, 26 miles in diameter, is entirely given to these cultures, and the rents attain and exceed £5 per acre. Nearly 300 steamers call at Roscoff to ship potatoes, onions and other vegetables to London and different English ports, as far north as Newcastle. Moreover, as much as 4,000 tons of vegetables are sent every year to Paris. And although the Roscoff peninsula enjoys a specially warm climate, small stone walls are erected everywhere, and rushes are grown on their tops in order to give still more protection and heat to the vegetables. The climate is improved as well as the soil.

At Ploustagel one hardly believes that he is in Brittany. Melons used to be grown at that spot, long since, in the open fields, with glass frames to protect them from the spring frost, and green peas were grown under the protection of rows of furze which sheltered them from the northern winds. Now, whole fields are covered with strawberries, roses, violets, cherries and plums, down to the very sea beach. Even the *landes* are reclaimed, and we are told that in five years or so there will be no more *landes* in that district. Nay, the marshes of the Dol – 'The Holland of Brittany' – protected from the sea by a wall (5,050 acres), have been turned into market-gardens, covered with cauliflowers, onions, radishes, haricot beans, and so on.

The neighbourhoods of Nantes could also be mentioned. Green peas are cultivated there on a very large scale. During the months of May and June quite an army of working people, especially women and children, are picking them. The roads leading to the great preserving factories are covered at certain hours with rows of carts, upon which the peas and onions are carted one way, while another row of carts are carrying the empty pods which are used for manure. For two months the children are missing in the schools; and in the peasant families of the neighbourhood, when the question comes about some expenditure to be made, the usual saying is: 'Wait till the season of the green peas has come.'

The fruit culture in the neighbourhoods of Paris is equally wonderful. At Montreuil, for instance, 750 acres, belonging

[89]

to 400 gardeners, are literally covered with stone walls, specially erected for growing fruit, and having an aggregate length of 400 miles. Upon these walls, peach trees, pear trees and vines are spread, and every year something like 12,000,000 peaches are gathered, as well as a considerable amount of the finest pears and grapes. The acre in such conditions brings in £56. This is how a 'warmer climate' was made, at a time when the greenhouse was still a costly luxury. All taken, 1,250 acres are given to peaches (25,000,000 peaches every year) in the close neighbourhood of Paris. Acres and acres are also covered with pear trees which yield 3 to 5 tons of fruit per acre, such crop being sold at from £50 to £60. Nay, at Angers, on the Loire, where pears are eight days in advance of the suburbs of Paris, Baltet knows an orchard of 5 acres, covered with pears (pyramid trees), which brings in £400 every year; and at a distance of thirty-three miles from Paris one pear plantation brings in £24 per acre – the cost of package, transport and selling being deducted. Likewise, the plantations of plums, of which 80,000 hundredweights are consumed every year at Paris alone, give an annual money income of from £29 to £48 per acre every year; and yet, pears, plums and cherries are sold at Paris, fresh and juicy, at such a price that the poor, too, can eat fresh home-grown fruit.

At Bennecour, a quite small village of 850 inhabitants, near Paris, one sees what man can make out of the most unproductive soil. Quite recently the steep slopes of its hills were only *mergers* from which stone was extracted for the pavements of Paris. Now these slopes are entirely covered with apricot and cherry trees, blackcurrant shrubs, and plantations of asparagus, green peas and the like.

It would take, however, a volume to describe the chief centres of market-gardening and fruit-growing in France; and I will mention only one region more, where vegetables and fruit-growing go hand in hand. It lies on the banks of the Rhône, about Vienne, where we find a narrow strip of land, partly composed of granite rocks, which has now become a garden of an incredible richness. The origin of that wealth, we are told by Ardouin Dumazet, dates from some thirty years ago, when the vineyards, ravaged by phylloxera, had to be destroyed and some new culture had to be found. The village of Ampuis became then renowned for its apricots. At the present time, for a full 100 miles along the Rhône, and in the lateral valleys of the Ardèche and the Drôme, the country is an admirable orchard, from which millions' worth of fruit is exported, and the land attains the selling price of from £325 to £400 the acre. Small plots of land are continually reclaimed for culture upon every crag. On both sides of the roads one sees the plantations of apricot and cherry trees, while between the rows of trees early beans and peas, strawberries and all sorts of early vegetables are grown. In the spring the fine perfume of the apricot trees in bloom floats over the whole valley. Strawberries, cherries, apricots, peaches and grapes follow each other in rapid succession, and at the same time cartloads of French beans, salads, cabbages, leeks and potatoes are sent towards the industrial cities of the region. It would be impossible to estimate the quantity and value of all that is grown in that region. Suffice it to say that a tiny commune, Saint Désirat, exported during Ardouin Dumazet's visit about 2,000 hundred-weight of cherries every day.

The exports of vegetables from Belgium have increased two-fold within the last twenty years of the nineteenth century, and whole regions, like Flanders, claim to be now the market-garden of England, even seeds of the vegetables preferred in this country being distributed free by one horticultural society in order to increase the export. Not only the best lands are appropriated for that purpose, but even the sand deserts of the Ardennes and peat-bogs are turned into rich market-gardens, while large plains (namely at Haeren) are irrigated for the same purpose. Scores of schools, experimental farms, and small experimental stations, evening lectures, and so on, are opened by the communes, the private societies, and the state, in order to promote horticulture, and hundreds of acres of land are covered with thousands of greenhouses.

Here we see one small commune exporting 5,500 tons of potatoes and £4,000 worth of pears to Stratford and Scotland, and keeping for that purpose its own line of steamers. Another

commune supplies the north of France and the Rhenish provinces with strawberries, and occasionally sends some of them
to Covent Garden as well. Elsewhere, early carrots, which are
grown amidst flax, barley and white poppies, give a considerable addition to the farmer's income.

The other country which must especially be recommended to
the attention of horticulturists is America. When we see the
mountains of fruit imported from America we are inclined to
think that fruit in that country grows by itself. 'Beautiful
climate'; 'virgin soil'; 'immeasurable spaces' – these words continually recur in the papers. The reality, however, is that
horticulture – that is, both market-gardening and fruit culture
– has been brought in America to a high degree of perfection.
Professor Baltet, a practical gardener himself, originally from
the classical *marais* (market-gardens) of Troyes, describes the
'truck farms' of Norfolk in Virginia as real 'model farms'. A
highly complimentary appreciation from the lips of a practical
maraîcher who has learned from his infancy that only in fairy-
land do the golden apples grow by the fairies' magic wand.
As to the perfection to which apple-growing has been brought
in Canada, the aid which the apple-growers receive from the
Canadian experimental farms, and the means which are resorted
to, on a truly American scale, to spread information amongst
the farmers and to supply them with new varieties of fruit trees
– all this ought to be carefully studied in this country, instead
of inducing Englishmen to believe that the American supremacy is due to the golden fairies' hands. If one-tenth part of
what is done in the States and in Canada for favouring agriculture and horticulture were done in this country, English fruit
would not have been so shamefully driven out of the market
as it was a few years ago.

However, a further advance is being made in order to
emancipate horticulture from climate. I mean the glasshouse
culture of fruit and vegetables.

Formerly the greenhouse was the luxury of the rich mansion.
It was kept at a high temperature, and was made use of for
growing, under cold skies, the golden fruit and the bewitching
flowers of the South. Now, and especially since the progress

[92]

of technics allows of making cheap glass and of having all the woodwork, sashes and bars of a greenhouse made by machinery, the glasshouse becomes appropriated for growing fruit for the million, as well as for the culture of common vegetables. The aristocratic hothouse, stocked with the rarest fruit trees and flowers, remains; nay, it spreads more and more for growing luxuries which become more and more accessible to the great number. But by its side we have the plebean greenhouse, which is heated for only a couple of months in winter and the still more economically built 'cool greenhouse', which is a simple glass shelter – a big 'cool frame' – and is stuffed with the humble vegetables of the kitchen garden: the potatoes, the carrot, the French beans, the peas and the like. The heat of the sun, passing through the glass, but prevented by the same glass from escaping by radiation, is sufficient to keep it a very high temperature during spring and early summer. A new system of horticulture – the market-garden under glass – is thus rapidly gaining ground.

Large vineries and immense establishments for growing flowers under glass are of an old standing in this country, and new ones are continually built on a grand scale. Entire fields are covered with glass at Cheshunt, at Broxburn (50 acres), at Finchley, at Bexley, at Swanley, at Whetstone, and so on, to say nothing of Scotland. Worthing is also a well-known centre for growing grapes and tomatoes; while the greenhouses given to flowers and ferns of Upper Edmonton, at Chelsea, at Orpington, and so on, have a world-wide reputation. And the tendency is, on the one side, to bring grape culture to the highest degree of perfection, and, on the other side, to cover acres and acres with glass for growing tomatoes, French beans and peas, which undoubtedly will soon be followed by the culture of still plainer vegetables. This movement, as will be seen further on, has been steadily continuing for the last twenty years.

However, the Channel Islands and Belgium still hold the lead in the development of glasshouse culture. The glory of Jersey is, of course, Mr Bashford's establishment. When I visited it in 1890, it contained 490,000 square feet under glass

– that is, nearly 13 acres – but 7 more acres under glass have been added to it since. A long row of glasshouses, interspersed with high chimneys, covers the ground – the largest of the houses being 900 feet long and 46 feet wide; this means that about 1 acre of land, in one piece, is under glass.

But it would be hardly possible to give an idea of all that is grown in such glasshouses, without producing photographs of their insides. In 1890, on 3 May, exquisite grapes began to be cut in Mr Bashford's vineries, and the crop was continued till October. In other houses, cartloads of peas had already been gathered, and tomatoes were going to take their place after a thorough cleaning of the house. The 20,000 tomato plants, which were going to be planted, had to yield no less than 80 tons of excellent fruit (8 to 10 pounds per plant). In other houses melons were grown instead of the tomatoes. Thirty tons of early potatoes, 6 tons of early peas, and 2 tons of early French beans had already been sent away in April. As to the vineries, they yielded no less than 25 tons of grapes every year. Mr W. Bear, who had visited the same establishment in 1886, was quite right to say that from these 13 acres they obtained money returns equivalent to what a farmer would obtain from 1,300 acres of land.

However, it is in the small 'vineries' that one sees, perhaps, the most admirable results. As I walked through such glass-roofed kitchen gardens, I could not but admire this recent conquest of man. I saw, for instance, three-fourths of an acre heated for the first three months of the year, from which about 8 tons of tomatoes and about 200 pounds of French beans had been taken as a first crop in April, to be followed by 2 crops more. In these houses 1 gardener was employed with 2 assistants, a small amount of coke was consumed, and there was a gas engine for watering purposes, consuming only 13s worth of gas during the quarter. I saw again, in cool green-houses – simple plank and glass shelters – pea plants covering the walls, for the length of one-quarter of a mile, which already had yielded by the end of April 3,200 pounds of exquisite peas and were yet as full of pods as if not one had been taken off.

[94]

I saw potatoes dug from the soil in a cool greenhouse, in April, to the amount of 5 bushels to the 21 feet square. And when chance brought me, in 1896, in company with a local gardener, to a tiny, retired 'vinery' of a veteran grower, I could see there, and admire, what a lover of gardening can obtain from so small a space as the two-thirds of an acre. Two small 'houses' about 40 feet long and 12 feet wide, and a third – formerly a pigsty – 20 feet by 12, contained vine trees which many a professional gardener would be happy to have a look at; especially the whilom pigsty, fitted with 'Muscats'! Some grapes (in June) were already in full beauty, and one fully understands that the owner would get in 1895, from a local dealer, £4 for 3 bunches of grapes (one of them was a 'Colmar', $13\frac{3}{4}$ pounds weight). The tomatoes and strawberries in the open air, as well as the fruit trees, all on tiny spaces, were equal to the grapes; and when one is shown on what a space half a ton of strawberries can be gathered under proper culture it is hardly believable.

It is especially in Guernsey that the simplification of the greenhouse must be studied. Every house in the suburbs of St Peter has some sort of greenhouse, big or small. All over the island, especially in the north, wherever you look, you see greenhouses. They rise amid the fields and from behind the trees; they are piled upon one another on the steep crags facing the harbour of St Peter; and with them a whole generation of practical gardeners has grown up. Every farmer is more or less of a gardener, and he gives free scope to his inventive powers for devising some cheap type of greenhouses. Some of them have almost no front and back walls – the glass roofs coming low down and the 2 or 3 feet of glass in front simply reaching the ground; in some houses the lower sheet of glass was simply plunged into a wooden trough standing on the ground and filled with sand. Many houses have only two or three planks, laid horizontally, instead of the usual stone wall, in the front of the greenhouse.

It is always difficult, of course, to know what are the money returns of the growers, first of all because Thorold Rogers's complaint about modern farmers keeping no accounts holds good, even for the best gardening establishments, and next because when the returns are known to me in all details, it would not be right for me to publish them. 'Don't prove too much; beware of the landlord!' a practical gardener once wrote to me.

As a rule, the Guernsey and Jersey growers have only three crops every year from their greenhouses. They will start, for instance, potatoes in December. The house will, of course, not be heated, fires being made only when a sharp frost is expected at night; and the potato crop (from 8 to 10 tons per acre) will be ready in April or May before the open-air potatoes begin to be dug out. Tomatoes will be planted next and be ready by the end of the summer. Various catch crops of peas, radishes, lettuce and other small things will be taken in the meantime. Or else the house will be 'started' in November with melons, which will be ready in April. They will be followed by tomatoes, either in pots, or trained as vines, and the last crop of tomatoes will be in October. Beans may follow and be ready for Christmas. I need not say that every grower has his preference method for utilising his houses, and it entirely depends upon his skill and watchfulness to have all sorts of small catch crops. These last begin to have a greater and greater importance, and one can already foresee that the growers under glass will be forced to accept the methods of the French *maraîchers*, so as to have 5 and 6 crops every year, so far as it can be done without spoiling the present high quality of the produce.

When I returned to Guernsey in 1903, I found that the industry of fruit-growing under glass had grown immensely since 1896, so that the whole system of export had to be reorganised. In 1896 it was the tourists' boats which transported the fruit and vegetables to Southampton, and the gardeners paid 1s for each basket taken at Guernsey and delivered at the Covent Garden market. In 1903 there was already a Guernsey Growers' Association, which had its own boats keeping, during the summer, a regular daily service direct from Guernsey to London. The Association had its own store-houses on the quay and its own cranes, which lifted immense cubic boxes containing on their shelves 20 or even 100 baskets, and carrying them to the boats. The cost of transport was thus reduced to 4d per basket. All this crop is sold every morning at Covent Garden to the London dealers and greengrocers. The importance of this export is seen from the fact that a special steamer has to leave Guernsey every morning with its cargo of fruit and vegetables.

All this is obtained from an island whose total area, rocks and barren hill-tops included, is only 16,000 acres, of which only 9,884 acres are under culture, and 5,189 acres are given to green crops and meadows. An island, moreover, on which 1,480 horses, 7,260 head of cattle and 900 sheep find their existence. How many men's food is, then, grown on these 10,000 acres?

I will not conclude this chapter without casting a glance on the progress that has been made in this country since the first edition of this book was published, in 1898, by fruit and flower farming, as also by culture under glass, and on the attempts recently made to introduce in different parts of England 'French Gardening' – that is, the *culture maraîchère* of the French gardeners.

There is not the slightest doubt that fruit-growing has notably increased – the area under fruit orchards having grown in Great Britain from 200,000 acres in 1888 to 250,000 acres in 1908; while the area under small fruit (gooseberries, currants, strawberries) has grown from 75,000 acres in 1901 to 85,000 in 1908. In fact, in some counties the acreage has trebled. Large plantations of fruit have grown lately round London and all the large cities, and the counties of Kent, Devon, Hereford, Somerset, Worcester and Gloucester have now more than 20,000 acres each under fruit orchards, a great proportion of them being of a recent origin. Not only was the area of fruit-growing considerably increased, but, owing to the experiments carried on since 1894 at the Woburn Experimental Farm, where different sorts of fruit-trees and small fruit are tested, new varieties have been introduced; and the system is spreading of growing fruit-trees of the pyramidal or 'bush' form (instead of the old-fashioned standards) – a step the advantages of

G

which I was enabled fully to appreciate in 1897 at the Agassiz Experimental Farm in British Columbia.

At the same time the culture of small fruit – gooseberries, raspberries, currants, and especially strawberries – took an immense development. Enormous quantities of strawberries are now grown in Mid- and South Kent, where we find the culture of fruit combined with large jam factories. One of such factories is connected with great fruit farms covering 2,000 acres at Swanley, ánd its yearly output attains 3,500 tons of jam, 850 tons of candied peel, and more than 100,000 bottles of bottled fruit. An extensive horticulture has also developed of late in Cambridgeshire, wherefrom fruit is sent partly fresh to London and Manchester, and partly is transformed on the spot in the jam factory at Histon.

I also ought to mention Essex, where fruit-growing has taken of late a notable development, and Hampshire, where the acreage under fruit has trebled since 1880. The same must be said of Worcestershire, and especially of the Evesham district. This last is a most instructive region. Owing to certain peculiarities of its soil, which render it very profitable for growing asparagus and plum trees, and partly owing to the maintenance in this region of the old 'Evesham custom' (according to which from times immemorial the ingoing tenant had to pay the outgoing tenant, not the landlord, for the agricultural improvements) – a custom maintained till nowadays – the small-holdings system and the culture of vegetables and fruit have developed to a remarkable extent. The result is that out of a rural area of 10,000 acres, 7,000 have already been taken in small holdings of under 50 acres each, and the demand for them, far from being satisfied, is still on the increase, so that in 1911 there were still nearly 400 farmers waiting for 2,000 acres. A new town has grown at Evesham, its population of 8,340 persons being almost entirely composed of gardeners and gardeners' labourers; its markets, held twice a week, remind one of markets in the south of France; and the export traffic on the railways radiating from that little town is as lively as if it were a busy industrial spot.

One cannot read the pages given by Mr Rider Haggard in

his *Rural England* to the Bewdley and Evesham districts without being impressed by what can be obtained from the soil in England, and by what has to be done by the nation and all those who care for its well-being in obtaining from the soil what it is ready to give, if only *labour* be applied to it.

Speaking of Catshill, Mr Haggard gives a very interesting instance of how a colony of people called 'Nailers', who lived formerly by making nails by hand, and compelled to abandon this trade when machine-made nails were introduced, took to agriculture, and how they succeed with it. Some intelligent people having bought a farm of 140 acres and divided it into small farms, from $2\frac{1}{2}$ to 8 acres, these small-holdings were offered to the nailers; and at the time of Mr Haggard's visit 'every instalment which was due had been paid up'. No able-bodied man out of them has gone on to the rates.

But the vale of Evesham is still more interesting. Suffice it to say, that while in most rural parishes the population is decreasing, it rose in the six parishes of the Evesham Union from 7,327 to 9,012 in the ten years, 1891–1901.

Although the soil of this district offers nothing extraordinary, and the conditions of sale are as bad as anywhere, owing to the importance acquired by the middlemen, we see that an extremely important industry of fruit-growing has developed; so important that in the year 1900 about 20,000 tons of fruit and vegetables were sent from the Evesham stations, in addition to large quantities exported from the small stations within a radius of ten miles round Evesham. The soil, of course, is improved by digging into it large quantities of all sorts of manure – soot, fish, guano, leather dust for cabbage (chamois dust being the best), and so on – and the most profitable sorts of fruit-trees and vegetables are continually tested; all this being, of course, not the work of some scientist or of one single man, but the product of the collective experience of the district.

Finally, I also ought to mention the recent development of fruit culture near the Broads of Norfolk, and especially in Ireland; but the examples just given will do to show what is obtained from the land in England where no obstacle is laid to the development of horticulture, and what amount of food

[99]

can be obtained in the climate and from the soil of this country whenever it is properly cultivated. Let me only add that a similar development of fruit culture has taken place within the last thirty years everywhere in the civilised countries; and that in France, in Belgium and in Germany the extension taken by horticulture during the last twenty or thirty years has been much greater than in this country.

As regards *market-gardening*, it has undoubtedly made remarkable progress in the United Kingdom within recent years. However, accurate data are failing, and those who have travelled over this country with the special purpose of studying its agriculture have not yet given sufficient attention to the recent developments of market-gardening; but it is quite certain that within the last five-and-twenty years it has taken a great development, especially in Ireland, but also in several parts of England, Scotland and Wales.

There are many interesting centres of market-gardening, especially in the neighbourhoods of all large cities, but I will mention only one – namely, Potton, in Huntingdonshire. It is – we are told by Mr Haggard – 'a stronghold of small cultivators who grow vegetables upon holdings of land varying in size from 1 up to 20 acres, or even more'. It has thus become an important centre for market-gardening. '120 trucks of produce leaving Potton daily during the season for London, in addition to 50 trucks which pass over the Great Northern line from Sandy station, together with much more from sidings and other stations'. This is the more interesting as within a short distance from this animated centre 'thousands of acres are quite or very nearly derelict, and the farmhouses, buildings and cottages are slowly rotting down'. The worst is that 'all this land was cultivated, and grew crops up to the 1880s'.

Another oasis of market-gardening is offered by the county of Bedfordshire. 'Being a county of natural small-holdings, carved out before the passing of the 1907 Act', it is rapidly becoming – we are told by Mr F. E. Green – 'a county of market-gardens'. The fertility of its soil, the fact that it can easily be worked at any time of the year, and that a race of skilled gardeners has developed there long since, have contri-

[100]

buted to that growth; but, of course, the whole is hampered by the heavy rents.

And yet all this progress still appears insignificant by the side of the demand for vegetables which grows every year (and necessarily *must* grow, as is seen by comparing the low consumption of vegetables in this country with the consumption of home-grown vegetables in Belgium, indicated by Mr Rowntree in his *Lessons from Belgium*). The result is a steadily increasing importation of vegetables to this country, which has attained now more than £8,000,000.

A branch of horticulture which has increased enormously since the first edition of this book was published, is the *growing of fruit and vegetables in greenhouses*, in the same way as it is done in the Channel Islands. Immense quantities of grapes, tomatoes, figs, and of all sorts of early vegetables are grown at Worthing, where 82 acres are covered now with glasshouses, as also in the parish of Cheshunt, in Herts where the area under hothouses is already 130 acres; while a careful estimate put in 1908 the area of individual hothouses in England at about 1,200 acres. The elements of this culture having been developed by the experience of the Channel Islands growers, and by the wide extension which hothouses for the growing of flowers had taken long since in this country, it may be concluded from the various evidence we have at hand that on the whole this sort of culture is finding its reward, and is now firmly established.

The same, however, cannot yet be said of the *culture maraîchère* of the French market-gardeners which is being introduced now into this country. Many attempts have been made in this direction in different parts of the country with varied degrees of success; but little or nothing is known about the results. An attempt on a large scale was made, as is known, by some Evesham gardeners. Having read about this sort of culture in France, and the wonderful results obtained by it, some of the Evesham gardeners went to Paris with the intention of learning that culture from the Paris *maraîchers*. Finding that impossible, they invited a French gardener to Evesham, gave him three-quarters of an acre, and, after he had brought from his Paris *marais* his glass-bells, frames and lights, and, above all, his knowledge, he began gardening under the eyes of his Evesham colleagues. 'Happily enough,' he said to an interviewer, 'I do not speak English; otherwise I should have had to talk all the time and give explanations, instead of working. So I show them my black trousers, and tell them in signs: "Begin by making the soil as black as these trousers, then everything will be all right."' Of course, the small amount of sunshine is a great obstacle for ripening the produce as early as it can be ripened in France, even in the suburbs of Paris. But home-grown fruit and vegetables have always many advantages in comparison with imported produce. Another disadvantage – the lack of horse manure – a disadvantage which will go on increasing with the spread of motor cars – is felt in France as well. This is why the French growers are eagerly experimenting with the direct heating of the soil with *thermosiphons*.

Let me add to these remarks that a decided awakening is to be noticed in this country for making a better use of the land than has been made for the last fifty years. There are a few counties where the County Councils, and still more so, the Parish Councils, are doing their best to break at last the land monopoly, and to permit those small farmers who intend to cultivate the soil to do so. Here and there we see a few timid attempts at imparting to the farmers and their children some knowledge of agriculture and horticulture. But all this is being made on too small a scale, and without a sincere desire to learn from other European nations, and still more so from the United States and Canada, what is being done in these countries to give to agriculture the new character of intensive culture combined with industry, which is imposed upon it by the recent progress of civilisation.

The various data which have been brought together on the preceding pages make short work of the over-population fallacy. It is precisely in the most densely populated parts of the world that agriculture has lately made such strides as hardly could have been guessed twenty years ago. A dense population, a high development of industry, and a high development of agriculture and horticulture, go hand in hand: they are inseparable. As to the future, the possibilities of agriculture are such that, in truth, we cannot yet foretell what would be the limit of the population which could live from the produce of a given area. Recent progress, already tested on a great scale, has widened the limits of agricultural production to a quite unforeseen extent; and recent discoveries, now tested on a small scale, promise to widen those limits still farther, to a quite unknown degree.

The present tendency of economical development in the world is – we have seen – to induce more and more every nation, or rather every region, taken in its geographical sense, to rely chiefly upon a home production of all the chief necessaries of life. Not to reduce, I mean, the world-exchange: it may still grow in bulk; but to limit it to the exchange of what really *must* be exchanged, and, at the same time, immensely to increase the exchange of novelties, produce of local or national art, new discoveries and inventions, knowledge and ideas. Such being the tendency of present development, there is not the slightest ground to be alarmed by it. There is not one nation in the world which, being armed with the present powers of agriculture, could not grow on its cultivable area all the food and most of the raw materials derived from agriculture which are required for its population, even if the requirements of that population were rapidly increased as they certainly ought to be. Taking the powers of man over the land and over the forces of nature – *such as they are at the present day* – we can maintain that 2 to 3 inhabitants to each cultivable acre of land would not yet be too much. But neither in this densely populated country nor in Belgium are we yet in such numbers. In this country we have, roughly speaking, 1 acre of the cultivable area per inhabitant.

Supposing, then, that each inhabitant of Great Britain were compelled to live on the produce of his own land, all he would have to do would be, first, to consider the land of this country as a common inheritance, which must be disposed of to the best advantage of each and all – this is, evidently, an absolutely necessary condition. And next, he would have to cultivate his

[103]

soil, not in some extravagant way, but no better than land is already cultivated upon thousands and thousands of acres in Europe and America. He would not be bound to invent some new methods, but could simply generalise and widely apply those which have stood the test of experience. He can do it; and in so doing he would save an immense quantity of the work which is now given for buying his food abroad, and for paying all the intermediaries who live upon this trade. Under a rational culture, those necessaries and those luxuries which must be obtained from the soil, undoubtedly *can* be obtained with much less work than is required now for buying these commodities. I have made elsewhere (in *The Conquest of Bread*) approximate calculations to that effect, but with the data given in this book everyone can himself easily test the truth of this assertion. If we take, indeed, the masses of produce which are obtained under rational culture, and compare them with the amount of labour which must be spent for obtaining them under an irrational culture, for collecting them abroad, for transporting them, and for keeping armies of middlemen, we see at once how few days and hours need be given, under proper culture, for growing man's food.

For improving our methods of culture to that extent, we surely need not divide the land into one-acre plots, and attempt to grow what we are in need of by everyone's separate individual exertions, on everyone's separate plot with no better tools than the spade; under such conditions we inevitably should fail. Those who have been so much struck with the wonderful results obtained in the *petite culture*, that they go about representing the small culture of the French peasant, or *maraîcher*, as an ideal for mankind, are evidently mistaken. They are as much mistaken as those other extremists who would like to turn every country into a small number of huge Bonanza farms, worked by militarily organised 'labour battalions'. In Bonanza farms human labour is certainly reduced, but the crops taken from the soil are far too small, and the whole system is robbery-culture, taking no heed of the exhaustion of the soil. This is why the Bonanza farms have disappeared from their former home, Ohio; and when I crossed part of this state in 1901 I saw its plains thickly dotted with medium-sized farms, from 100 to 200 acres, and with windmills pumping water for the orchards and the vegetable gardens. On the other side, in the spade culture, on isolated small plots, by isolated men or families, too much human labour is wasted, even though the crops are heavy; so that real economy – of both space and labour – requires different methods, representing a combination of machinery work with hand work.

In agriculture, as in everything else, associated labour is the only reasonable solution. Two hundred families of 5 persons each, owning 5 acres per family, having no common ties between the families, and compelled to find their living, each family on its 5 acres, almost certainly would be an economical failure. Even leaving aside all *personal* difficulties resulting from different education and tastes and from the want of knowledge as to what has to be done with the land, and admitting for the sake of argument that these causes do not interfere, the experiment would end in a failure, merely for *economical*, for *agricultural* reasons. Whatever improvement upon the present conditions such an organisation might be, that improvement would not last; it would have to undergo a further transformation or disappear.

But the same 200 families, if they consider themselves, say, as tenants of the nation, and treat the 1,000 acres as a common tenancy – again leaving aside the *personal* conditions – would have, economically speaking, from the point of view of the agriculturist, every chance of succeeding, *if they know what is the best use to make of that land.*

In such case they probably would first of all associate for permanently improving the land which is in need of immediate improvement, and would consider it necessary to improve more of it every year, until they had brought it all into a perfect condition. On an area of 340 acres they could most easily grow all the cereals – wheat, oats, etc. – required for both the thousand inhabitants and their livestock, without resorting for that purpose to replanted or planted cereals. They could grow on 400 acres, properly cultivated, and irrigated if necessary and possible, all the green crops and fodder re-

[105]

quired to keep the 30 to 40 milch cows which would supply them with milk and butter, and, let us say, the 300 head of cattle required to supply them with meat. On 20 acres, two of which would be under glass, they would grow more vegetables, fruit and luxuries than they could consume. And supposing that half an acre of land is attached to each house for hobbies and amusement (poultry-keeping, or any fancy culture, flowers, and the like) – they would still have some 140 acres for all sorts of purposes: public gardens, squares, manufactures and so on. The labour that would be required for such an intensive culture would not be the hard labour of the serf or slave. It would be accessible to everyone, strong or weak, town bred or country born; it would also have many charms besides. And its total amount would be far smaller than the amount of labour which every thousand persons, taken from this or from any other nation, have now to spend in getting their present food, much smaller in quantity and of worse quality. I mean, of course, the technically necessary labour, without even considering the labour which we now have to give in order to maintain all our middlemen, armies, and the like. The amount of labour required to grow food under a rational culture is so small, indeed, that our hypothetical inhabitants would be led necessarily to employ their leisure in manufacturing, artistic, scientific, and other pursuits.

From the technical point of view there is no obstacle whatever for such an organisation being started tomorrow with full success. The obstacles against it are not in the imperfection of the agricultural art, or in the infertility of the soil, or in climate. They are entirely in our institutions, in our inheritances and survivals from the past – in the 'Ghosts' which oppress us. But to some extent they lie also – taking society as a whole – in our phenomenal ignorance. We, civilised men and women, know everything, we have settled opinions upon everything, we take an interest in everything. We only know nothing about whence the bread comes which we eat – even though we pretend to know something about that subject as well – we do not know how it is grown, what pains it costs to those who grow it, what is being done to reduce their pains, what sort of men those

[106]

feeders of our grand selves are . . . we are more ignorant than savages in this respect, and we prevent our children from obtaining this sort of knowledge – even those of our children who would prefer it to the heaps of useless stuff with which they are crammed at school.

EDITOR'S APPENDIX

In the three chapters condensed to form Chapter 2 of this edition, Kropotkin sought to demonstrate that the United Kingdom in his day could, from its own soil, feed 24,000,000 instead of a mere 17,000,000 people, simply if the land were still cultivated as it was in the period of 'high farming' before the agricultural collapse of the 1870s; that it could feed 37,000,000 people if it were cultivated as Belgium was; and that it could feed 90,000,000 people if the soil were cultivated to the standards of the best farms in England, Flanders and Lombardy, coupled with an increase in horticultural production.

This view was held to be over-optimistic even by Kropotkin's fellow anarchists. Vernon Richards notes that Errico Malatesta

'always pointed out that the characteristic of capitalism is under- rather than over-production, and that it was a mistake to believe that the stocks of food and essential goods in the large cities was sufficient to feed the people for more than a few days. When pressed by Malatesta to investigate the true position, Kropotkin who, in all his writings on the subject, had been a partisan of the *prise au tas* (taking from the storehouses) view, discovered that if the imports of food into England were stopped for four weeks everybody in the country would die of starvation; and that in spite of all the warehouses in London, the capital city was never provisioned for much more than three days.'[1]

Malatesta himself describes the origins of Kropotkin's inquiry in these terms:

'. . . Kropotkin set about studying the problems at first hand and arrived at the conclusion that such abundance did not exist and that some countries were continually threatened by shortages. But he recovered (his optimism) by thinking of the great potentialities of agriculture aided by science. He took as examples the results obtained by a few cultivators and gifted agronomists over limited areas and drew the most encouraging conclusions without thinking of the difficulties that would be put in the way by the ignorance and aversion of peasants to what is change, and in any case to the time that would be needed to achieve general acceptance of the new forms of cultivation and of distribution. As always, Kropotkin saw things as he would have wished them to be and as we all hope they will be one day; he considered as existing or immediately realisable that which must be won through long and bitter struggle.'[2]

Malatesta was right about Kropotkin's covert motives, which are not made apparent in this book. His interest in agricultural self-sufficiency grew out of his preoccupation with revolutionary strategy. In the course of *The Conquest of Bread*, written for a French readership, he sought to show that, isolated by a counter-revolution, just as the Paris Commune had been, the Departments of the Seine and Seine-et-Oise could, with the aid of intensive horticultural methods, feed Paris. Here, however, we are concerned with the validity of his conclusions in terms of the general argument of this book.

Kropotkin's observations of British agriculture were made in the early decades of the agricultural depression which began in the 1870s and in spite of a slight revival in the Edwardian period, a hectic plough-up in the First World War, and a short-lived boom in the years immediately after it, continued until 1939. Any middle-aged British reader will remember the dereliction and decay, the fields full of thistles, and the blocked ditches of the picturesque pre-war countryside. On the eve of the First World War, with a population of 40,000,000, Britain was dependent on imports for four-fifths of her wheat and two-fifths of her meat. On the eve of the Second World War, with a population of 47,700,000 Britain produced about one-third of her total food requirements from her own soil. The vicissitudes of home production between Kropotkin's day and ours are best shown in the two tables overleaf derived by Angela Edwards and Gerald Wibberley[3] from official statistics.

The production figures of each commodity tell their own story, which any account of British farming will explain.[4] The rise and fall may be due to prices, to marketing policy, to policies of Imperial Preference, to the need to protect the export sugar trade of the West Indies. What they are *not* related to is the productive capacity of the soil. The dramatic expansion of arable farming in the Second World War through the necessities of a siege situation illustrated the enormous potential for change, which had nothing at all to do with the myths of some traditional wisdom of the soil handed down from father to son.[5] (The Agricultural Executive Committees in some counties had to import ploughmen from East Anglia to

The Share of Home Production in Total Food Supplies in the United Kingdom 1900–1945

(Home production as a per cent of the total supplies)

	1905–9	1924–7	1936/7–8/9	1944/5
Wheat	24·8	21·0	22·7	44·8
Barley	59·8	57·3	46·2	100·0
Sugar	—	6·2	17·9	23·5
Potatoes	92·0	88·0	95·9	100·0
Beef and Veal	52·6	43·2	49·1	65·4
Mutton and Lamb ...	51·5	44·2	35·9	25·3
Pork } ...	35·8	32·1	77·1	10·4
Bacon and Ham }			29·3	26·9
Butter	13·0	13·0	8·9	9·7
Cheese	24·2	23·1	24·1	7·5
Eggs	32·4	44·6	61·2	43·7

Source: M.A.F.F. 1968, *A Century of Agricultural Statistics*

The Share of Home Production in Total Food Supplies in the United Kingdom 1953/4–1967/8

(Home production as a per cent of total U.K. supplies)

	1953/4	1960/1	1965/6	1967/8
Wheat	40·9	39·8	47·2	49·0
Barley	66·8	81·7	97·7	98·8
Sugar	19·4	29·5	28·5	30·0
Potatoes	97·8	96·2	96·2	95·3
Beef and Veal	65·8	65·4	72·1	78·6
Mutton and Lamb ...	35·4	38·4	44·4	54·1
Pork	88·3	95·2	96·9	97·4
Bacon and Ham ...	43·0	32·6	46·4	34·3
Butter	9·2	10·6	8·2	9·3
Cheese	27·5	47·3	43·8	40·6
Eggs	80·2	92·5	96·4	96·4

Sources: M.A.F.F. 1968, *A Century of Agricultural Statistics*;
M.A.F.F. 1969, *Annual Review and Determination of Guarantees*

teach their craft to farmers who had become mere graziers or 'dog-and-stick' farmers in the decades of neglect.)

The enormous increases in yields that seemed to be such optimistic forecasts to Kropotkin's contemporaries have in many instances become normal in Britain and in other European countries. (The countries of the original European Economic Community were virtually self-supporting in almost all foods, and in fact were embarrassed by surplus, and the percentage of self-sufficiency is almost as great in the enlarged community.)[6] The great increase in productivity has happened in spite of a decline in the arable acreage and of an enormous decline in the agricultural labour force. The empty fields Kropotkin noticed when he first came to England are considerably emptier today. The same land, Nan Fairbrother remarked,

'is now worked swiftly and impersonally by machines – one day the grain is ripe, the next it is gone, and there must now be thousands of acres of arable where no one has walked for years. It is probably true, in fact, that fewer people now set *foot* on our farmland than at any time since prehistory. Industry has made our truly rural landscape more solitary, more remote and countrified; it is a difference we notice travelling the poorer parts of Europe – how small the hand-worked fields are, and how like vegetable gardens covering the land.'[7]

But it was precisely Kropotkin's expectation that *our* farms would become like vegetable gardens covering the land. He had, so to speak, a horticultural approach to agriculture and saw labour-intensive, but mechanised farming as the key to increased production – together with the application of experimental science to plant- and animal-breeding and to soil fertility.

The kind of agricultural development Kropotkin envisaged has occurred more in the continental countries from which he drew much of his data on intensive development than in Britain. Denmark is a net exporter by 79 per cent, and Holland with the greatest population density in Europe manages to produce about 25 per cent by value above her own food requirements. Gavin McCrone, emphasising the importance of spending liberally on research and new equipment, remarked:

'There seems little doubt that it is this sort of approach which has enabled countries such as Denmark and Holland, with their limited area and intensive methods, to compete with the extensive producers of Australia and the New World and yet to be able to attain a high standard of living. Had Denmark been part of Great Britain, and had she been subject to British policy, it is most doubtful if her costs of production would be as low as they are.'[8]

When Peter Self and H. J. Storing wrote *The State and the Farmer* they found that there were in Britain 13,000 holdings with more than 300 acres, 64,000 with from 100 to 300 acres, and over 200,000 with from 5 to 100 acres, and they noted:

'The small farms cover under a third of the agricultural area, but they account for a considerably higher proportion of total output. Shortage of space compels the small farmer to work his limited area more intensively to earn a livelihood. Larger farms tend to become progressively more extensive, as interest shifts from output per acre to output per worker.'[9]

The paradox is that while in the U.K. the industry has a higher output per worker than most European countries, its output per acre is among the lowest. Self and Storing explain that:

'The high output per man is largely the result of substituting machinery for the labour which left the industry in the years of depression, and the low output per acre is an inheritance from the time when conditions were not favourable for intensive production.'[10]

Their observations were based on the agricultural statistics of 1955. In the thirteen years following the publication of those figures there was a marked increase in average farm size. Holdings of over 300 acres increased by 25 per cent, those of 100–300 acres decreased by 11 per cent, those of 50–100 acres decreased by 17 per cent, and those of under 50 acres decreased by 30 per cent.

In a developed economy the trend is for real incomes in the industrial sector to rise in relation to agricultural incomes.

'If then the incomes of the farming population are to bear any relation to those of the rest of the population this can be achieved only by artificial means, that is by government intervention or by some contraction of the resources devoted to food production. In practice, it will probably be achieved by a combination of both. As the proportion of the national income spent upon food decreases and the technical ability to produce it increases, the labour force contracts through a gradual transfer to new occupations. But it never seems to decline

[112]

fast enough to catch up with the proportionate fall in demand and so equalise earnings in agriculture and elsewhere.'[11]

Government support policies, universal in the Western world in one form or another, are a recognition that food production is more than just an industry and is an absolutely essential service, but in practice governments favour the large capital-intensive producer, and in both Europe and America it is found cheaper to pay the small producer not to produce than to find a market for his product.

Kropotkin, with his functional, Veblenite assumption that the purpose of food production was to produce food, never understood the game of agricultural economics as played in capitalist society. The paradox is that in both the two World Wars (at one stage in each of them the blockade brought Britain within a few weeks of starvation), in spite of rationing and shortages, dietary standards actually rose, precisely because market forces were ignored in determining food production and distribution. A post-war study by Royston Lambert demonstrated that in the 1950s the diet of certain groups, for instance wage-earning families with three or more children, actually deteriorated 'The indications are that at least a quarter, and probably a third, of the people of Britain live in households which fail to attain all the desirable levels of dietary intake'[12] by the standards defined by the British Medical Association. In the world as a whole, the proportion of the population living on 2,220 or less calories a day was 49 per cent in the 1930s and increased to 66 per cent in the 1960s. The 'food problem' in both Europe and America is a problem of over-production, but if in some sudden growth of a global sense of social responsibility, whether through prudence, military strategy, altruism or long-term self-interest, the surpluses were diverted on a really effective scale to the Third World countries, this would bring new and enormous economic problems. When the American government made a token gesture of a gift of surplus grain to India, Australian producers protested at the potential threat to their markets. And as Lord de la Warr once said: 'When the crumbs cease to fall from the rich man's table, the beneficiaries are not only as hungry but as helpless as they were before.' Neither a market economy nor charity will solve the world's food problems.

A country which illustrates very well some of Kropotkin's contentions, as well as their limitations in capitalist society, is Japan, the most densely populated country in the Far East, and the most densely populated country in the world in terms of the ratio of population to agricultural land. Its *agricultural* area is only about a third of that of the United Kingdom and its population (90 million) is about 80 per cent higher. Gavin McCrone, after enumerating the difficulties of a country in Japan's situation, observes that

'it will be clear that even in Japan, where conditions might be imagined to be as difficult as anywhere, it has been possible to increase the output of food considerably faster than population. There is every reason to suppose that the methods employed by the Japanese to obtain this increase would be applicable in other countries. Increased agricultural output can be obtained either from improvements in yields or by reclaiming more land; but with their very limited area the Japanese concentrated on the former.'[13]

He shows how Japanese yields per acre are at least double those for almost all the other Far Eastern countries, even though they are still low compared with those of several countries in Europe. He also notes that 'if it is assumed that the Far East, though obliged to rely mainly on its own food supplies at present, will ultimately become industrialised, a situation might develop which could be of much more consequence to the food supplies of the rest of the world.' Japan, he says, has more or less reached this stage now:

'Although she is able to provide most of her own food from her limited agricultural resources, she finds that the productivity of her labour is much higher in industry. . . . So long as Japan has to supply most of her own food, she will find that, at the conditions of price and exchange which make her agriculture competitive, her industry will be able to undercut the prices of other nations. Conversely, if the prices of her industrial products were to rise to the levels which would be comparable to other countries, her agriculture could not exist without heavy support. Because the cost in terms of real resources used to be so high in Japanese agriculture, it would obviously be worth while to expand the industrial sector and to import a larger part of the food supply. The argument applies to Japan with even more force than it ever did to the United Kingdom. Most probably she will gradually try to do this, but she is limited by the willingness of other countries to buy her goods. . . .'

Mr McCrone does not in fact believe that the consequent growth of Japan (or of the next country to reach Japan's level of industrial development) will cause greater competition for the exports of the primary producing countries, because 'if

[114]

present trends continue, Europe may be importing less and Australia, New Zealand and the Argentine may have been joined as major primary exporters by other South American countries and by parts of Africa'. (This is a prediction which is coming true.) But he states with great clarity the standard economist's argument against the views of Kropotkin. He does not mention that it was precisely this need to find markets which Britain solved by imperialist adventures and by economic imperialism in the nineteenth century, just as Japan did in the first half of the twentieth.

After defeat in the Second World War, with the consequent loss of its overseas conquests, Japan was obliged to make, and succeeded in making, a Kropotkinian effort to achieve agricultural self-sufficiency. But in the climate of economic expansion in the 1960s and 1970s this has resulted in massive trade imbalances. 'It is towards the other, U.S.-style "rationalis-ation" that Japanese monopoly capital is moving – elimination of the domestic "low-productive" agriculture and its replace-ment with profit-oriented, mechanised and systematised farm-ing by capitalist corporations and large, rich farmers

. . . For one thing, domestic rice production is now being positively discouraged, to the extent that in 1970 the govern-ment was paying out 68 yen to the farmers for each kilo of rice they did *not* produce, with the result that 10 per cent of the country's rice fields were left uncultivated. . . . All in all, the agricultural problem may be expected to worsen greatly in the future; levels of discontent are rising among the farmers, who have so long been urged to produce as much rice as pos-sible and are now being urged to stop producing it at all, and who on the whole have never made a decent living out of their back-breaking work anyway. . . .'[14]

Nevertheless, the Japanese experience – the evolution from domestic insufficiency, through self-sufficiency, to an embarrass-ing 'over-production' – illustrates the technical feasibility of Kropotkin's claims for the enormous productivity of labour-intensive agriculture. The modern horticultural industry in Britain and in the continental countries fully lives up to his expectations – so much so that it is haunted by the fear of surpluses.

Kropotkin was by no means the only student of British agri-culture to claim that the soil of Britain could feed the entire population. Self-sufficiency has been advocated from a variety of motives, and through a variety of techniques.[15] What emerges from the evidence is the immense productivity per acre of the small unit (in spite of its growing economic 'non-viability'). This is almost ludicrously evident in the Communist countries. 'In 1963, private plots covered about 44,000 sq km or some 4 per cent of all the arable land of the collective farms. From this "private" land, however, comes about half of the vegetables produced in the U.S.S.R., while 40 per cent of the cows and 30 per cent of the pigs in the country are on them.'[16]

British experience of non-commercial food production certainly suports Kropotkin's optimism.

'It would be difficult to over-estimate the contribution which the produce of allotments made to the nation's food supply during the war years. On 15 March 1944, the government estimated that the food grown on allotments, private gardens and plots of land cultivated by service personnel totalled 10 per cent of all food produced in this country. In 1941 the Ministry of Agriculture assessed the total annual production from allotments alone at over 1,300,000 tons. . . .'[17]

The actual or potential contribution to food production of ordinary domestic gardens is another illustration of the productivity of domestic horticulture. The advocates of hight density housing have always cited the 'loss of valuable agricultural land' as a factor supporting their point of view. Sir Frederic Osborn, with equal persistence, has always argued that the produce of the ordinary domestic garden, even though a small area of gardens is devoted to food production, more than equalled in value the produce of the land lost to commercial food production. Surveys conducted by the government and by university departments in the 1950s proved him right.[18]

One implication of Kropotkin's line of argument is that, at present assumptions of population growth, nobody *need* starve. Hunger in the world today is not because of the soil's insufficiency, nor will it be in the conceivable future. Our concern about over-population is justifiable in terms of the finite nature of resources and energy, rather than in terms of potential food production. But there is an obvious objection to this reasoning. The enormous expansion of agricultural productivity has not been achieved by labour-intensive soil conservation, but by capital-intensive exploitation of the soil, which will inevitably reach a point of diminishing returns. Kropotkin himself had a mechanistic nineteenth-century attitude to the land, was as cavalier about crop rotation systems as the modern British cereal farmer, and would probably have regarded contemporary factory-farming methods as just another indication of the indefinite expansion of production on a given area of land.

Those who are worried about questions of conservation and pollution in the countryside will have little difficulty in pinpointing the farmer as the most serious polluter, through the use of herbicides, fungicides and pesticides and through the discharge of untreated farm effluents, and would ask whether the modern extension of Kropotkin's ideas would depend upon the exploitation and exhaustion of the soil. They would point to the dangers documented in the report *Modern Farming and the Soil*[19] which investigated the effects of continuous cereal growing on soil structure. The committee which produced this report was actually more worried about the damage caused by heavy machinery on poorly drained land, but it certainly indicated that modern farming practice in certain areas and on certain soils was causing deterioration of soil structure. Some of the dangers mentioned in this report would be avoided by a return to rotational systems, like the ley farming advocated for years by Sir George Stapleton (widely used in the postwar years until notions of 'an adequate return on capital invested' took its place), or to the Norfolk rotation,

'perhaps the most perfectly balanced rotation in farming history (in which) the beauty of the system was that each crop contributed to the welfare of the next: the build-up of weeds, disease and pests was avoided because susceptible crops were followed by non-susceptible, and the orderly sequence of winter and spring planting balanced the work throughout the year.'[20]

Latter-day Kropotkins, with an eye to the maximum utilisation of resources, would certainly point out that: 'Only a decade or two ago, when livestock was housed on straw, farmyard manure was a valued by-product that played a recognised role in the maintenance of fertility and soil structure. Now the same annual wastes of dung and urine, but wtthout the straw, have become a health hazard and a social nuisance.'[21] In 1968 the consumption of artificial fertilisers in England and Wales amounted to about 600,000 tons of nitrogen and 350,000 tons of both phosphate and potash. Estimates predict that by 1980 the corresponding figure will be 900,000 tons of nitrogen and 450,000 tons of both phosphate and potash. The farm industry produces 120,000,000 tons of animal wastes annually, mostly in the form of strawless slurry. John L. Jones points out that a proper use of these wastes could play an important part in reducing the country's annual fertiliser import bill of £40 million. 'The United Kingdom's dairy cow population alone has a yearly output of 180,000 tons of nitrogen, 120,000 tons of phosphates and 370,000 tons of potash.'[22]

A report on the disposal of sewage from urban Britain is at pains to indicate that

'utilisation of all the available sewage sludge represents only about 4·5 per cent of our present annual nitrogen and phosphate consumption and under 1 per cent of the potash consumption. But since about half of the 1·1 million tons of sewage sludge is already available as manure, the nutrients potentially available in the sludge which is as yet unused are only about half the percentages used above. In addition to the plant nutrients present in sewage sludge, its organic matter forms humus which is a useful soil conditioner. But here again we find it can be shown that the quantity normally available is only a few per cent of that normally added as a result of good farming practice.'[23]

However, these estimates ignore the fact that, as the same report indicates, 'the sewage and trade waste from a population of about 6 million is discharged directly into the sea or to estuaries with only partial or no treatment.' To dismiss these wasted resources as insignificant or 'uneconomical' (quite apart from questions of pollution) is to misread our future.

But the dominant trend today, both in agriculture and horticulture, is undoubtedly *away* from the labour-intensive small-scale productive unit that Kropotkin envisaged. The drift from the land is even more evident than it was in his day and is being vigorously promoted by government policy in Britain and by the European Common Agricultural Policy. Kropotkin's account of American agriculture must seem like a nostalgic idyll to readers in the United States today. For as Sheldon Greene remarks: 'We know that each year 100,000 farms are abandoned and that rural America has sustained a population loss of 40 million people in the last fifty years. Concomitant with the abandonment of small farms and the migration to the cities of a heretofore agriculturally dependent rural population has been the increasing entry into agriculture of multi-purpose business interests, bringing with it an increase in farm size and absentee ownership of the land. Once-populous areas occupied by independent small land-holders interspersed with small rural service communities are being transformed into feudalistic estates – possibly one of the most significant economic and social transformations to be experienced in our history.'[24]

And, of course, the inherent income differences and inequalities between industrial and agricultural work are still evident. Kropotkin's solution, in his next chapter, is the integration of agriculture.

[118]

Editor's Notes

1 Vernon Richards (ed.), *Errico Malatesta: Life and Ideas* (London, Freedom Press, 1965)

2 *Ibid.* Kropotkin's own account of his change from the *prise au tas* to the *mis au tas* position is given in his postscript to the 1921 edition of his *Words of a Rebel* (Moscow and Petrograd, 1921). A translation of this by Nicolas Walter appeared in *Freedom*, Anarchist Pamphlet No. 5 (London, Freedom Press, 1970)

3 A. M. Edwards and G. P. Wibberley, *An Agricultural Land Budget for Britain, 1965–2000* (Ashford, Kent, Wye College Studies in Rural Land Use, No. 10, 1971)

4 See, for example, J.G.S. and Frances Donaldson, *Farming in Britain Today* (Harmondsworth, Penguin, 1972)

5 See Keith A. H. Murray, *Agriculture* and R. J. Hammond, *Food* (Vol. 2) in the *History of the Second World War*, U.K. Civil Series London, H.M.S.O., 1955 and 1956)

6 See Table 50 in Donaldson, *op. cit.*

7 Nan Fairbrother, *New Lives, New Landscapes* (London, Architectural Press, 1970; New York, Knopf, 1971)

8 Gavin McCrone, *The Economics of Subsidising Agriculture* (London, Allen & Unwin, 1962)

9 Peter Self and H. J. Storing, *The State and the Farmer* (London, Allen & Unwin, 1962)

10 *Ibid.*

11 Donaldson, *op. cit.*

12 Royston Lambert, *Nutrition in Britain* (London, 1964)

13 McCrone, *op. cit.*

14 Jon Halliday and Gavan Cormack, *Japanese Imperialism Today* (Harmondsworth, Penguin, 1973)

15 See George P. Pollitt, *Britain Can Feed Herself* (London, Macmillan, 1942); Philip Oyler, *Feeding Ourselves* (London, Hodder & Stoughton, 1951); H. J. Massingham and Edward Hyams, *Prophesy of Famine* (London, Thames & Hudson, 1953); and *Feeding the Fifty Millions*, Report of the Rural Reconstruction Association (London, Hollis & Carter, 1955)

16 J. P. Cole, *A Geography of the U.S.S.R.* (Harmondsworth, Penguin, 1967)

17 *Report* of the Departmental Committee of Inquiry into Allotments (London, H.M.S.O., 1969)

18 See Robin H. Best and J. T. Ward, *The Garden Controversy* (Ashford, Kent, Wye College Studies in Rural Land Use, No. 2, 1956)

and G. P. Wibberley, *Agriculture and Urban Growth* (London, Michael Joseph, 1959). Also Robin H. Best and J. T. Coppock, *The Changing Use of Land in Britain* (London, Faber, 1962)

19 *Modern Farming and the Soil*, Report of the Agricultural Advisory Council on Soil Structure and Soil Fertility (London, H.M.S.O., 1970)

20 Donaldson, *op. cit.*

21 'Slurry: Asset or Liability?', *Country Life* (5 October 1972)

22 'Slurry: Problem or Profit?, *Country Life* (29 March 1973)

23 *Taken for Granted*, Report of the Working Party on Sewage Disposal (London, H.M.S.O., 1970)

24 Sheldon Greene, addressing the National Conference on Land Reform (San Francisco, April 1973)

Chapter 3

Small Industries and
Industrial Villages

The two sister arts of agriculture and industry were not
always so estranged from one another as they are now. There
was a time, and that time is not so far back, when both were
thoroughly combined; the villages were then the seats of a
variety of industries, and the artisans in the cities did not
abandon agriculture; many towns were nothing else but industrial villages. If the medieval city was the cradle of those
industries which bordered upon art and were intended to supply
the wants of the richer classes, still it was the rural manufacture which supplied the wants of the million, as it does until
the present day in Russia, and to a very great extent in Germany and France. But then came the water-motors, steam,
the development of machinery, and they broke the link which
formerly connected the farm with the workshop. Factories
grew up and they abandoned the fields. They gathered where
the sale of their produce was easiest, or the raw materials
and fuel could be obtained with the greatest advantage. New
cities rose, and the old ones rapidly enlarged; the fields were
deserted. Millions of labourers, driven away by sheer force
from the land, gathered in the cities in search of labour, and
soon forgot the bonds which formerly attached them to the
soil. And we, in our admiration of the prodigies achieved
under the new factory system, overlooked the advantages of
the old system under which the tiller of the soil was an industrial worker at the same time. We doomed to disappearance
all those branches of industry which formerly used to prosper
in the villages; we condemned in industry all that was not a
big factory.

True, the results were grand as regards the increase of the

productive powers of man. But they proved terrible as regards the millions of human beings who were plunged into misery and had to rely upon precarious means of living in our cities. Moreover, the system, as a whole, brought about those abnormal conditions which I have endeavoured to sketch in the two first chapters. We were thus driven into a corner; and while a thorough change in the present relations between labour and capital is becoming an imperious necessity, a thorough re-modelling of the whole of our industrial organisation has also become unavoidable. The industrial nations are bound to re-vert to agriculture, they are compelled to find out the best means of combining it with industry, and they must do so with-out loss of time.

To examine the special question as to the possibility of such a combination is the aim of the following pages. Is it possible, from a technical point of view? Is it desirable? Are there, in our present industrial life, such features as might lead us to presume that a change in the above direction would find the necessary elements for its accomplishment? Such are the ques-tions which rise before the mind. And to answer them, there is, I suppose, no better means than to study that immense but overlooked and underrated branch of industries which are described under the names of rural industries, domestic trades, and petty trades: to study them, not in the works of the econo-mists who are too much inclined to consider them as obsolete types of industry, but in their life itself, in their struggles, their failures and achievements.

The variety of forms of organisation which is found in the small industries is hardly suspected by those who have not made them a subject of special study. There are, first, two broad categories: those industries which are carried on in the villages, in connection with agriculture; and those which are carried on in towns or in villages, with no connection with the land – the workers depending for their earnings exclusively upon their industrial work.

In Russia, in France, in Germany, in Austria, and so on, millions and millions of workers are in the first case. They are owners or occupiers of the land, they keep one or two cows, very often horses, and they cultivate their fields, or their orchards, or gardens, considering industrial work as a by-occupation. In those regions, especially, where the winter is long and no work on the land is possible for several months every year, this form of small industries is widely spread. In this country, on the contrary, we find the opposite extreme. Few small industries have survived in England in connection with land-culture; but hundreds of petty trades are found in the suburbs and the slums of the great cities, and large portions of the populations of several towns, such as Sheffield and Birmingham, find their living in a variety of petty trades. Between these two extremes there is evidently a mass of intermediate forms, according to the more or less close ties which continue to exist with the land. Large villages, and even towns, are thus peoples with workers who are engaged in small trades, but most of whom have a small garden, or an orchard, or a field, or only retain some rights of pasture on the commons, while part of them live exclusively upon their industrial earnings.

With regard to the sale of the produce, the small industries offer the same variety of organisation. Here again there are two great branches. In one of them the worker sells his produce directly to the wholesale dealer; cabinet-makers, weavers, and workers in the toy trade are in this case. In the other great division the worker works for a 'master' who either sells the produce to a wholesale dealer, or simply acts as a middle-man who himself receives his orders from some big concern. This is the 'sweating system', properly speaking, under which we find a mass of small trades. Part of the toy trade, the tailors who work for large clothing establishments – very often for those of the state – the women who sew and embroider the 'uppers' for the boot and shoe factories, and who as often deal with the factory as with an intermediary 'sweater', and so on, are in this case. All possible gradations of feudalisation and sub-feudalisation of labour are evidently found in that organisation of the sale of the produce.

Again, when the industrial, or rather technical aspects of

[123]

the small industries are considered, the same variety of types is soon discovered. Here also there are two great branches: those trades, on the one side, which are purely domestic – that is, those which are carried on in the house of the worker, with the aid of his family, or of a couple of wage-workers; and those which are carried on in separate workshops – all the just-mentioned varieties, as regards connection with land and the divers modes of disposing of the produce, being met with in both these branches. All possible trades – weaving, workers in wood, in metals, in bone, in india-rubber, and so on – may be found under the category of purely domestic trades, with all possible gradations between the purely domestic form of production and the workshop and the factory.

Thus, by the side of the trades which are carried on entirely at home by one or more members of the family, there are the trades in which the master keeps a small workshop attached to his house and works in it with his family, or with a few 'assistants' – that is, wage-workers. Or else the artisan has a separate workshop, supplied with wheel-power, as is the case with the Sheffield cutlers. Or several workers come together in a small factory which they maintain themselves, or hire in association, or where they are allowed to work for a certain weekly rent. And in each of these cases they work either directly for the dealer or for a small master, or for a middleman.

A further development of this system is the big factory, especially of ready-made clothes, in which hundreds of women pay so much for the sewing-machine, the gas, the gas-heated irons, and so on, and are paid themselves so much for each piece of the ready-made clothes they sew, or each part of it. Immense factories of this kind exist in England, and it appeared from testimony given before the 'Sweating Committee' that women are fearfully 'sweated' in such workshops – the full price of each slightly spoiled piece of clothing being deducted from their very low piecework wages.

And, finally, there is the small workshop (often with hired wheel-power) in which a master employs 3 to 10 workers, who are paid in wages, and sells his produce to a bigger employer or merchant – there being all possible gradations between such

[124]

a workshop and the small factory in which a few time workers (5, 10 to 20) are employed by an independent producer. In the textile trades, weaving is often done either by the family or by a master who employs 1 boy only, or several weavers, and after having received the yarn from a big employer, pays a skilled workman to put the yarn in the loom, invents what is necessary for weaving a given, sometimes very complicated pattern, and after having woven the cloth or the ribbons in his own loom or in a loom which he hires himself, he is paid for the piece of cloth according to a very complicated scale of wages agreed to between masters and workers. This last form, we shall see presently, is widely spread up to the present day, especially in the woollen and silk trades; it continues to exist by the side of big factories in which 50, 100 or 5,000 wage-workers, as the case may be, are working with the employers' machinery and are paid in time-wages so much the day or the week.

The small industries are thus quite a world, which, remarkable enough, continues to exist even in the most industrial countries, side by side with the big factories. Into this world we must now penetrate to cast a glimpse upon it: a glimpse only, because it would take volumes to describe its infinite variety of pursuits and organisation, and its infinitely varied connection with agriculture as well as with other industries.

Most of the petty trades, except some of those which are connected with agriculture, are, we must admit, in a very precarious position. The earnings are very low, and the employment is often uncertain. The day of labour is by two, three, or four hours longer than it is in well-organised factories, and at certain seasons it reaches an almost incredible length. The crises are frequent and last for years. Altogether, the worker is much more at the mercy of the dealer or the employer, and the employer is at the mercy of the wholesale dealer. Both are liable to become enslaved to the latter, running into debt to him. In some of the petty trades, especially in the fabrication of the plain textiles, the workers are in dreadful misery. But those who pretend that such misery is the rule are totally wrong. Anyone who has lived among, let us say, the watch-makers in Switzerland and knows their inner family life, will recognise that the condition of these workers was out of all comparison superior, in every respect, material and moral, to the conditions of millions of factory hands. Even during such a crisis in the watch trade as was lived through in 1876–80, their condition was preferable to the condition of factory hands during a crisis in the woollen or cotton trade; and the workers perfectly well knew it themselves.

Whenever a crisis breaks out in some branch of the petty trades, there is no lack of writers to predict that that trade is going to disappear. During the crisis which I witnessed in 1877, living amidst the Swiss watch-makers, the impossibility of a recovery of the trade in the face of the competition of machine-made watches was a current topic in the press. The same was said in 1882 with regard to the silk trade of Lyons, and, in fact, wherever a crisis has broken out in the petty trades. And yet, notwithstanding the gloomy predictions, and the still gloomier prospects of the workers, that form of industry does not disappear. Even when some branch of it disappears, there always remains something of it; some portions of it continue to exist as small industries (watch-making of a high quality, best sorts of silks, high quality velvets, etc.), or new connected branches grow up instead of the old ones, or the small industry, taking advantage of a mechanical motor, assumes a new form. We thus find it endowed with an astonishing vitality. It undergoes various modifications, it adapts itself to new conditions, it struggles without losing hope of better times to come. Anyhow, it has not the characteristics of a decaying institution. In some industries the factory is undoubtedly victorious; but there are other branches in which the petty trades hold their own position. Even in the textile industries – especially in consequence of the wide use of the labour of children and women – which offer so many advantages for the factory system, the hand-loom still competes with the power-loom.

As a whole, the transformation of the petty trades into great industries goes on with a slowness which cannot fail to astonish even those who are convinced of its necessity. Nay, sometimes we may even see the reverse movement going on – occasionally, of course, and only for a time. I cannot forget my amazement when I saw at Verviers, some thirty years ago, that most of the woollen cloth factories – immense barracks facing the streets by more than a hundred windows each – were silent, and their costly machinery was rusting, while cloth was woven in hand-looms in the weavers' houses, for the owners of those very same factories. Here we have, of course, but a temporary fact, fully explained by the spasmodic character of the trade and the heavy losses sustained by the owners of the factories when they cannot run their mills all the year round. But it illustrates the obstacles which the transformation has to comply with. As to the silk trade, it continues to spread over Europe in its rural industry shape; while hundreds of new petty trades appear every year, and when they find nobody to carry them on in the villages – as is the case in this country – they shelter themselves in the suburbs of the great cities, as we have lately learned from the inquiry into the 'sweating system'

Now, the advantages offered by a large factory in comparison with hand work are self-evident as regards the economy of labour, and especially – *this is the main point* – the facilities both for sale and for having the raw produce at a lower price. How can we then explain the persistence of the petty trades? Many causes, however, most of which cannot be valued in shillings and pence, are at work in favour of the petty trades, and these causes will be best seen from the following illustrations. I must say, however, that even a brief sketch of the countless industries which are carried on on a small scale in this country, and on the Continent, would be far beyond the scope of this chapter. When I began to study the subject some thirty years ago, I never guessed, from the little attention devoted to it by the orthodox economists, what a wide, complex, important, and interesting organisation would appear at the end of a closer inquiry.

We have not for the United Kingdom such statistical data as are obtained in France and Germany by periodical censuses of all the factories and workshops, and the numbers of the workpeople, foremen and clerks, employed on a given day in

[127]

each industrial and commercial establishment. Consequently, up to the present time all the statements made by economists about the so-called 'concentration' of the industry in this country, and the consequent 'unavoidable' disappearance of the small industries, have been based on mere impressions of the writers – not on statistical data. It is only since factory inspection has been introduced by the Factory Act of 1895 that we begin to find, in the reports published since 1900 by the Factory Inspectors, information which permits us to get a general idea about the distribution of working men in factories of different sizes, and the extension that the petty trades have retained in this country up till now.

Let me remark that the Factory Inspectors consider as a *workshop* every industrial establishment which has no mechanican motive power, and as a *factory* every establishment provided with steam, gas, water or electric power.

On the basis of these reports we can say that *nearly one-fourth (24 per cent) of all the industrial workers of this country are working in workshops having less than 8 to 10 workers per establishment.* One-fifth part of all the industrial workers of this country were girls and boys, and more than two-fifths (41 per cent) were either women or children. All the industrial production of the United Kingdom, with its immense exports, was thus *giving work to less than 3,000,000 adult men* – 2,983,000 – out of a population of 42,000,000, to whom we must add 972,200 persons working in the mines. As to the textile industry, which supplies almost one-half of the English exports, *there are less than 300,000 adult men who find employment in it.* The remainder is the work of children, boys, girls and women.

It is true that the Factory Inspectors represent each separate branch of a given industry as a special establishment. Thus, if an employer or a society owns a spinning mill, a weaving factory, and a special building for dressing and finishing, the three are represented as separate factories. But this is precisely what is wanted for giving us an exact idea about the degree of concentration of a given industry. Besides, it is also known that, for instance, in the cotton industry, in the neigh-

[128]

bourhood of Manchester, the spinning, the weaving, the dressing, and so on belong very often to different employers, who send to each other the stuffs at different degrees of fabrication; those factories which combine under the same management all the three or four consecutive phases of the manufacture are an exception.

But it is especially in the division of the non-textile industries that we find an enormous development of small factories. The 2,755,460 workpeople who are employed in all the non-textile branches, with the exception of mining, are scattered in 79,059 factories, each of which has only an average of 35 workers. Moreover, the Factory Inspectors had on their lists 676,776 workpeople employed in 88,814 workshops (without mechanical power), which makes an average of 8 persons only per workshop. These last figures are, however, as we saw, below the real ones, as another 60,000 workshops occupying 500,000 more workpeople were not yet tabulated.

Such averages as *93 and 35 workpeople per factory, and 8 per workshop,* distributed over 178,756 industrial establishments, destroy already the legend according to which the big factories have already absorbed most of the small ones. The figures show, on the contrary, what an immense number of small factories and workshops resist the absorption by the big factories, and how they multiply by the side of the great industry in various branches, especially those of recent origin.

Let us take, first of all, the *textile* industries, which include cotton, wool, silk, linen, jute and hemp, as well as machine-made lace and knitting. Many of my readers will probably be astonished to learn that even in the cotton industry a great number of quite small factories continue to exist up to the present day.

This could have been foreseen by everyone who has some practical knowledge of industry, but it is overlooked by the theorists, who know industry mostly from books. In every country of the world there are by the side of the large factories a great number of small ones, the success of which is due to the variety of their produce and the facilities they offer to follow the vagaries of fashion.

All the important branches of the British textile industry, which give work to more than 240,000 men and women, have thus remained up till now at the stage of a small and middle-sized industry.

If we take now the *non-textile* industries, we find on the one side an immense number of small industries which have grown up around the great ones, and owing to them; and, on the other side, a large part of the fundamental industries have remained in the stage of small establishments. The average for all these branches, which give occupation to three-fourths of all the industrial workers of the United Kingdom – that is, 2,755,460 workers – hardly attains, we saw, 35 persons per factory – the workshops being not yet included in this division. However, it is especially when we go into details, and analyse the figures which I have calculated for each separate branch, that we fully realise the importance of the petty trades in England. This is what we are going to do, mentioning first what belongs here to the great industry, and studying next the small one.

Following the classification adopted by the Factory Inspectors, we see first that the gasworks belong to the domain of the fairly big establishments (78 people on the average). The india-rubber factories belong to the same category (125 workers on the average); and amidst the 456 glass-works of the United Kingdom there must be some big ones, as the average is 87 workpeople.

Next come mining and metallurgy, which are carried on, as a rule, on a great scale; but already in the iron foundries we find a great number of establishments belonging to the middle-sized and small industry. Thus at Sheffield I saw myself several foundries employing only from 5 to 6 workmen. For the making of huge machinery there is, of course, a number of very large works. But it is very instructive to see how very small works prosper by the side of big ones; they are numerous enough to reduce the average to 70 workers per establishment for the 5,318 works of this category.

Shipbuilding and the manufacture of metallic tubes evidently belong to the great industry (averages, 243 and 156 persons per establishment).

Going over to the chemical works, we find again a great industry in the fabrication of alkalies and of matches (only 25 works); but, on the contrary, the fabrication of soap and candles, as well as manures and all other sorts of chemical produce, which represents nearly 2,000 factories, belongs almost entirely to the domain of the small industry. The average is only 29 workpeople per factory. There are, of course, half a dozen of very large soap works – one knows them only too well by their advertisements on the cliffs and in the fields; but the low average of 29 workmen proves how many small factories must exist by the side of the soap kings. The 2,500 works engaged in the fabrication of furniture, both in wood and in iron, belong again chiefly to the small industry. The small and very small factories swarm by the side of a few great ones, to say nothing of the thousands of the still smaller workshops. The great storehouses of our cities are for the most part mere exhibitions of furniture made in very small factories and workshops.

In the fabrication of food produce we find several great sugar, chocolate and preserves works; but by their side we find also a very great number of small establishments, which seem not to complain of the proximity of the big ones, as they occupy nearly two-thirds of the workers employed in this branch. I do not speak, of course, of the village windmills, but one cannot fail to be struck by the immense number of small breweries (2,076 breweries have on the average only 24 workmen each).

In calico-printing we enter once more the domain of great factories; but by their side we find a pretty large number of small ones; so that the average for all this category is 144 workpeople per factory.

In the making of ready-made clothing and the fabrication of hats, linen, boots and shoes, and gloves, we see the averages for the factories of this description going up to 80, 100 and 150 persons per factory. But it is here also that countless small workshops come in. It must also be noticed that most of the factories of ready-made clothing have their own special character. The factory buys the cloth and makes the cutting by

[131]

means of special machinery; but the sewing is done by women, who come to work in the factory. They pay so much for the sewing-machine, so much for the motor power (if there is one), so much for the gas, so much for the iron, and so on, and they are on piece work. Very often this becomes a 'sweating system' on a large scale. Round the big factories a great number of small workshops are centred.

And, finally, we find great factories for the fabrication of gunpowder and explosives (they employ less than 12,000 workpeople), stuff buttons, and umbrellas (only 6,000 employees). But we find also in the table of workshops that in these last two branches there are thousands of them by the side of a few great factories.

In this brief enumeration we have gone over all that belongs to the great industry. The remainder belongs almost entirely to the domain of the small, and often the very small industry. Such are all the factories for woodwork, which have on the average only 15 men per establishment, but represent a contingent of more than 100,000 workmen and more than 6,000 employers. The tanneries, the manufacture of all sorts of little things in ivory and bone, and even the brick-works and the potteries, representing a total of 260,000 workpeople and 11,200 employers, belong, with a very few exceptions, to the small industry.

Then we have the factories dealing with the burnishing and enamelling of metals, which also belong chiefly to the small industry – the average being only 28 workpeople per factory. But what is especially striking is the development of the small and very small industry in the fabrication of agricultural machinery (32 workers per factory), of all sorts of tools (22 on the average), needles and pins (43), ironmongery, sanitary apparatus, and various instruments (25), even of boilers (48 per factory), chains, cables and anchors (in many districts this work, as also the making of nails, is made by hand by *women*).

Needless to say that the fabrication of furniture, which occupies nearly 64,000 operatives, belongs chiefly – more than three-fourths of it – to the small industry. The average for the 1,979 factories of this branch is only 21 workpeople, the work-

[132]

shops not being included in this number. The same is true of the factories for the curing of fish, machine-made pastry, and so on, which occupy 38,030 workpeople in more than 2,700 factories, having thus an average of 14 operatives each.

Jewellery and the manufacture of watches, photographic apparatus, and all sorts of luxury articles, again belong to the small and very small industry, and give occupation to 54,000 persons.

All that belongs to printing, lithography, bookbinding, and stationery again represents a vast field occupied by the small industry, which prospers by the side of a small number of very large establishments. More than 120,000 are employed in these branches in more than 6,000 factories (workshops not yet included).

And, finally, we find a large domain occupied by saddlery, brush-making, the making of sails, basket-making, and the fabrication of a thousand little things in leather, paper, wood, metal, and so on. This class is certainly not insignificant, as it contains more than 4,300 employers and nearly 130,000 workpeople, employed in a mass of very small factories by the side of a few very great ones, the average being only from 25 to 35 persons per factory.

In short, in the different non-textile industries, the Inspectors have tabulated *32,042 factories employing, each of them, less than 10 workpeople.*

All taken, we find 270,000 workpeople employed in small factories having less than 50 and even 20 workers each, the result being that the very great industry (the factories employing more than 1,000 workpeople per factory) and the very small one (less than 10 workers) employ nearly the same number of operatives.

The important part played by small industry in this country fully appears from this rapid sketch. And I have not yet spoken of the workshops. The Factory Inspectors mentioned, as we saw, in their first report, 88,814 workshops, in which 676,776 workpeople (356,098 women) were employed in 1897. But, as we have already seen, these figures are incomplete. The number of workshops is about 147,000, and there must be about 1,200,000 persons employed in them (820,000 men and about 356,000 women and children).

It is evident that this class comprises a very considerable number of bakers, small carpenters, tailors, cobblers, cartwrights, village smiths, and so on. But there is also in this class an immense number of workshops belonging to industry, properly speaking – that is, workshops which manufacture for the great commercial market. Some of these workshops may of course employ 50 persons or more, but the immense majority employ only from 5 to 20 workpeople each.

We thus find in this class 1,348 small establishments, scattered both in the villages and the suburbs of great cities, where nearly 14,000 persons make lace, knitting, embroidery, and weaving in hand-looms; more than 100 small tanneries, more than 20,000 cartwrights, and 746 small bicycle-makers. In cutlery, in the fabrication of tools and small arms, nails and screws, and even anchors and anchor chains, we find again many thousands of small workshops employing something like 60,000 workmen. All that, let us remember, without counting those workshops which employ no women or children, and therefore are not submitted to the Factory Inspectors. As to the fabrication of clothing, which gives work to more than 350,000 men and women, distributed over nearly 45,000 workshops, let it be noted that it is not small tailors that is spoken of here, but that mass of *workshops* which swarm in Whitechapel and the suburbs of all great cities, and where we find them 5 to 50 women and men making clothing for the tailor shops, big and small. In these shops the measure is taken, and sometimes the cutting is made; but the clothing is sewn in the small workshops, which are very often somewhere in the country. Even parts of the commands of linen and clothing for the army find their way to workshops in country places. As to the underclothing and mercery which are sold in the great stores, they are fabricated in small workshops, which must be counted by the thousand.

We thus see that even in this country, which may be considered as representing the highest development of the great

[134]

industry, the number of persons employed in the small trade continues to be immense. The small industries are as much a distinctive feature of the British industry as its few immense factories and ironworks.

Going over now to what is known about the small industries of this country from direct observation, we find that the suburbs of London, Glasgow and other great cities swarm with small workshops, and that there are regions where the petty trades are as developed as they are in Switzerland or in Germany. Sheffield is a well-known example in point. The Sheffield cutlery – one of the glories of England – is *not* made by machinery: it is chiefly made by hand. There are at Sheffield a number of firms which manufacture cutlery right through from the making of steel to the finishing tools, and employ wage-workers, and yet even these firms – I am told by Edward Carpenter, who kindly collected for me information about the Sheffield trade – let out some part of their work to the 'small masters'. But by far the greatest number of the cutlers work in their homes with their relatives, or in small workshops supplied with wheel-power, which they rent for a few shillings a week. Immense yards are covered with buildings, which are sub-divided into numbers of small workshops. Some of these cover but a few square yards and there I saw smiths hammering, all the day long, blades of knives on a small anvil, close by the blaze of their fires; occasionally the smith may have 1 helper, or 2.

When I walked through these workshops I easily imagined myself in a Russian cutlery village, like Pavlovo or Vorsma. The Sheffield cutlery has thus maintained its olden organisation, and the fact is the more remarkable as the earnings of the cutlers are low as a rule; but, even when, they are reduced to a few shillings a week, the cutler prefers to vegetate on his small earnings than to enter as a waged labourer in a 'house'.

The variety of domestic industries carried on in the Lake District is much greater than might be expected, but they still wait for careful explorers. I will only mention the hoop-makers, the basket trade, the charcoal-burners, the bobbin-makers, the

[135]

small iron furnaces working with charcoal at Backbarrow, and so on. As a whole, we do not well know the petty trades of this country, and therefore we sometimes come across quite unexpected facts. Few Continental writers on industrial topics would guess, indeed, that twenty-five years ago nails were made by hand by thousands of men, women and children in the Black Country of South Staffordshire, as also in Derbyshire, and that some of this industry remains still in existence, or that the best needles are made by hand at Redditch.

The Birmingham gun and rifle trades, which also belong to the same domain of small industries, are well known. As to the various branches of dress, there are still important divisions of the United Kingdom where a variety of domestic trades connected with dress is carried on on a large scale. I need only mention the cottage industries of Ireland, as also some of them which have survived in the shires of Buckingham, Oxford, and Bedford; hosiery is a common occupation in the villages of the counties of Nottingham and Derby; and several great London firms send out cloth to be made into dress in the villages of Sussex and Hampshire. Woollen hosiery is at home in the villages of Leicester, and especially in Scotland; straw-plaiting and hat-making in many parts of the country; while at Northampton, Leicester, Ipswich and Stafford shoe-making was, till quite lately, a widely spread domestic occupation, or was carried on in small workshops; even at Norwich it remains a petty trade to some extent, notwithstanding the competition of the factories.

The petty trades are thus an important factor of industrial life even in Great Britain, although many of them have gathered into the towns. But if we find in this country so many fewer rural industries than on the Continent, we must not imagine that their disappearance is due only to a keener competition of the factories. The chief cause was the compulsory exodus from the villages.

As everyone knows from Thorold Rogers's work, the growth of the factory system in England was intimately connected with that enforced exodus. Whole industries, which prospered till then, were killed downright by the forced clearing of estates.

[136]

The workshops, much more even than the factories, multiply wherever they find cheap labour; and the specific feature of this country is, that the cheapest labour – that is, the greatest number of destitute people – is to be found in the great cities. The agitation raised (with no result) in connection with the 'Dwellings of the Poor', the 'Unemployed', and the 'Sweating System', has fully disclosed that characteristic feature of the economic life of England and Scotland; and the painstaking researches made by Mr Charles Booth have shown that one-quarter of the population of London – that is, 1,000,000 out of the 3,800,000 who entered within the scope of his inquest – would be happy if the heads of their families could have regular earnings of something like £1 a week all the year round. Half of them would be satisfied with even less than that. The same state of things was found by Mr Seebohm Rowntree at York. Cheap labour is offered in such quantities in the suburbs of all the great cities of Great Britain, that the petty and domestic trades, which are scattered on the Continent in the villages, gather in this country in the cities.

Exact figures as to the small industries are wanting, but a simple walk through the suburbs of London would do much to realise the variety of petty trades which swarm in the metropolis, and, in fact, in all chief urban agglomerations. The evidence given before the 'Sweating System Committee' has shown how far the furniture and ready-made clothing palaces and the 'Bonheur des Dames' bazaars of London are mere exhibitions of samples, or markets for the sale of the produce of the small industries. Thousands of sweaters, some of them having their own workshops, and others merely distributing work to sub-sweaters who distribute it again amidst the destitute, supply those palaces and bazaars with goods made in the slums or in very small workshops. The commerce *is* centralised in those bazaars – not the industry. The furniture palaces and bazaars are thus merely playing the part which the feudal castle formerly played in agriculture: they centralise the profits – not the production.

In reality, the extension of the petty trades, side by side with the great factories, is nothing to be wondered at. It is an

[137]

economic necessity. The absorption of the small workshops by bigger concerns is a fact which had struck the economists in the forties of the last century, especially in the textile trades. It is continued still in many other trades, and is especially striking in a number of very big concerns dealing with metals and war supplies for the different states. But there is another process which is going on parallel with the former, and which consists in the continuous creation of new industries, usually making their start on a small scale. Each new factory calls into existence a number of small workshops, partly to supply its own needs and partly to submit its produce to a further transformation. Thus, to quote but one instance, the cotton mills have created an immense demand for wooden bobbins and reels, and thousands of men in the Lake District set to manufacture them – by hand first, and later on with the aid of some plain machinery. Only quite recently, after years had been spent in inventing and improving the machinery, the bobbins began to be made on a larger scale in factories. And even yet, as the machines are very costly, a great quantity of bobbins are made in small workshops, with but little aid from machines, while the factories themselves are relatively small, and seldom employ more than 50 operatives – chiefly children. As to the reels of irregular shape, they are still made by hand, or partly with the aid of small machines, continually invented by the workers. New industries thus grow up to supplant the old ones; each of them passes through a preliminary stage on a small scale before reaching the great factory stage; and the more active the inventive genius of a nation is, the more it has of these budding industries. The countless small bicycle works which have lately grown up in this country, and are supplied with ready-made parts of the bicycle by the larger factories, are an instance in point. The domestic and small workshops fabrication of boxes for matches, boots, hats, confectionery, grocery, and so on is another familiar instance.

Besides, the large factory stimulates the birth of new petty trades by creating new wants. The cheapness of cottons and woollens, of paper and brass, has created hundreds of new small industries. Our households are full of their produce –

mostly things of quite modern invention. And while some of them already are turned out by the million in the great factory, all have passed through the small workshop stage, before the demand was great enough to require the great factory organisation. The more we may have of new inventions, the more shall we have of such small industries; and again, the more we have of them, the more shall we have of the inventive genius, the want of which is so justly complained of in this country (by W. Armstrong, amongst many others). We must not wonder, therefore, if we see so many small trades in this country; but we must regret that the great number have abandoned the villages in consequence of the bad conditions of land tenure, and that they have migrated in such numbers to the cities, to the detriment of agriculture.

In England, as everywhere, the small industries are an important factor in the industrial life of the country; and it is chiefly in the infinite variety of the small trades, which utilise the half-fabricated produce of the great industries, that inventive genius is developed, and the rudiments of the future great industries are elaborated. The small bicycle workshops, with the hundreds of small improvements which they introduced, have been under our very eyes the primary cells out of which the great industry of the motor cars, and later on of the aeroplanes, has grown up. The small village jam-makers were the precursors and the rudiments of the great factories of preserves which now employ hundreds of workers. And so on.

Consequently, to affirm that the small industries are doomed to disappear, while we see new ones appear every day, is merely to repeat a hasty generalisation that was made in the earlier part of the nineteenth century by those who witnessed the absorption of hand-work by machinery work in the cotton industry – a generalisation which, as we saw already, and are going still better to see on the following pages, find no confirmation from the study of industries, great and small, and is upset by the censuses of the factories and workshops. Far from showing a tendency to disappear, the small industries show, on the contrary, a tendency towards making a further development,

[139]

since the municipal supply of electrical power – such as we have, for instance, in Manchester – permits the owner of a small factory to have a cheap supply of motive power, exactly in the proportion required at a given time, and to pay only for what is really consumed.

Small industries are met with in France in a very great variety, and they represent a most important feature of national economy. It is estimated, in fact, that while one-half of the population of France live upon agriculture, and one-third upon industry, this third part is equally distributed between the great industry and the small one.

A considerable number of peasants who resort to small industries without abandoning agriculture would have to be added, and the additional earnings which these peasants find in industry are so important that in several parts of France peasant proprietorship could not be maintained without the aid derived from the rural industries.

The small peasants know what they have to expect the day they become factory hands in a town; and so long as they have not been dispossessed by the money-lender of their lands and houses, and so long as the village rights in the communal grazing grounds or woods have not been lost, they cling to a combination of industry with agriculture. Having, in most cases, no horses to plough the land, they resort to an arrangement which is widely spread, if not universal, among small French landholders, even in purely rural districts. One of the peasants who keep a plough and a team of horses tills all the fields in turn. At the same time, owing to a wide maintenance of the communal spirit, which I have described elsewhere, further support is found in the communal shepherd, the communal wine-press, and various forms of 'aids' amongst the peasants. And wherever the village-community spirit is maintained, the small industries persist, while no effort is spared to bring the small plots under higher culture.

Market-gardening and fruit culture often go hand in hand with small industries. And wherever well-being is found on a relatively unproductive soil, it is nearly always due to a combination of the two sister arts.

The most wonderful adaptations of the small industries to new requirements, and substantial technical progress in the methods of production, can be noted at the same time. In the woody regions of the Perche and the Maine we find all sorts of wooden industries which evidently could only be maintained owing to the communal possession of the woods. Near the forest of Perseigne there is a small burg, Fresnaye, which is entirely peopled with workers in wood.

At Theirs, where the cheapest sorts of cutlery are made, the division of labour, the cheapness of rent for small workshops supplied with motive power from the Durolle river, or from small gas motors, the aid of a great variety of specially invented machine tools, and the existing combination of machine work with hand-work have resulted in such a perfection of the technical part of the trade that it is considered doubtful whether the factory system could further economise labour. For twelve miles round Thiers, in each direction, all the streamlets are dotted with small workshops, in which peasants, who continue to cultivate their fields, are at work.

Basket-making is again an important cottage industry in several parts of France, namely in Aisne and in Haute Marne. In this last department, at Villaines, everyone is a basket-maker, 'and all the basket-makers belong to a co-operative society', Ardouin Dumazet remarks. 'There are no employers; all the produce is brought once a fortnight to the co-operative stores and there it is sold for the association. About 150 families belong to it, and each owns a house and some vineyards.' At Fays-Billot, also in Haute Marne, 1,500 basket-makers belong to an association; while at Thiérache, where several thousand men are engaged in the same trade, no association has been formed, the earnings being in consequence extremely low.

In Héricourt, a variety of small industries has grown by the side of the great ironmongery factories. The city spreads into the villages, where the population are making coffee-mills, spice-mills, machines for crushing the grain for the cattle, as well as saddlery, small ironmongery, or even watches. Else-

[141]

where the fabrication of different small parts of the watch having been monopolised by the factories, the workshops began to manufacture the small parts of the bicycles, and later on of the motor cars. In short, we have here quite a world of industries of modern origin, and with them of inventions made to simplify the work of the hand.

Each peasant house, each farm and *métayerie* in the hilly tracts of the Beaujolais and the Forez were small workshops at that time, and one could see, Reybaud wrote (in 1863), the lad of 20 embroidering fine muslin after he had finished cleaning the farm stables, without the work suffering in its delicacy from a combination of two such varied pursuits. On the contrary, the delicacy of the work and the extreme variety of patterns were a distinctive feature of the Tarare muslins and a cause of their success. All testimonies agreed at the same time in recognising that, while agriculture found support in the industry, the agricultural population enjoyed a relative well-being.

What most deserves admiration is not so much the development of the great industries – which, after all, here as elsewhere, are to a great extent international in their origins – as the creative and inventive powers and capacities of adaptation which appear amongst the great mass of these industrious populations. At every step, in the field, in the garden, in the orchard, in the dairy, in the industrial arts, in the hundreds of small inventions in these arts, one sees the creative genius of the folk. In these regions one best understands why France, taking the mass of its population, is considered the richest country of Europe.

The chief centre for petty trades in France is, however, Paris. There we find, by the side of the large factories, the greatest variety of petty trades for the fabrication of goods of every description, both for the home market and for export. The petty trades at Paris so much prevail over the factories that the average number of workmen employed in the 98,000 factories and workshops of Paris is less than *six*, while the number of persons employed in workshops which have less than five operatives is almost twice as big as the number of persons employed in the larger establishments. In fact, Paris is a great

[142]

bee-hive where hundreds of thousands of men and women fabricate in small workshops all possible varieties of goods which require skill, taste and invention. These small work-shops, in which artistic finish and rapidity of work are so much praised, necessarily stimulate the mental powers of the producers; and we may safely admit that if the Paris workmen are generally considered, and really are, more developed intellectually than the workers of any other European capital, this is due to a great extent to the character of the work they are engaged in – a work which implies artistic taste, skill, and especially inventiveness, always wide awake in order to invent new patterns of goods and steadily to increase and to perfect the technical methods of production. It also appears very probable that if we find a highly developed working population in Vienna and Warsaw, this depends again to a very great extent upon the very considerable development of similar small industries, which stimulate invention and so much contribute to develop the worker's intelligence.

The conclusion to be drawn is thus worded by M. Lucien March: 'To sum up, during the last fifty years a notable concentration of the factories took place in the big establishments' but *'this concentration does not prevent the maintenance of a mass of small enterprises, the average sizes of which increase but very slowly.'* This last is, in fact, what we have just seen from our brief sketch for the United Kingdom, and we can only ask ourselves whether – such being the facts – the word 'concentration' is well chosen. What we see in reality is, the appearance, *in some branches of industry*, of a certain number of large establishments, and especially of middle-sized factories. But this does not prevent in the least that very great numbers of small factories should continue to exist, either in other branches, or in the very same branches where large factories have appeared (the textiles, work in metal), or in branches connected with the main ones, which take their origin in these main ones, as the industry of clothing takes its origin from that of the textiles. As to the large deductions about 'concentration' made by certain economists, they are mere *hypotheses* – useful, of course, for stimulating research, but becoming quite noxious when they are represented *as economical laws*, when in reality they are not confirmed at all by the testimony of carefully observed facts.

Unhappily, the discussion upon this important subject has often taken in Germany a passionate and even a personally aggressive character. On the one hand, the ultra-conservative elements of German politics tried, and succeeded to some extent, in making of the petty trades and the domestic industries an arm for securing a return to the 'olden good times'. They even passed a law intended to prepare a re-introduction of the old-fashioned, closed and patriarchal corporations which could be placed under the close supervision and tutorship of the state, and they saw in such a law a weapon against social democracy. On the other hand, the social democrats, justly opposed to such measures, but themselves inclined, in their turn, to take too abstract a view of economical questions, bitterly attack all those who do not merely repeat the stereotyped phrases to the effect that 'the petty trades are in decay', and 'the sooner they disappear the better', as they will give room to capitalist centralisation, which, according to the social democratic creed, 'will soon achieve its own ruin'. In this dislike of the small industries they are, of course, at one with the economists of the orthodox school, whom they combat on nearly all other points.

The foundation for this creed is contained in one of the concluding chapters of Marx's *Kapital* (the last but one), in which the author spoke of the concentration of capital and saw in it the 'fatality of a natural law'. In the 'forties', this idea of 'concentration of capital', originated from what was going on in the textile industries, was continually recurring in the writings of all the French socialists, especially Considérant, and their German followers, and it was used by them as an argument in favour of the necessity of a social revolution. But Marx was too much of a thinker that he should not have taken notice of the subsequent developments of industrial life, which were not foreseen in 1848; if he had lived now, he surely would *not* have shut his eyes to the formidable growth of the numbers of small capitalists and to the middle-class fortunes

[144]

which are made in a thousand ways under the shadow of the modern 'millionaires'. Very likely he would have noticed also the extreme slowness with which the wrecking of small industries goes on – a slowness which could not be predicted fifty or forty years ago, because no one could foresee at that time the facilities which have been offered since for transport, the growing variety of demand, nor the cheap means which are now in use for the supply of motive power in small quantities. Being a thinker, he would have studied these facts, and very probably he would have mitigated the absoluteness of his earlier formulae, as in fact he did once with regard to the village community in Russia. It would be most desirable that his followers should rely less upon abstract formulae – easy as they may be as watchwords in political struggles – and try to imitate their teacher in his analysis of *concrete* economical phenomena.

It is evident that a number of petty trades in Germany are already now doomed to disappear; but there are others, on the contrary, which are endowed with a great vitality, and all chances are in favour of their continuing to exist and to take a further development for many years to come. In the fabrication of such textiles as are woven by millions of yards, and can be best produced with the aid of a complicated machinery, the competition of the hand-loom against the power-loom is evidently nothing but a survival, which may be maintained for some time by certain local conditions, but finally must die away.

The same is true with regard to many branches of the iron industries, hardware fabrication, pottery, and so on. But wherever the direct intervention of taste and inventiveness are required, wherever new patterns of goods requiring a continual renewal of machinery and tools must continually be introduced in order to fed the demand, as is the case with all fancy textiles, even though they be fabricated to supply the millions; wherever a great variety of goods and the uninterrupted invention of new ones goes on, as is the case in the toy trade, in instrument-making, watch-making, bicycle-making, and so on; and finally, wherever the artistic feeling of the individual worker makes the best part of his goods, as is the case in hundreds

K

of branches of small articles of luxury, there is a wide field for petty trades, rural workshops, domestic industries, and the like. More fresh air, more ideas, more general conceptions, and more co-operation are evidently required in those industries. But where the spirit of initiative has been awakened in one way or another, we see the petty industries taking a new development in Germany, as we have just seen that being done in France.

Now, in nearly all the petty trades in Germany, the position of the workers is unanimously described as most miserable, and the many admirers of centralisation which we find in Germany always insist upon this misery in order to predict, and to call for, the disappearance of 'those medieval survivals' which 'capitalist centralisation' must supplant for the benefit of the worker. The reality is, however, that when we compare the miserable conditions of the workers in the petty trades with the conditions of the wage-workers in the factories, in the same regions and in the same trades, we see that the very same misery prevails among the factory workers. They live upon wages of from 9s to 11s a week, in town slums instead of the country. They work eleven hours a day, and they also are subject to the extra misery thrown upon them during the frequently recurring crises. It is only after they have undergone all sorts of sufferings in their struggles against their employers that some factory workers succeed, more or less, here and there, to wrest from their employers a 'living wage' – and this again only in certain trades.

To welcome all these sufferings, seeing in them the action of a 'natural law' and a *necessary* step towards the *necessary* concentration of industry, would be simply absurd. While to maintain that the pauperisation of all workers and the wreckage of all village industries are a *necessary* step towards a higher form of industrial organisation would be, not only to affirm much more than one is entitled to affirm under the present imperfect state of economical knowledge, but to show an absolute want of comprehension of the sense of both natural and economic laws. Everyone, on the contrary, who has studied the question of the growth of great industries on its own merits, will undoubtedly agree with Thorold Rogers, who considered the sufferings inflicted upon the labouring classes for that purpose as having been of *no necessity whatever*, and simply having been inflicted to suit the temporary interests of the few – by no means those of the nation.

One fact dominates all the investigations which have been made into the conditions of the small industries. We find it in Germany, as well as in France or in Russia. In an immense number of trades it is not the superiority of the *technical* organisation of the trade in a factory, nor the economies realised on the prime-motor, which militate against the small industry in favour of the factories, but the more advantageous conditions for *selling* the produce and for *buying* the raw produce which are at the disposal of big concerns. Wherever this difficulty has been overcome, either by means of association, or in consequence of a market being secured for the sale of the produce, it has always been found – first, that the conditions of the workers or artisans immediately improve; and next, that a rapid progress was realised in the technical aspects of the respective industries. New processes were introduced to improve the produce or to increase the rapidity of its fabrication; new machine-tools were invented; or new motors were resorted to; or the trade was reorganised so as to diminish the cost of production.

On the contrary, wherever the helpless, isolated artisans and workers continue to remain at the mercy of the wholesale buyers, who always – since Adam Smith's time – 'openly or tacitly' agree to act as one man to bring down the prices almost to a starvation level – and such is the case for the immense number of the small and village industries – their condition is so bad that only the longing of the workers after a certain relative independence, and their knowledge of what awaits them in the factory, prevent them from joining the ranks of the factory hands. Knowing that in most cases the advent of the factory would mean no work at all for most men, and the taking of the children and girls to the factory, they do the utmost to prevent it from appearing at all in the village.

[147]

As to combinations in the villages, co-operation and the like, one must never forget how jealously the German, the French, the Russian and the Austrian governments have hitherto prevented the workers, *and especially the village workers*, from entering into any sort of combination for economical purposes. In France the peasant syndicates were permitted only by the law of 1884. To keep the peasant at the lowest possible level, by means of taxation, serfdom, and the like, has been, and is still, the policy of most continental states. It was only in 1876 that some extension of the association rights was granted in Germany, and even now a mere co-operative association for the sale of the artisans' work is soon reported as a 'political association' and submitted as such to the usual limitations, such as the exclusion of women and the like. A striking example of that policy as regards a village association was given by Professor Issaieff, who also mentioned the severe measures taken by the wholesale buyers in the toy trade to prevent the workers from entering into direct intercourse with foreign buyers.

When one examines with more than a superficial attention the life of the small industries and their struggles for life, one sees that when they perish, they perish – not because 'an economy can be realised by using a hundred horse-power motor, instead of a hundred small motors'. This in conveniency never fails to be mentioned, although it is easily obviated in Sheffield, in Paris, and many other places by hiring workshops with wheel-power, supplied by a central machine, and, still more, as was so truly observed by Professor W. Unwin, by the electric transmission of power. They do not perish because a substantial economy can be realised in the factory production – in many more cases than is usually supposed, the fact is even the reverse – but because the capitalist who establishes a factory emancipates himself from the wholesale and retail dealers in raw materials; and especially, because he emancipates himself from the buyers of his produce and can deal directly with the wholesale buyer and exporter; or else he concentrates in one concern the different stages of fabrication of a given produce. The pages which Schulze-Gäwernitz gave to the organisation of the cotton industry in England, and to the difficulties which the German cotton-mill owners had to contend with, so long as they were dependent upon Liverpool for raw cotton, are most instructive in this direction. And what characterises the cotton trade prevails in all other industries as well.

If the Sheffield cutlers who now work in their tiny workshops, in one of the above-mentioned buildings supplied with wheel-power, were incorporated in one big factory, the chief advantage which would be realised in the factory would *not* be an economy in the costs of production, in comparison to the quality of the produce; with a shareholders' company the costs might even increase. And yet the profits (including wages) probably would be greater than the aggregate earnings of the workers, in consequence of the reduced costs of purchase of iron and coal, and the facilities for the sale of the produce. The great concern would thus find its advantages not in such factors as are imposed by the *technical* necessities of the trade at the time being, but in such factors as could be eliminated by co-operative organisation. All these are elementary notions among practical men.

It hardly need be added that a further advantage which the factory owner has is, that he can find a sale even for produce of the most inferior quality, provided there is a considerable quantity of it to be sold. All those who are acquainted with commerce know, indeed, what an immense bulk of the world's trade consists of 'shoddy', *patraque*, 'Red Indians' blankets', and the like, shipped to distant countries. Whole cities – we just saw – produce nothing but 'shoddy'.

Altogether, it may be taken as one of the fundamental facts of the economical life of Europe that the defeat of a number of small trades, artisan work and domestic industries, came through their being incapable of organising the *sale* of their produce – not from the *production* itself. The same thing recurs at every page of economical history. The incapacity of organising the sale, without being enslaved by the merchant, was the leading feature of the medieval cities, which gradually fell under the economical and political yoke of the guild-merchant, *simply because they were not able to maintain the sale of their manu-*

[149]

factures by the community as a whole, or to organise the sale of a new produce in the interest of the community. When the markets for such commodities came to be Asia on the one side, and the New World on the other side, such was fatally the case; since commerce had ceased to be *communal*, and had become *individual*, the cities became a prey for the rivalries of the chief merchant families.

Even nowadays, when we see the co-operative societies beginning to succeed in their productive workshops, while fifty years ago they invariably failed in their capacity of producers, we may conclude that the cause of their previous failures was not in their incapacity of properly and economically organising *production*, but in their inability of acting as *sellers* and exporters of the produce they had fabricated. Their present successes, on the contrary, are fully accounted for by the network of distributive societies which they have at their command. The sale has been simplified, and production has been rendered possible *by first organising the market*.

Such are a few conclusions which may be drawn from a study of the small industries in Germany and elsewhere. And it may be safely said, with regard to Germany, that if measures are not taken for driving the peasants from the land on the same scale as they have been taken in this country; if, on the contrary, the numbers of small landholders multiply, they necessarily will turn to various small trades, in addition to agriculture, as they have done, and are doing, in France. Every step that may be taken, either for awakening intellectual life in the villages, or for assuring the peasants' or the country's rights upon the land, will necessarily further the growth of industries in the villages.

If it were worth extending our inquiry to other countries, we should find a vast field for most interesting observations in Switzerland. There we should see the same vitality in a variety of petty industries, and we could mention what has been done in the different cantons for maintaining the small trades by three different sets of measures: the extension of co-operation; a wide extension of technical education in the schools and the introduction of new branches of semi-artistic production in different parts of the country; and the supply of cheap motive power in the houses by means of a hydraulic or an electric transmission of power borrowed from the waterfalls. A separate book of the greatest interest and value could be written on this subject, especially on the impulse given to a number of petty trades, old and new, by means of a cheap supply of motive power. Such a book would also offer a great interest in that it would show to what an extent that mingling together of agriculture with industry, which I described in the first edition of this book as 'the factory amidst the fields', has progressed of late in Switzerland. It strikes at the present time even the casual traveller.

The facts which we have briefly passed in review show, to some extent, the benefits which could be derived from a combination of agriculture with industry, if the latter could come to the village, not in its present shape of a capitalist factory, but in the shape of a socially organised industrial production, with the full aid of machinery and technical knowledge. In fact, the most prominent feature of the petty trades is that a relative well-being is found only where they are combined with agriculture: where the workers have remained in possession of the soil and continue to cultivate it. Even amidst the weavers of France or Moscow, who have to reckon with the competition of the factory, relative well-being prevails so long as they are not compelled to part with the soil. On the contrary, as soon as high taxation or the impoverishment during a crisis has compelled the domestic worker to abandon his last plot of land to the usurer, misery creeps into his house. The sweater becomes all-powerful, frightful overwork is resorted to, and the whole trade often falls into decay.

Such facts, as well as the pronounced tendency of the factories towards migrating to the villages, which becomes more and more apparent nowadays, and found of late its expression in the 'Garden Cities' movement, are very suggestive. Of course, it would be a great mistake to imagine that industry ought to return to its hand-work stage in order to be combined with agriculture. Whenever a saving of human labour can be obtained by means of a machine, the machine is welcome and

[151]

will be resorted to; and there is hardly one single branch of industry into which machinery work could not be introduced with great advantage, at least at some of the stages of the manufacture. In the present chaotic state of industry, nails and cheap pen-knives can be made by hand, and plain cottons be woven in the hand-loom; but such an anomaly will not last. The machine will supersede hand-work in the manufacture of plain goods. But at the same time, hand-work very probably will extend its domain in the artistic finishing of many things which are now made entirely in the factory; and it will always remain an important factor in the growth of thousands of young and new trades.

But the question arises: Why should not the cottons, the woollen cloth and the silks, now woven by hand in the villages, be woven by machinery in the same villages, without ceasing to remain connected with work in the fields? Why should not hundreds of domestic industries, now carried on entirely by hand, resort to labour-saving machines, as they already do in the knitting trade and many others? There is no reason why the small motor should not be of a much more general use than it is now, wherever there is no need to have a factory; and there is no reason why the village should not have its small factory, wherever factory work is preferable, as we already see it occasionally in certain villages in France.

More than that. There is no reason why the factory, with its motive force and machinery, should not belong to the community, as is already the case for motive power in the above-mentioned workshops and small factories in the French portion of the Jura hills. It is evident that now, under the capitalist system, the factory is the curse of the village, as it comes to overwork children; and to make paupers out of its male inhabitants; and it is quite natural that it should be opposed by all means by the workers, if they have succeeded in maintaining their olden trades' organisations (as at Sheffield, or Solingen), or if they have not yet been reduced to sheer misery (as in the Jura). But under a more rational social organisation, the factory would find no such obstacles: it would be a boon to the village. And there is already unmis-

[152]

takable evidence to show that a move in this direction *is being made* in a few village communities.

The moral and physical advantages which man would derive from dividing his work between the field and the workshop are self-evident. But the difficulty is, we are told, in the necessary centralisation of the modern industries. In industry, as well as in politics, centralisation has so many admirers! But in both spheres the ideal of the centralisers badly needs revision. In fact, if we analyse the modern industries, we soon discover that for some of them the co-operation of hundreds, or even thousands, of workers gathered at the same spot is really necessary. The great iron works and mining enterprises decidedly belong to that category; oceanic steamers cannot be built in village factories. But very many of our big factories are nothing else but agglomerations under a common management, of several distinct industries; while others are mere agglomerations of hundreds of copies of the very same machine; such are most of our gigantic spinning and weaving establishments.

The manufacture being a strictly private enterprise, its owners find it advantageous to have all the branches of a given industry under their own management; they thus cumulate the profits of the successive transformations of the raw material. And when several thousand power-looms are combined in one factory, the owner finds his advantage in being able to hold the command of the market. But from a *technical* point of view the advantages of such an accumulation are trifling and often doubtful. Even so centralised an industry as that of the cottons does not suffer at all from the division of production of one given sort of goods at its different stages between several separate factories: we see it at Manchester and its neighbouring towns. As to the petty trades, no inconvenience is experienced from a still greater subdivision between the workshops in the watch trade and very many others.

We often hear that one horse-power costs so much in a small engine, and so much less in an engine ten times more powerful; that the pound of cotton yarn costs much less when

[153]

the factory doubles the number of its spindles. But, in the opinion of the best engineering authorities, such as Professor W. Unwin, the hydraulic, and especially the electric, distribution of power from a central station sets aside the first part of the argument. As to its second part, calculations of this sort are only good for those industries which prepare the half-manufactured produce for further transformations. As to those countless descriptions of goods which derive their value chiefly from the intervention of skilled labour they can be best fabricated in small factories which employ a few hundreds, or even a few scores of operatives. This is why the 'concentration' so much spoken of is often nothing but an amalgamation of capitalists for the purpose of *dominating the market*, not for cheapening the technical process.

Even under the present conditions the leviathan factories offer great inconveniences, as they cannot rapidly reform their machinery according to the constantly varying demands of the consumers. How many failures of great concerns, too well known in this country to need to be named, were due to this cause during the crisis of 1886–90. As for the new branches of industry which I have mentioned at the beginning of the previous chapter, they always must make a start on a small scale; and they can prosper in small towns as well as in big cities, if the smaller agglomerations are provided with institutions stimulating artistic taste and the genius of invention. The progress achieved of late in toy-making, as also the high perfection attained in the fabrication of mathematical and optical instruments, of furniture, of small luxury articles, of pottery, and so on, are instances in point. Art and science are no longer the monopoly of the great cities, and further progress will be in scattering them over the country.

The geographical distribution of industries in a given country depends, of course, to a great extent upon a complexus of natural conditions; it is obvious that there are spots which are best suited for the development of certain industries. The banks of the Clyde and the Tyne are certainly most appropriate for shipbuilding yards, and shipbuilding yards must be surrounded by a variety of workshops and factories. The industries will always find some advantages in being grouped, to some extent, according to the natural features of separate regions. But we must recognise that now they are *not at all* grouped according to those features. Historical causes – chiefly religious wars and national rivalries – have had a good deal to do with their growth and their present distribution; still more so the employers were guided by considerations as to the facilities for sale and export – that is, by considerations which are already losing their importance with the increased facilities for transport, and will lose it still more when the producers produce for themselves, and not for customers far away.

Why, in a rationally organised society, ought London to remain a great centre for the jam and preserving trade, and manufacture umbrellas for nearly the whole of the United Kingdom? Why should the countless Whitechapel petty trades remain where they are, instead of being spread all over the country? There is no reason whatever why the mantles which are worn by English ladies should be sewn at Berlin and in Whitechapel, instead of in Devonshire or Derbyshire. Why should Paris refine sugar for almost the whole of France? Why should one-half of the boots and shoes used in the United States be manufactured in the 1,500 workshops of Massachusetts? There is absolutely no reason why these and like anomalies should persist. The industries must be scattered all over the world; and the scattering of industries amidst all civilised nations will be necessarily followed by a further scattering of factories over the territories of each nation.

In the course of this evolution, the natural produce of each region and its geographical conditions certainly will be *one* of the factories which will determine the character of the industries going to develop. in this region. But when we see that Switzerland has become a great exporter of steam engines, railway engines, and steamboats – although she has no iron ore and no coal for obtaining steel, and even has no sea-port to import them; when we see that Belgium has succeeded in being a great exporter of grapes, and that Manchester has managed to become a sea-port – we understand that in the geographical distribution of industries, the two factors of local

[155]

produces and of an advantageous position by the sea are not yet the dominant factors. We begin to understand that, all taken, it is the *intellectual* factor – the spirit of invention, the capacity of adaptation, political liberty, and so on – which counts for more than all others.

That all the industries find an advantage in being carried on in close contact with a great variety of other industries the reader has seen already from numerous examples. Every industry requires *technical surroundings*. But the same is also true of agriculture.

Agriculture cannot develop without the aid of machinery, and the use of a perfect machinery cannot be generalised without industrial surroundings: without mechanical workshops, easily accessible to the cultivator of the soil, the use of agricultural machinery is not possible. The village smith would not do. If the work of a threshing-machine has to be stopped for a week or more, because one of the cogs in a wheel has been broken, and if to obtain a new wheel one must send a special messenger to the next province – then the use of a threshing-machine is not possible. But this is precisely what I saw in my childhood in Central Russia; and quite lately I have found the very same fact mentioned in an English autobiography in the first half of the nineteenth century. Besides, in all the northern part of the temperate zone, the cultivators of the soil must have some sort of industrial employment during the long winter months. This is what has brought about the great development of rural industries, of which we have just seen such interesting examples. But this need is also felt in the soft climate of the Channel Islands, notwithstanding the extension taken by horticulture under glass. 'We need such industries. Could you suggest us any?' wrote to me one of my correspondents in Guernsey.

But this is not yet all. Agriculture is so much in need of aid from those who inhabit the cities, that every summer thousands of men leave their slums in the towns and go to the country for the season of crops. The London destitutes go in thousands to Kent and Sussex as hay-makers and hop-pickers, it being estimated that Kent alone requires 80,000 additional men and women for hop-picking; whole villages in France and their

[156]

cottage industries are abandoned in the summer, and the peasants wander to the more fertile parts of the country; hundreds of thousands of human beings are transported every summer to the prairies of Manitoba and Dakota. Every summer many thousands of Poles spread at harvest time over the plains of Mecklenburg, Westphalia, and even France; and in Russia there is every year an exodus of several millions of men who journey from the north to the southern prairies for harvesting the crops; while many St Petersburg manufacturers reduce their production in the summer, because the operatives return to their native villages for the culture of their allotments.

Agriculture cannot be carried on without additional hands in the summer; but it still more needs temporary aids for *improving* the soil, for tenfolding its productive powers. Steam-digging, drainage, and manuring would render the heavy clays in the north-west of London a much richer soil than that of the American prairies. To become fertile, those clays want only plain, unskilled human labour, such as is necessary for digging the soil, laying in drainage tubes, pulverising phosphorites, and the like; and that labour would be gladly done by the factory workers if it were properly organised in a free community for the benefit of the whole society. The soil claims that sort of aid, and it would have it under a proper organisation, even if it were necessary to stop many mills in the summer for that purpose. No doubt the present factory-owners would consider it ruinous if they had to stop their mills for several months every year, because the capital engaged in a factory is expected to pump money every day and every hour, if possible. But that is the capitalist's view of the matter, not the community's view.

As to the workers, who ought to be the real managers of industries, they will find it healthy *not* to perform the same monotonous work all the year round, and they will abandon it for the summer, if indeed they do not find the means of keeping the factory running by relieving each other in groups.

The scattering of industries over the country – so as to bring the factory amidst the fields, to make agriculture derive all those profits which it always finds in being combined with industry (see the eastern states of America) and to produce a combination of industrial with agricultural work – is surely the next step to be made, as soon as a reorganisation of our present conditions is possible. It is being made already, here and there, as we saw on the preceding pages. This step is imposed by the very necessity of *producing for the producers themselves*; it is imposed by the necessity for each healthy man and women to spend a part of their lives in manual work in the free air; and it will be rendered the more necessary when the great social movements, which have now become unavoidable, come to disturb the present international trade, and compel each nation to revert to her own resources for her own maintenance. Humanity as a whole, as well as each separate individual, will be gainers by the change, and the change will take place.

However, such a change also implies a thorough modification of our present system of education. It implies a society composed of men and women, each of whom is able to work with his or her hands, as well as with his or her brain, and to do so in more directions than one. This 'integration of capacities' and 'integral education' I am now going to analyse.

EDITOR'S APPENDIX

Kropotkin, whom one imagines was never without his notebook when visiting a field, factory or workship (which he did more frequently than most economic theorists), felt a certain exasperation at the assumption, whether by capitalists or Marxists, that there was a necessary and inevitable process of industrial concentration which all right-thinking people took for granted. When the Chief Inspector of Factories began publishing statistics on the numbers of industrial undertakings of various sizes, Kropotkin was delighted because they so amply confirmed his observations, and entered into correspondence with the Chief Inspector on the further elucidation of the figures. His friend and fellow-exile, Cherkesov, wrote a pamphlet, *The Concentration of Capital: A Marxian Fallacy*,[1] which, in terms of the distribution of ownership, supported his point of view.

Today we would ask more complicated questions. Are we talking about the number of employees, the capital value of the undertaking, the value of the product, its profitability, or the ownership of the capital invested in its production? The economist's attempt to evaluate the significance of scale in industry is characterised by Michael Utton's *Industrial Concentration*[2] in which he concludes that 'the amount of evidence on the economies of scale that can be achieved by large *firms* (as opposed to large plants) is very sparse . . . and what evidence there is tends to suggest that such economies are not universal throughout manufacturing industry nor significant in reducing costs'. But the reader's dilemma, in considering the validity of Kropotkin's point of view, is most readily resolved by looking around the room he is sitting in. Will he not find that most of the artefacts it contains, from clothing to furniture, are in fact the output of industry on a minute scale? Even his transistor radio ('sophisticated product of advanced technology', etc.) was probably made from components produced in tiny factories and assembled by women and children on the very pavements of Hong Kong.[3]

The worship of bigness in industry makes us exaggerate its actual extent, as Kropotkin found. My own experience, confined to the building industry, predisposes me towards his point of view. I remember working on a building designed from industrialised components where it was said to be essential (to reap the benefits of industrialisation) that the structure should be confined to standardised parts. When I actually went to the

[159]

factory where they were made, I found that these lattice beams were being made by a single old man, using a Staffa bending machine by hand, and could be varied simply by telling him to make the next one longer or shorter. We just assume that industry *ought* to be big.

We are in fact hypnotised by the cult of bigness in industry, even though the actual size of the industrial unit relates neither to technical complexity nor to functional efficiency, but rather to the cult of sheer size and of power and profit: the inevitable by-products of authoritarian society. This used to be reflected in the building of uneconomically over-sized ships like the giant Cunarders, and, since their demise, has been expressed in the building of grotesquely uneconomical planes, of which Concorde is simply the last of a long line. (Remember the Brabazon – whole villages were swept away to make a runway for it; then it rusted in its million-pound hanger until it was finally broken up for scrap.)

In the 1950s, Professor S. R. Dennison made the same discovery, declaring that the relief that modern industry *inevitably* leads to larger units of production was a Marxist fallacy:

'Over a wide range of industry the productive efficiency of small units was at least equal to, and in some cases surpassed that of the industrial giants. About 92 per cent of the businesses in the United Kingdom employed fewer than 250 people and were responsible for by far the greater part of the total national production. The position in the United States was about the same.'[4]

Again, those who think of industry as one great assembly line would be surprised by Dr Mark Abrams's observation that:

'In spite of nationalisation and the growth of large private firms, the proportion of the total working population employed by large organisations (i.e. concerns with over 1,000 employees) is still comparatively small. Such people constitute only 36 per cent of the working population and are far outnumbered by those who hold jobs as members of comparatively small organisations where direct personal contact throughout the group is a practical everyday possibility.'[5]

It is also revealing to study the nature of the industrial giants and to reflect on how few of them owe their size to considerations of industrial efficiency. H. P. Barker distinguished between two essentially different types of motive: the industrial and the non-industrial. By the industrial motive he meant,

[160]

'the normal commercial development of a product or a service which the public wants; for instance the motor-car industry or the chain store. There is also the vertical type of growth in which a seller expands downwards towards his raw materials, or a primary producer expands upwards towards the end products of his primary material. The soap and oil industries are such cases. Then there is the kind of expansion in which a successful firm seeks to diversify its business and its opportunities and to carry its financial eggs in several baskets – and lastly there is the type of expansion by which whole industries are aggregated under a single control because they cannot effectively be operated in any other way. Electricity and railways are an example.'[6]

But the very examples that he chose as cases of industrially necessary concentration, are ones which not only anarchists would query. I am not alone in thinking he is wrong about electricity. For example, an editorial in *New Scientist* commenting on the appalling complexity of the present system, prophesied that 'in future there will be a tendency to return to more or less local generation of electricity' and a correspondent of the *Guardian* castigates the Central Electricity Generating Board for 'spinning a web of electrical transmission lines without much reference to any other interests than its own' thus 'prejudicing the development of a more flexible and useful power system'. I know he is wrong about railways, where the history ever since the nationalisation of railways in Britain has pointed to the desirability of regional autonomy rather than of central control. The international co-ordination, without central control, of railways was one of Kropotkin's standard arguments for the success of non-hierarchical federation. Paul Goodman noted that: 'It is just such a situation that Kropotkin points to as an argument for anarchism – the example he uses is the railroad-network of Europe, laid down and run to perfection with no plan imposed from above.' I suspect that he is wrong about the motor industry. We know, from the much-publicised experience of Volvo, that manufacturers in the interests of 'job-enlargement' find it perfectly feasible to abandon the giant assembly-line in favour of small working groups. We know too that, in Colin Buchanan's words, 'two-thirds of the factory value of a car is represented by components brought by the actual manufacturer from *outside suppliers*. Brake drums, water pumps, oil seals, fuses, gaskets, connection rods, dynamos, petrol tanks, shock absorbers, carburettors, ball bearings, axles, cam-shafts, road springs and a couple of hundred other items

L

[161]

in car assembly are in fact made by a very large number of specialist firms scattered all over the country.'[7]

When Mr Barker turned to what he called the non-industrial and less healthy types of growth, he was describing familiar territory.

'Among these there is the type which starts and ends in the Stock Exchange and where the sole reason is the prospect of making a profitable flotation. Then there is the type of adiposity which often occurs when a successful company becomes possessed of large resources from past profits. The directors then look round for ways of investing the surplus fat merely because they have it. Then there is the type of large business born only out of doctrinaire or political considerations. Last of all there is the industrial giant created primary to satisfy the megalomania of one man.'[8]

He was writing before the wave of take-over bids and government-supported mergers of the late 1960s, for which the usual explanation was that of the economies of scale that would result and the argument that larger units would enable British industry to compete effectively in international markets. But since then, a study by the Industrial Policy Group itself has stressed the importance of small-scale enterprise and has dismissed the theory that Britain's industrial weakness stems from an inadequate number of large firms,[9] while Gerald Newbould concludes in his book, *Management and Merger Activity*, that while the declared aims of mergers and take-overs was industrial efficiency, the real objects were the creation or reinforcement of market dominance or defence against competitors.[10]

A growing number of such mergers are, of course, sheer financial piracy: the activity known as asset-stripping, when a company is acquired with the intention of making a profit, not from its productive activities, but by closing it down and selling off its assets – real property and capital goods. This certainly affects any attempt to draw contemporary conclusions from Kropotkin's analysis. In a debate in the House of Commons on the subject, Mr Arthur Blenkinsop said: "In 1960, 100 of our largest firms were responsible for 22 per cent of the nation's net industrial assets. By 1970 there had been a dramatic change, and the 100 largest firms were responsible for 50 per cent of our industrial assets. That is a much heavier concentration than that in the United States of America.' In the same debate, Mr T. H. Skeet remarked:

[162]

'In 1949 the top ten companies accounted for 25 per cent of the pre-taxed profits of all British industrial and commercial companies. By 1969 the figure was about 50 per cent. Therefore, the concentration had doubled in twenty years. . . . The Bolton Report also indicated that small firms, as a share of manufacturing output, accounted in 1924 for 42 per cent and in 1951 for 32 per cent, and that in 1968 the figure had gone down to 25 per cent.'[11]

The figures are different, of course, if you argue, like Kropotkin, in terms of the number of workers:

'Small firms – with 500 employees or less – still constitute more than 90 per cent of Britain's manufacturing industry, for instance. In the United States there are more than 300,000 companies with 500,000 factories, employing 16 million people and producing half the world's manufactured goods. The majority are quite small.'[12]

The confusion about definitions which arises in any discussion of the issue can be seen by comparing these conclusions with those of Jonathan Boswell, who says:

'there may be around 45,000 private and independent manufacturing firms employing fewer than 500 – responsible for about 20 per cent of total manufacturing employment, and a rather lower percentage of net manufacturing output. For practical purposes, therefore, small firms as I define them can be said to be responsible for around one-fifth of economic activity in British manufacturing: by any standards an appreciable share.'[13]

The Bolton Report, referred to by Mr Skeet, was the report of a government inquiry, which concluded: 'In manufacturing the share of small firms in employment and output has fallen substantially and almost continuously since the mid-1920s. There was also a dramatic fall in the number of small manufacturing firms up to 1948 and a slower but continual decline has been going on since then.'[14]

The Bolton Report saw the small-firm sector as 'the traditional breeding-ground for new industries – that is for innovation writ large' – and noted that technological changes could make small-scale operation highly economic. But what about automation? The word itself is simply the current jargon for a more intensive application of machines, particularly transfer machines, but it is seen as yet another factor which makes greater industrial concentration inevitable. This is simply another expression of the centralist mentality, for as Dr J. Langdon Goodman says:

'Automation can be a force either for concentration or dispersion. There is a tendency today for automation to develop along with larger and larger production units, but this may only be a phase through which the present technological advance is passing. The comparatively large sums of money which are needed to develop automation techniques, together with the amount of technological knowledge and unique quality of management, are possibly found more in the large units than in the smaller ones. Thus the larger units will proceed more quickly towards automation. When this knowledge is dispersed more widely and the small units take up automation, the pattern may be quite different. Automation, being a large employer of plant and a relatively small employer of labour, allows plants to be taken away from large centres of population. Thus one aspect of the British scene may change.' And he goes on in a truly Kropotkinian vein:

'Rural factories, clean, small, concentrated units will be dotted about the countryside. The effects of this may be far-reaching. The Industrial Revolution caused a separation of large numbers of people from the land and concentrated them in towns. The result has been a certain standardisation of personality, ignorance of nature, and lack of imaginative power. Now we may soon see some factory-workers moving back into the country and becoming part of a rural community.'[15]

The very technological developments which, in the hands of people with statist, centralising, authoritarian habits of mind, as well as in the hands of mere exploiters, demand greater concentration of industry, are also those which could make possible a local, intimate, decentralised society. When tractors were first made, they were giants, suitable only for prairie-farming. Now you can get them scaled down to a Rotivator for a smallholding. Power tools, which were going to make all industry one big Dagenham, are commonplace for every do-it-yourself enthusiast.

The most striking evidence, within industry as we know it today, in favour of reducing the scale of industrial organisation, comes from the experiments conducted by industrial psychologists, sociologists, and so on, who in the interests of morale, health or increased productivity, have sought to break down large units into small groups. Thus Professor Norman C. Hunt remarked that the problems arising from the growth of industrial enterprises were such that:

'A number of larger companies have recently decentralised their organisations and established smaller, largely autonomous units, each to some extent a managerial entity in itself. A few years ago the President of the General Electric Company of America, one of the companies which has followed such a policy, said: "With fewer people we find that management can do a better job of organising facilities and personnel. This results in lower management costs and better production control." It may be that the current interest in and apparent tendency towards the decentralisation of large undertakings is a somewhat belated recognition of the importance of *people* in organisations. One can only hope that at long last we are beginning to think about the pressures which traditional forms of organisation put upon the people who are required to work in them.'[16]

He concluded by reflecting on the possibility of reversing the trend of so-called scientific management:

'decentralising rather than centralising; increasing the significant content of jobs rather than subdividing them further; harnessing group solidarity rather than trying to break it up; putting more satisfaction into the work situation rather than expecting workers to find it outside their jobs; in short, making it possible for workers to utilise their capacities more fully and thus truly earning their keep.'

Notice his last phrase, which tells us why the industrialists employ the psychologists.

And how have Kropotkin's decentralist and regionalist ideas fared? Once again the evidence is equivocal. On one side, we have a stream of advocates of decentralist planning: Ebenezer Howard, Patrick Geddes and Lewis Mumford, who have had some influence on official policy. But on the other, we have the 'natural' movements of capital and labour which have contradicted the trends which he predicted. Howard's immensely inventive and influential book was first published under the title *Tomorrow: A Peaceful Path to Real Reform* in the same year as Kropotkin's book. When it was re-issued as *Garden Cities of Tomorrow* in 1902, Howard made use of Kropotkin's findings.[17] His disciples, from Thomas Adams,[18] first Secretary of the Garden Cities Association (later the T.C.P.A.), through Lewis Mumford,[19] to Paul and Percival Goodman,[20] have acknowledged the fertile influence of Kropotkin's work. Howard's book was a creative synthesis of decentralist ideas which, as Mumford declared, lay the foundation 'for a new cycle in urban civilisation: one in which the means of life will be subservient

[165]

to the purposes of living, and in which the pattern needed for biological survival and economic efficiency will likewise lead to social and personal fulfilment'. Kropotkin's similar vision can be traced in an American,[21] a Russian,[22] or a Chinese[23] context. In Israel the importance of Kropotkin's ideas on the decentralisation of industry (in a context which has nothing to do with Zionist nationalism) can be seen in the work of a variety of thinkers from Martin Buber to Haim Halperin.[24]

But at the same time we can see a world-wide tendency towards urbanisation. 'In 1850 there were four cities of the world with more than one million people. In 1950 there were about a hundred cities with a million or more population. By 2000 – less than three decades away – there will be over 1,000 cities of this magnitude.'[25] In the British context, there has been a *decline* in the population of the big cities, due partly to the implementation in the New Towns of Howard's proposals for decentralising both residence and work, but more to the growth of commuting and the increase in secondary occupations.

In the context of the Third World countries, there is one significant exception:

'The development of industry, education, health and cultural life has naturally tended to concentrate in cities all over the Third World. China's example is the reverse of this picture. The "inevitable" drift of population to growing industrial centres was firmly countered in the late 1950s by a new policy of developing agriculture as the "foundation" of the Chinese economy, with the commune its basic unit. The commune provides a variety of jobs, social services, education and cultural life – all the attractions which draw people away from "backward" villages to "advanced" city life. It offers the first real alternative to the usual pattern of industrialisation: the growth of huge, unmanageable cities which drain the countryside of its "best" people and leave agriculture impoverished and stagnant.'[26]

The urgency of the task of developing industry on a village scale has been stressed in India by Gandhi, Vinoba Bhave and Jayaprakash Narayan, and in Africa by Julius Nyerere.[27] It was the intention behind the experiments sponsored by Leonard and Dorothy Elmhirst of Dartington Hall,[28] and is brilliantly expressed in E. F. Schumacher's *Small is Beautiful*,[29] a book which marvellously complements Kropotkin's work.

Editor's Notes

1   W. Cherkesov, *The Concentration of Capital: A Marxian Fallacy* (London, Freedom Press, 1896)

2   Michael Utton, *Industrial Concentration* (Harmondsworth, Penguin, 1970)

3   Chuen-Yan Lai, 'Small Industries in Hong Kong', *Town-Planning Review*, Vol. 44, No. 2 (April 1973)

4   S. R. Dennison, addressing the conference of the British Institute of Management and the Institute of Industrial Administration (14 February 1953)

5   Mark Abrams, 'Bigness in Industry', *Socialist Commentary* (June 1956)

6   H. P. Barker, 'Have Large Firms an Advantage in Industry?', *The Listener* (1957)

7   Colin Buchanan, *Mixed Blessing: The Motor in Britain* (London, Leonard Hill, 1958)

8   Barker, op. cit.

9   Industrial Policy Group, *Paper No. 6* (London, 1970)

10 Gerald Newbould, *Management and Merger Activity* (London, 1970)

11 House of Commons debate on 24 November 1972 on 'Take-overs and Mergers', *Parliamentary Debates*, Vol. 846, No. 19)

12 David Hamilton, *Technology, Man and the Environment* (London, Faber, 1973)

13 Jonathan Boswell, *The Rise and Decline of Small Firms* (London, Allen & Unwin, 1972)

14 *Report of the Committee of Inquiry on Small Firms* (London, H.M.S.O., 1971)

15 L. Langdon Goodman, *Man and Automation* (Harmondsworth, Penguin, 1957)

16 Norman C. Hunt in *The Listener* (1958)

17 Ebenezer Howard, *Garden Cities of Tomorrow*, edited with a preface by Lewis Mumford (London, Faber, 1945)

18 Thomas Adams, *Garden City and Agriculture* (London, Simkin Marshall, 1905)

19 For example in *Technics and Civilisation* (London, Routledge, 1946; in *The Culture of Cities* (London, Secker & Warburg, 1938); and in *The City in History* (London, Secker & Warburg, 1961; Harmondsworth, Penguin, 1963)

20 Paul and Percival Goodman, *Communitas: Means of Livelihood*

and Ways of Life (Chicago University Press, 1947; New York, Vintage Books, 1960; London, Wildwood House, 1973)

21 See, for example, Ralph Borsodi, *Flight from the City* (New York, Harper, 1933, 1972); and Ralph L. Woods, *America Reborn: A Plan for Decentralisation of Agriculture and Industry* (London, Longmans, 1939)

22 See Paul Avrich, *The Russian Anarchists* (Princeton University Press, 1967)

23 See, for example, Robert A. Scalapino and George T. Yu, *The Chinese Anarchist Movement* (Berkeley, Cal., 1961)

24 See Martin Buber, *Paths in Utopia* (London, Routledge, 1949; Haim Halperin, *Agrindus: Integration of Agriculture and Industries* (London, Routledge, 1963)

25 Gwen Bell and Jaqueline Tyrwhitt, *Human Identity in the Urban Environment* (Harmondsworth, Penguin, 1973)

26 Harriet Ward, 'China and the Third World', notes for slide set *China – Another Way* (London, Voluntary Committee for Overseas Aid and Development, 1973). See Jerome Ch'en, *Mao and the Chinese Revolution* (London, O.U.P., 1965)

27 See G. Dhawan, *The Political Philosophy of Mahatma Gandhi* (Ahmedabad, Navajivan, 1957); Jayaprakash Narayan, *A Picture of Sarvodaya Social Order* (Tanjore, Sarvodaya Prachuralaya, 1961); Julius K. Nyerere, *Ujamaa – Essays on Socialism* (London, O.U.P. 1968)

28 Victor Bonham-Carter, *Dartington Hall* (London, Phoenix House, 1958; Dulverton, Exmoor Press, 1970); John Saville, *Rural Depopulation in England and Wales, 1851–1951* (London, Routledge, 1957)

29 E. F. Schumacher, *Small is Beautiful: A Study of Economics as if People Mattered* (London, Blond & Briggs, 1973)

Chapter 4

Brain Work and Manual Work

In olden times men of science, and especially those who have done most to forward the growth of natural philosophy, did not despise manual work and handicraft. Galileo made his telescopes with his own hands. Newton learned in his boyhood the art of managing tools; he exercised his young mind in contriving most ingenious machines, and when he began his researches in optics he was able himself to grind the lenses for his instruments, and himself to make the well-known telescope, which, for its time, was a fine piece of workmanship. Leibnitz was fond of inventing machines: windmills and carriages to be moved without horses preoccupied his mind as much as mathematical and philosophical speculations. Linnæus became a botanist while helping his father – a practical gardener – in his daily work. In short, with our great geniuses handicraft was no obstacle to abstract researches – it rather favoured them. On the other hand, if the workers of old found but few opportunities for mastering science, many of them had, at least, their intelligences stimulated by the very variety of work which was performed in the then unspecialised workshops; and some of them had the benefit of familiar intercourse with men of science. Watt and Rennie were friends with Professor Robinson; Brindley, the road-maker, despite his fourteenpence-a-day wages, enjoyed intercourse with educated men, and thus developed his remarkable engineering faculties; the son of a well-to-do family could 'idle' at a wheelwright's shop, so as to become later on a Smeaton or a Stephenson.

We have changed all that. Under the pretext of division of labour, we have sharply separated the brain worker from the manual worker. The masses of the workmen do not receive more scientific education than their grandfathers did; but they have been deprived of the education of even the small workshop, while their boys and girls are driven into a mine or a factory from the age of 13 and there they soon forget the little they may have learned at school. As to the men of science, they despise manual labour. How few of them would be able to make a telescope, or even a plainer instrument! Most of them are not capable of even designing a scientific instrument, and when they have given a vague suggestion to the instrument-maker, they leave it with him to invent the apparatus they need. Nay, they have raised the contempt of manual labour to the height of a theory. 'The man of science', they say, 'must discover the laws of nature, the civil engineer must apply them, and the worker must execute in steel or wood, in iron or stone, the patterns devised by the engineer. He must work with machines invented for him, not by him. No matter if he does not understand them and cannot improve them: the scientific man and the scientific engineer will take care of the progress of science and industry.'

It may be objected that nevertheless there is a class of men who belong to none of the above three divisions. When young they have been manual workers, and some of them continue to be; but, owing to some happy circumstances, they have succeeded in acquiring some scientific knowledge, and thus they have combined science with handicraft. Surely there are such men; happily enough there is a nucleus of men who have escaped the so-much-advocated specialisation of labour, and it is precisely to them that industry owes its chief recent inventions. But in old Europe, at least, they are the exceptions; they are the irregulars – the Cossacks who have broken the ranks and pierced the screens so carefully erected between the classes. And they are so few, in comparison with the ever-growing requirements of industry – and of science as well, as I am about to prove – that all over the world we hear complaints about the scarcity of precisely such men.

What is the meaning, in fact, of the outcry for technical education which has been raised, at one and the same time in England, in France, in Germany, in the States, and in Russia, if it does not express a general dissatisfaction with the present division into scientists, scientific engineers, and workers?

[170]

Listen to those who know industry, and you will see that the substance of their complaints is this:

'The worker whose task has ben specialised by the permanent division of labour has lost the intellectual interest in his labour, and it is especially so in the great industries: he has lost his inventive powers. Formerly, he invented very much. Manual workers – not men of science nor trained engineers – have invented, or brought to perfection, the prime motors and all that mass of machinery which has revolutionised industry for the last hundred years. But since the great factory has been enthroned, the worker, depressed by the monotony of his work, invents no more. What can a weaver invent who merely supervises four looms, without knowing anything either about their complicated movements or how the machines grew to be what they are? What can a man invent who is condemned for life to bind together the ends of two threads with the greatest celerity, and knows nothing beyond making a knot?

'At the outset of modern industry, three generations of workers *have* invented; now they cease to do so. As to the inventions of the engineers, specially trained for devising machines, they are either devoid of genius or not practical enough. Those "nearly to nothings", of which Sir Frederick Bramwell spoke once at Bath, are missing in their inventions – those nothings which can be learned in the workshop only, and which permitted a Murdoch and the Soho workers to make a practical engine of Watt's schemes. None but he who knows the machine – not in its drawings and models only, but in its breathing and throbbings – who unconsciously thinks of it while standing by it, can really improve it. Smeaton and Newcomen surely were excellent engineers; but in their engines a boy had to open the steam valve at each stroke of the piston; and it was one of those boys who once managed to connect the valve with the remainder of the machine so as to make it open automatically, while he ran away to play with other boys. But in the modern machinery there is no room left for naïve improvements of that kind. Scientific education on a wide scale has become necessary for further inventions, and that education is refused to the workers. So that there is no issue out of the difficulty, unless scientific education and handicraft are combined together – unless integration of knowledge takes the place of the present divisions.'

Such is the real substance of the present movement in favour of technical education. But, instead of bringing to public consciousness the, perhaps, unconscious motives of the present discontent, instead of widening the views of the discontented and discussing the problem to its full extent, the mouthpieces of the movement do not mostly rise above the shopkeeper's view of the question. Some of them indulge in jingo talk about crushing all foreign industries out of competition, while the others see in technical education nothing but a means of somewhat improving the flesh-machine of the factory and of transferring a few workers into the upper class of trained engineers.

Such an ideal may satisfy them, but it cannot satisfy those who keep in view the combined interests of science and industry, and consider both as a means for raising humanity to a higher level. We maintain that in the interests of both science and industry, as well as of society as a whole, every human being, without distinction of birth, ought to receive such an education as would enable him, or her, to combine a thorough knowledge of science with a thorough knowledge of handicraft. We fully recognise the necessity of specialisation of knowledge, but we maintain that specialisation must follow general education, and that general education must be given in science and handicraft alike. To the division of society into brain workers and manual workers we oppose the combination of both kinds of activities; and instead of 'technical education', which means the maintenance of the present division between brain work and manual work, we advocate the *éducation intégrale*, or complete education, which means the disappearance of that pernicious distinction.

Plainly stated, the aims of the school under this system ought to be the following: to give such an education that on leaving school at the age of 18 or 20, each boy and each girl should be endowed with a thorough knowledge of science – such

[172]

a knowledge as might enable them to be useful workers in science – and, at the same time, to give them a general knowledge of what constitutes the bases of technical training, and such a skill in some special trade as would enable each of them to take his or her place in the grand world of the manual production of wealth. I know that many will find that aim too large, or even impossible to attain, but I hope that if they have the patience to read the following pages, they will see that we require nothing beyond what can be easily attained. In fact, *it has been attained*; and what has been done on a small scale could be done on a wider scale, were it not for the economical and social causes which prevent any serious reform from being accomplished in our miserably organised society.

Waste of time is the leading feature of our present education. Not only are we taught a mass of rubbish, but what is not rubbish is taught so as to make us waste over it as much time as possible. Our present methods of teaching originate from a time when the accomplishments required from an educated person were extremely limited; and they have been maintained, notwithstanding the immense increase of knowledge which must be conveyed to the scholar's mind since science has so much widened its former limits. Hence the over-pressure in schools, and hence, also, the urgent necessity of totally revising both the subjects and the methods of teaching, according to the new wants and to the examples already given here and there, by separate schools and separate teachers.

It is evident that the years of childhood ought not to be spent so uselessly as they are now. German teachers have shown how the very plays of children can be made instrumental in conveying to the childish mind some concrete knowledge in both geometry and mathematics. The children who have made the squares of the theorem of Pythagoras out of pieces of coloured cardboard, will not look at the theorem, when it comes in geometry, as on a mere instrument of torture devised by the teachers; and the less so if they apply it as the carpenters do. Complicated problems of arithmetic, which so much harassed us in our boyhood, are easily solved by children 7 and 8 years old if they are put in the shape of interesting puzzles.

[173]

And if the *Kindergarten* – German teachers often make of it a kind of barrack in which each movement of the child is regulated beforehand – has often become a small prison for the little ones, the idea which presided at its foundation is nevertheless true. In fact, it is almost impossible to imagine, without having tried it, how many sound notions of nature, habits of classification, and taste for natural sciences can be conveyed to the children's minds; and, if a series of concentric courses adapted to the various phases of development of the human being were generally accepted in education, the first series in all sciences, save sociology, could be taught before the age of 10 or 12, so as to give a general idea of the universe, the earth and its inhabitants, the chief physical, chemical, zoological and botanical phenomena, leaving the discovery of the *laws* of those phenomena to the next series of deeper and more specialised studies.

On the other side, we all know how children like to make toys themselves, how they gladly imitate the work of full-grown people if they see them at work in the workshop or the building-yard. But the parents either stupidly paralyse that passion, or do not know how to utilise it. Most of them despise manual work and prefer sending their children to the study of Roman history, or of Franklin's teachings about saving money, to seeing them at a work which is good for the 'lower classes only'. They thus do their best to render subsequent learning the more difficult.

And then come the school years, and time is wasted again to an incredible extent. Take, for instance, mathematics, which every one ought to know, because it is the basis of all subsequent education, and which so few really learn in our schools. In geometry, time is foolishly wasted by using a method which merely consists in committing geometry to memory. In most cases, the boy reads again and again the proof of a theorem till his memory has retained the succession of reasonings. Therefore, nine boys out of ten, if asked to prove an elementary theorem two years after having left the school, will be unable to do it, unless mathematics is their speciality. They will forget which auxiliary lines to draw, and they never have been taught

[174]

to *discover* the proofs by themselves. No wonder that later on they find such difficulties in applying geometry to physics, that their progress is despairingly sluggish, and that so few master higher mathematics.

There is, however, the other method which permits the pupil to progress, as a whole, at a much speedier rate, and under which he who once has learned geometry will know it all his life long. Under this system, each theorem is put as a problem; its solution is never given beforehand, and the pupil is induced to find it by himself. Thus, if some preliminary exercises with the rule and the compass have been made, there is not one boy or girl, out of twenty or more, who will not be able to find the means of drawing an angle which is equal to a given angle, and to prove their equality, after a few suggestions from the teacher; and if the subsequent problems are given in a systematic succession (there are excellent textbooks for the purpose), and the teacher does not press his pupils to go faster than they can go at the beginning, they advance from one problem to the next with an astonishing facility, the only difficulty being to bring the pupil to solve the first problem, and thus to acquire confidence in his own reasoning.

Moreover, each abstract geometrical truth must be impressed on the mind in its concrete form as well. As soon as the pupils have solved a few problems on paper, they must solve them in the playing-ground with a few sticks and a string, and they must apply their knowledge in the workshop. Only then will the geometrical lines acquire a concrete meaning in the children's minds; only then will they see that the teacher is playing no tricks when he asks them to solve problems with the rule and the compass without resorting to the protractor; only then will they *know* geometry.

'Through the eyes *and* the hand to the brain' – this is the true principle of economy of time in teaching. I remember, as if it were yesterday, how geometry suddenly acquired for me a new meaning, and how this new meaning facilitated all ulterior studies. It was as we were mastering at school a Montgolfier balloon, and I remarked that the angles at the summits of each of the twenty strips of paper out of which

[175]

we were going to make the balloon must cover less than the fifth part of a right angle each. I remember, next, how the sinuses and the tangents ceased to be mere cabalistic signs when they permitted us to calculate the length of a stick in a working profile of a fortification; and how geometry in space became plain when we began to make on a small scale a bastion with embrasures and barbettes – an occupation which obviously was soon prohibited on account of the state into which we brought our clothes. 'You look like navvies', was the reproach addressed to us by our intelligent educators, while we were proud precisely of being navvies, and of discovering the use of geometry.

By compelling our children to study real things from mere graphical representations, instead of *making* those things themselves, we compel them to waste the most precious time; we uselessly worry their minds; we accustom them to the worst methods of learning; we kill independent thought in the bud; and very seldom we succeed in conveying a real knowledge of what we are teaching. Superficiality, parrot-like repetition, slavishness and inertia of mind are the results of our method of education. We do not teach our children how to learn.

The very beginnings of science are taught on the same pernicious system. In most schools even arithmetic is taught in the abstract way, and mere rules are stuffed into the poor little heads. In this country, the United States and Russia, instead of accepting the decimal system, which is the system of our numeration, they still torture the children by making them learn a system of weights and measures which ought to have been abandoned long since.

The waste of time in physics is simply revolting. While young people very easily understand the principles of chemistry and its formulae, as soon as they themselves make the first experiments with a few glasses and tubes, they mostly find the greatest difficulties in grasping the mechanical introduction into physics, partly because they do not know geometry, and especially because they are merely shown costly machines instead of being induced to make themselves plain apparatus for illustrating the phenomena they study.

[176]

Instead of learning the laws of force with plain instruments which a boy of 15 can easily make, they learn them from mere drawings, in a purely abstract fashion. Instead of making themselves an Atwood's machine with a broomstick and the wheel of an old clock, or verifying the laws of falling bodies with a key gliding on an inclined string, they are shown a complicated apparatus, and in most cases the teacher himself does not know how to explain to them the principle of the apparatus, and indulges in irrelevant details. In reality, all *apparatus used to illustrate the fundamental laws of physics ought to be made by the children themselves.*

If waste of time is characteristic of our methods of teaching science, it is characteristic as well of the methods used for teaching handicraft. We know how years are wasted when a boy serves his apprenticeship in a workshop; but the same reproach can be addressed, to a great extent, to those technical schools which endeavour at once to teach some special handicraft, instead of resorting to the broader and surer methods of systematical teaching.

Each machine, however complicated, can be reduced to a few elements – plates, cylinders, discs, cones, and so on – as well as to a few tools – chisels, saws, rollers, hammers, etc.; and, however complicated its movements, they can be decomposed into a few modifications of motion, such as the transformation of circular motion into a rectilinear, and the like, with a number of intermediate links. So also each handicraft can be decomposed into a number of elements. In each trade one must know how to make a plate with parallel surfaces, a cylinder, a disc, a square, and a round hole; how to manage a limited number of tools, all tools being mere modifications of less than a dozen types; and how to transform one kind of motion into another. This is the foundation of all mechanical handicrafts; so that the knowledge of how to make in wood those primary elements, how to manage the chief tools in wood-work, and how to transform various kinds of motion ought to be considered as the very basis for the subsequent teaching of all possible kinds of mechanical handicraft. The pupil who has acquired that skill already knows one good half of all possible trades.

M

Be it handicraft, science or art, the chief aim of the school is not to make a specialist from a beginner, but to teach him the elements of knowledge and the good methods of work, and, above all, to give him that general inspiration which will induce him, later on, to put in whatever he does a sincere longing for truth, to like what is beautiful, both as to form and contents, to feel the necessity of being a useful unit amidst other human units, and thus to feel his heart at unison with the rest of humanity.

As for avoiding the monotony of work which would result from the pupil always making mere cylinders and discs, and never making full machines or other useful things, there are thousands of means for avoiding that want of interest, and one of them, in use at Moscow, is worthy of notice. It was, not to give work for mere exercise, but to utilise everything which the pupil makes, from his very first steps. Do you remember how you were delighted, in your childhood, if your work was utilised, be it only as a part of something useful? So they did at the Moscow Technical School. Each plank planed by the pupils was utilised as a part of some machine in some of the other workshops. When a pupil came to the engineering workshop, and was set to make a quadrangular block of iron with parallel and perpendicular surfaces, the block had an interest in his eyes, because, when he had finished it, verified its angles and surfaces, and corrected its defects, the block was not thrown under the bench – it was given to a more advanced pupil, who made a handle to it, painted the whole, and sent it to the shop of the school as a paper-weight. The systematical teaching thus received the necessary attractiveness. (The sale of the pupils' work was not insignificant, especially when they reached the higher classes, and made steam engines. Therefore the Moscow school, when I knew it, was one of the cheapest in the world. It gave boarding and education at a very low fee. But imagine such a school connected with a farm school, which grows food and exchanges it at its cost price. What will be the cost of education then?)

It is evident that celerity of work is a most important factor in production. So it might be asked if, under the above system, the necessary speed of work could be obtained. But there are two kinds of celerity. There is the celerity which I saw in a Nottingham lace-factory: full-grown men, with shivering hands and heads, were feverishly binding together the ends of two threads from the remnants of cotton-yarn in the bobbins; you hardly could follow their movements. But the very fact of requiring such kind of rapid work is the condemnation of the factory system. What has remained of the human being in those shivering bodies? What will be their outcome? Why this waste of human force, when it could produce ten times the value of the odd rests of yarn? This kind of celerity is required exclusively because of the cheapness of the factory slaves; so let us hope that no school will ever aim at this kind of quickness in work.

But there is also the time-saving celerity of the well-trained worker, and this is surely achieved best by the kind of education which we advocate. However plain his work, the educated worker makes it better and quicker than the uneducated. Observe, for instance, how a good worker proceeds in cutting anything – say a piece of cardboard – and compare his movements with those of an improperly trained worker. The latter seizes the cardboard, takes the tool as it is, traces a line in a haphazard way, and begins to cut; half-way he is tired, and when he has finished, his work is worth nothing; whereas, the former will examine his tool and improve it if necessary; he will trace the line with exactitude, secure both cardboard and rule, keep the tool in the right way, cut quite easily, and give you a piece of good work.

This is the true time-saving celerity, the most appropriate for economising human labour; and the best means for attaining it is an education of the most superior kind. The great masters painted with an astonishing rapidity; but their rapid work was the result of a great development of intelligence and imagination, of a keen sense of beauty, of a fine perception of colours. And that is the kind of rapid work of which humanity is in need.

Much more ought to be said as regards the duties of the school, but I hasten to say a few words more as to the desirability of the kind of education briefly sketched in the preceding pages. Certainly, I do not cherish the illusion that a thorough reform in education, or in any of the issues indicated in the preceding chapters, will be made as long as the civilised nations remain under the present narrowly egotistic system of production and consumption. All we can expect, as long as the present conditions last, is to have some microscopical attempts at reforming here and there on a small scale – attempts which necessarily will prove to be far below the expected results, because of the impossibility of reforming on a small scale when so intimate a connection exists between the manifold functions of a civilised nation. But the energy of the constructive genius of society depends chiefly upon the depths of its conception as to what ought to be done, and how; and the necessity of recasting education is one of those necessities which are most comprehensive to all, and are most appropriate for inspiring society with those ideals, without which stagnation or even decay are unavoidable.

So let us suppose that a community – a city, or a territory which has, at least, a few millions of inhabitants – gives the above-sketched education to all its children, without distinction of birth (and we *are* rich enough to permit us the luxury of such an education), without asking anything in return from the children but what they will give when they have become producers of wealth. Suppose such an education is given, and analyse its probable consequences.

I will not insist upon the increase of wealth which would result from having a young army of educated and well-trained producers; nor shall I insist upon the social benefits which would be derived from erasing the present distinction between the brain workers and the manual workers, and from thus reaching the concordance of interest and harmony so much wanted in our times of social struggles. I shall not dwell upon the fullness of life which would result for each separate individual, if he were enabled to enjoy the use of both his mental and bodily powers; nor upon the advantages of raising manual labour to the place of honour it ought to occupy in society, instead of being a stamp of inferiority, as it is now.

Nor shall I insist upon the disappearance of the present misery and degradation, with all their consequences – vice, crime, prisons, price of blood, denunciation, and the like – which necessarily would follow. In short, I will not touch now the great social question, upon which so much has been written and so much remains to be written yet. I merely intend to point out in these pages the benefits which science itself would derive from the change.

Some will say, of course, that to reduce men of science to the *rôle* of manual workers would mean the decay of science and genius. But those who will take into account the following considerations probably will agree that the result ought to be the reverse – namely, such a revival of science and art, and such a progress in industry, as we only can faintly foresee from what we know about the times of the Renaissance. It has become a commonplace to speak with emphasis about the progress of science during the nineteenth century; and it is evident that our century, if compared with centuries past, has much to be proud of. But, if we take into account that most of the problems which our century has solved already had been indicated, and their solutions foreseen, a hundred years ago, we must admit that the progress was not so rapid as might have been expected, and that something hampered it.

The mechanical theory of heat was very well foreseen in the last century by Rumford and Humphry Davy, and even in Russia it was advocated by Lomonosoff. However, much more than half a century elapsed before the theory reappeared in science. Lamarck, and even Linnæus, Geoffroy Saint-Hilaire, Erasmus Darwin, and several others were fully aware of the variability of species; they were opening the way for the construction of biology on the principles of variation; but here, again, half a century was wasted before the variability of species was brought again to the front; and we all remember how Darwin's ideas were carried on and forced on the attention of university people, chiefly by persons who were not professional scientists themselves; and yet in Darwin's hands the theory of evolution surely was narrowed, owing to the overwhelming importance given to only one factor of evolution.

In short, there is not one single science which does not suffer in its development from a want of men and women endowed with a philosophical conception of the universe, ready to apply their forces of investigation in a given field, however limited, and having leisure for devoting themselves to scientific pursuits. In a community such as we suppose, thousands of workers would be ready to answer any appeal for exploration. Darwin spent almost thirty years in gathering and analysing facts for the elaboration of the theory of the origin of species. Had he lived in such a society as we suppose, he simply would have made an appeal to volunteers for facts and partial exploration, and thousands of explorers would have answered his appeal. Scores of societies would have come to life to debate and to solve each of the partial problems involved in the theory, and in ten years the theory would have been verified; all those factors of evolution which only now begin to receive due attention would have appeared in their full light. The rate of scientific progress would have been tenfold; and if the individual would not have the same claims on posterity's gratitude as he has now, the unknown mass would have done the work with more speed and with more prospect for ulterior advance than the individual could do in his lifetime.

However, there is another feature of modern science which speaks more strongly yet in favour of the change we advocate. While industry, especially by the end of the last century and during the first part of the present, has been inventing on such a scale as to revolutionise the very face of the earth, science has been losing its inventive powers. Men of science invent no more, or very little. Is it not striking, indeed, that the steam engine, even in its leading principles, the railway engine, the steamboat, the telephone, the phonograph, the weaving-machine, the lace-machine, the lighthouse, the macadamised road, photography in black and in colours, and thousands of less important things, *have* not been invented by professional men of science, although none of them would have refused to associate his name with any of the above-named inventions? Men who hardly had received any education at school, who had merely picked up the crumbs of knowledge from the tables

[182]

of the rich, and who made their experiments with the most primitive means – the attorney's clerk Smeaton, the instrument-maker Watt, the brakesman Stephenson, the jeweller's apprentice Fulton, the millwright Rennie, the mason Telford, and hundreds of others whose very names remain unknown, were, as Mr Smiles justly says, 'the real makers of modern civilisation'; while the professional men of science, provided with all means for acquiring knowledge and experimenting, have invented little in the formidable array of implements, machines, and prime-motors which has shown to humanity how to utilise and to manage the forces of nature. (Chemistry is, to a great extent, an exception to the rule. Is it not because the chemist is to such an extent a manual worker? Besides, during the last ten years we see a decided revival in scientific inventiveness, especially in physics – that is, in a branch in which the engineer and the man of science meet so much together.) The fact is striking, but its explanation is very simple: those men – the Watts and the Stephensons – knew something which the savants do not know – they knew the use of their hands; their surroundings stimulated their inventive powers; they knew machines, their leading principles, and their work; they had breathed the atmosphere of the workshop and the building yard.

We know how men of science will meet the reproach. They will say: 'We discover the laws of nature, let others apply them; it is a simple division of labour.' But such a rejoinder would be utterly untrue. The march of progress is quite the reverse, because in a hundred cases against one the mechanical invention comes before the discovery of the scientific law. It was not the dynamical theory of heat which came before the steam engine – it followed it.

When thousands of engines already were transforming heat into motion under the eyes of hundreds of professors, and when they had done so for half a century, or more; when thousands of trains, stopped by powerful brakes, were disengaging heat and spreading sheaves of sparks on the rails at their approach to the stations; when all over the civilised world heavy hammers and perforators were rendering burning hot the masses of iron they were hammering and perforating – then,

[183]

and then only, Séguin, senior, in France, and a doctor, Mayer, in Germany, ventured to bring out the mechanical theory of heat with all its consequences: and yet the men of science ignored the work of Séguin and almost drove Mayer to madness by obstinately clinging to their mysterious caloric fluid. Worse than that, they described Joule's first determination of the mechanical equivalent of heat as 'unscientific'.

It was not the theory of electricity which gave us the telegraph. When the telegraph was invented, all we knew about electricity was but a few facts more or less badly arranged in our books; the theory of electricity is not ready yet; it still waits for its Newton, notwithstanding the brilliant attempts of late years. Even the empirical knowledge of the laws of electrical currents was in its infancy when a few bold men laid a cable at the bottom of the Atlantic Ocean, despite the warnings of the authorised men of science.

The name of 'applied science' is quite misleading, because, in the great majority of cases, invention, far from being an application of science, on the contrary creates a new branch of science. The American bridges were no application of the theory of elasticity; they came before the theory, and all we can say in favour of science is that, in this special branch, theory and practice developed in a parallel way, helping one another. It was not the theory of the explosives which led to the discovery of gunpower; gunpowder was in use for centuries before the action of the gases in a gun was submitted to scientific analysis. And so on.

Of course, we have a number of cases in which the discovery, or the invention, was a mere application of a scientific law (cases like the discovery of the planet Neptune), but in the immense majority of cases the discovery, or the invention, is unscientific to begin with. It belongs much more to the domain of art – art taking the precedence over science, as Helmholtz has so well shown in one of his popular lectures – and only after the invention has been made, science comes to interpret it. It is obvious that each invention avails itself of the previously accumulated knowledge and modes of thought; but in most cases it makes a start in advance upon what is known; it

[184]

makes a leap in the unknown, and thus opens a quite new series of facts for investigation. This character of invention, which is to make a start in advance of former knowledge; instead of merely applying a law, makes it identical, as to the processes of mind, with discovery; and, therefore, people who are slow in invention are also slow in discovery.

In most cases, the inventor, however inspired by the general state of science at a given moment, starts with a very few settled facts at his disposal. The scientific facts taken into account for inventing the steam engine, or the telegraph, or the phonograph were strikingly elementary. So that we can affirm that what we presently know is already sufficient for resolving any of the great problems which stand in the order of the day — prime-motors without the use of steam, the storage of energy, the transmission of force, or the flying-machine. If these problems are not yet solved, it is merely because of the want of inventive genius, the scarcity of educated men endowed with it, and the present divorce between science and industry. (I leave on purpose these lines as they were in the first edition All these desiderata are already accomplished facts.) On the one side, we have men who are endowed with capacities for invention, but have neither the necessary scientific knowledge nor the means for experimenting during long years; and, on the other side, we have men endowed with knowledge and facilities for experimenting, but devoid of inventive genius, owing to their education, too abstract, too scholastic, too bookish, and to the surroundings they live in – not to speak of the patent system, which divides and scatters the efforts of the inventors instead of combining them.

The flight of genius which has characterised the workers at the outset of modern industry has been missing in our professional men of science. And they will not recover it as long as they remain strangers to the world, amidst their dusty bookshelves; as long as they are not workers themselves, amidst other workers, at the blaze of the iron furnace, at the machine in the factory, at the turning-lathe in the engineering workshop, sailors amidst sailors on the sea, and fishers in the fishing-boat, woodcutters in the forest, tillers of the soil in the field.

Our teachers in art – Ruskin and his school – have repeatedly told us of late that we must not expect a revival of art as long as handicraft remains what it is; they have shown how Greek and medieval art were daughters of handicraft, how one was feeding the other. The same is true with regard to handicraft and science; their separation is the decay of both. As to the grand inspirations which unhappily have been so much neglected in most of the recent discussions about art – and which are missing in science as well – these can be expected only when humanity, breaking its present bonds, shall make a new start in the higher principles of solidarity, doing away with the present duality of moral sense and philosophy.

It is evident, however, that all men and women cannot equally enjoy the pursuit of scientific work. The variety of inclinations is such that some will find more pleasure in science, some others in art, and others again in some of the numberless branches of the production of wealth. But, whatever the occupations preferred by everyone, everyone will be the more useful in his own branch if he is in possession of a serious scientific knowledge. And, whosoever he might be – scientist or artist, physicist or surgeon, chemist or sociologist, historian or poet – he would be the gainer if he spent a part of his life in the workshop or the farm (the workshop *and* the farm), if he were in contact with humanity in its daily work, and had the satisfaction of knowing that he himself discharges his duties as an unprivileged producer of wealth.

How much better the historian and the sociologist would understand humanity if they knew it, not in books only, not in a few of its representatives, but as a whole, in its daily life, daily work, and daily affairs! How much more medicine would trust to hygiene, and how much less to prescriptions, if the young doctors were the nurses of the sick and the nurses received the education of the doctors of our time! And how much the poet would gain in his feeling of the beauties of nature, how much better would he know the human heart, if he met the rising sun amidst the tillers of the soil, himself a tiller; if he fought against the storm with the sailors on board ship;

[186]

if he knew the poetry of labour and rest, sorrow and joy, struggle and conquest?

The so-called 'division of labour' has grown under a system which condemned the masses to toil all the day long, and all the life long, at the same wearisome kind of labour. But if we take into account how few are the real producers of wealth in our present society, and how squandered is their labour, we must recognise that Franklin was right in saying that to work five hours a day would generally do for supplying each member of a civilised nation with the comfort now accessible for the few only.

But we have made some progress since Franklin's time, and some of that progress in the hitherto most backward branch of production – agriculture – has been indicated in the preceding pages. Even in that branch the productivity of labour can be immensely increased, and work itself rendered easy and pleasant. If everyone took his share of production, and if production were socialised – as political economy, if it aimed at the satisfaction of the ever-growing needs of all, would advise us to do – then more than one half of the working day would remain to everyone for the pursuit of art, science, or any hobby he or she might prefer; and his work in those fields would be the more profitable if he spent the other half of the day in productive work – if art and science were followed from more inclination, not for mercantile purposes. Moreover, a community organised on the principles of all being workers would be rich enough to conclude that every man and woman, after having reached a certain age – say of 40 or more – ought to be relieved from the moral obligation of taking a direct part in the performance of the necessary manual work, so as to be able entirely to devote himself or herself to whatever he or she chooses in the domain of art, or science, or any kind of work. Free pursuit in new branches of art and knowledge, free creation, and free development thus might be fully guaranteed. And such a community would not know misery amidst wealth. It would not know the duality of conscience which permeates our life and stifles every noble effort. It would freely take its flight towards the highest regions of progress compatible with human nature.

EDITOR'S APPENDIX

There is a well-known passage in Marx's *German Ideology* in which he envisages the abolition of the division of labour in a Communist society where, since 'nobody has one exclusive sphere of activity but each can become accomplished in any branch he wishes, production as a whole is regulated by society, thus making it possible for me to do one thing today and another tomorrow, to hunt in the morning, fish in the afternoon, rear cattle in the evening, criticise after dinner. . . .' Kropotkin too wanted the 'moral and physical advantages which man would derive from dividing his work between the field and the workshop'.

It does happen in our society, of course, but hardly in the way Marx and Kropotkin envisaged. Studying the combination of farm-work and factory-work in Belgium, René Dumont concluded that 'the part-time farmer leads a life of virtual slavery'[1] precisely because the farmers he met did their work *after* an eight-hour day in a factory. Kropotkin's vision has shrunk to a footnote from Peter Self and H. S. Storing: 'As a spare-time activity, it should be repeated, the importance of small-scale farming, in conjunction with employment in de-centralised industries, may well grow.'[2] The nearest thing to Kropotkin's industrial villages are the Chinese communes. J. K. Galbraith stresses their significance for the countries of the Third World:

'Hsu Hang Commune has 20,500 inhabitants and roughly 4,200 acres of land, all irrigated. This is no great amount of land – less than an irrigated acre per family. The crops are grain (2 crops of rice a year, plus 1 of wheat), cotton, hogs and a variety of factory enterprises. . . . The families we visited, in addition to private, tiny vegetable plots, also each had their personal pig. Then we went to the factories. These, including some we did not see, make elementary threshing machines, furniture, basket-ware, boxes, light bulbs, chemicals and steel pipe. The factories are small – at most a few dozen workers in those we saw – and there is not much attempt at line pro-duction. Men and women are mostly either making a whole item or a substantial component. Still, they are serious operations – not a show. The justification is not efficiency but the employment of labour that would otherwise have little to do – technically it is the Chinese answer to one of the greatest

[188]

problems of rural Asia, that of recurrent and disguised unemployment.'³

What would have amazed Kropotkin most about changes in Western industry, just as it would have amazed a dozen other prophets who, as a result of the same kind of careful analysis, predicted the three-hour day, the three-day week, or the three-week month, is that working hours have scarcely diminished. In Britain, although the unions were demanding an eight-hour day eighty years ago, a report issued in 1971 found factories with a twelve-hour shift system in which employees were working a seventy-two hour week. It found that more than 250,000 men in the country were working for more than seventy hours a week, and that whereas the standard working week has dropped to forty hours, overtime has increased. An overwhelming majority of the workers interviewed said that they preferred more money to more leisure. In the United States the number of people working more than forty-eight hours a week rose from 13 per cent of the work force in 1948 to 20 per cent in 1965, while the number of people who were moonlighting, or holding more than one job, has doubled since 1950. The reason, of course, is not that people prefer work to leisure, but that in order to enjoy their leisure they feel the need to earn more, and consequently to work longer. Or it may be just to get the money to pay the rent.

We are, in fact, further than ever from Kropotkin's dreams of a leisured society and of the integration of work. Even the making of cuckoo-clocks or jack-in-the-boxes is no longer a sideline of the forestry trades, but a by-product of the plastics industry. Gypsy clothes-pegs are dearer than their industrial equivalent. The typical combinations of village industry and agriculture that existed in Kropotkin's day have tended to wither away. The rural craftsman, except in the specialised 'art' market, is beset with economic difficulties.⁴

Still less do we see the combination of brainwork and manual work that Kropotkin anticipated. In both manufacturing and service industries the intellectual content of most jobs has been systematically reduced so that most jobs require neither skill nor training, neither ingenuity nor creativity, merely the ability to 'switch off' until clocking-out time. The people who do have creative or rewarding jobs, far from taking their share of the routine chores, demand assistants, ancillaries, auxiliaries – minions in fact – to relieve them of the brainless aspects of the work.

In a manuscript written as early as 1873, Kropotkin himself wrote:

'Repeating the formulation of Proudhon, we say: if a naval academy is not itself a ship with sailors who enjoy equal rights and receive a theoretical education, then it will produce not sailors but officers to supervise sailors; if a technical academy is not itself a factory, not itself a trade school, then it will produce foremen and managers and not workmen, and so on. We do not need these privileged establishments; we need neither universities nor technical academies nor naval academies created for the few; we need the hospital, the factory, the chemical works, the ship, the productive trade school for workers, which, having become available to all, will with unimaginable speed exceed the standard of present universities and academies. In eliminating all the unnecessary ballast of useless occupations, in devising accelerated methods of education (which always appear only when a demand for them arises which cannot be put off), the school will train healthy workers equally capable of both further intellectual and physical work.'[5]

These ideas remained at the heart of Kropotkin's educational thought, and are still relevant. (One hundred years after they were written, India had 20,000 unemployed graduate engineers, and was training 72,000 more every year.)

From one point of view, Kropotkin's ideas about the nature of education in this chapter are the conventional wisdom of progressive education. 'Through the eyes *and* the hand to the brain' he says, and we are reminded of the old adage, 'I hear, and I forget. I see, and I remember. I do, and I understand.' Like many in both his generation and ours, Kropotkin was full of an optimistic faith in the capacity of education to change society. He hoped, one might say, to give the industrial worker a theoretical grounding in his trade so that he comprehends the principles behind the operations he performs, and to give the scientist a taste of practical craftsmanship, with the aim that their their two functions might become interchangeable. Now in fact, in the history of technical education in Britain, there has been a tradition of lone voices, from Lyon Playfair to Lord Eustace Percy, who, like Kropotkin, urged an *integral* education. This was in fact the basis of the polytechnic ideal, though the academics who run our polytechnics probably never knew it. For in practice there has been, as Stephen Cotgrove said, a conflict 'between the needs of an industrial society for a scientific and technological élite, and the ideals of a liberal education derived from a society in which such an education was appropriate for a predominantly governing and administrative élite'.[6] Certainly both these Two Cultures are élitist. In the academic status race, every technical institution, with quite shameless haste, has shed its 'low-level work' (this is the actual phrase used today for the practical training Kropotkin was demanding) on to colleges lower in the hierarchy. Craft training is for the 'thickies', degree courses for the technocrats.

Similarly in the schools, however comprehensive they may be in name, craft subjects are rapidly dropped by the academically gifted in favour of those subjects whose examinations lead to university entrance. And as to the idea that the school itself might be partially self-supporting through productive work, this has been laughed out of existence long ago in the West, just as it has been ignored in India, where it was one of the cornerstones of Gandhi's programme of Basic Education.

There is in Britain one tiny and unlikely venture which throws light on this notion and on Kropotkin's ideas in Chapter 2. At Coity Mawr in Wales, an organisation called the Society for Training in Rural Industries and Village Enterprises maintains a farm with the intention 'of bringing young people from developing countries and teaching them farming methods that will improve their own standard of living and those of their villages'.[7] The students, straight from school, are divided into 'families' of two boys and two girls who must aim at self-sufficiency using traditional agricultural and livestock-rearing methods. The home farm where the students meet for lessons and social activities is also the place where they share cereal production using slightly more sophisticated tools and implements of an 'intermediate technology' type.

If the reader saw on television the young Tibetan refugees who were the first batch of students, one of the things which will have stayed in his mind will be the statement that the 'external' cost of maintaining a student at Coity Mawr was 5p a day. If he compares this with the £40 or more a week which it costs a local authority to keep 'in care' a child from a family that our advanced-technology society has pauperised and rendered homeless, and concludes that such welfare waifs are likely to be the next generation of unskilled unemployed, he might reflect on the importance of Kropotkin's and Gandhi's educational philosophy. For the normal education systems of both the rich nations and the poor have one thing in common: they are an infallible recipe for robbing the poor to feed the rich.[8]

As to the relationship between education and industry – Kropotkin's preoccupation in this chapter – Ken Coates has pointed to the way in which every advance in technology raises the question: 'How can education better serve industry?' But to see things the right way up, and to begin the pursuit of *education*, we should be asking: 'What sort of factories do our schools need?' He concludes, just as Kropotkin would:

'Free development of each personality to its outer limits means the systematic encouragement and fostering of talents, and this will never begin until factories begin to be schools, and self-governing schools at that. Only then will schools cease to be factories for the engineering of human beings into employees. Perhaps a hundred years ago, this was a utopian message. Today it is direly practical: the only resource which we possess in virtual abundance is that of human potential, and yet it is that resource which we squander with even greater profligacy than we eat up the Earth's finite material resources.'[9]

Editor's Notes

1 René Dumont, *Types of Rural Economy* (London, Methuen, 1957)

2 Peter Self and H. J. Storing, *The State and the Farmer* (London, Allen & Unwin, 1962)

3 John Kenneth Galbraith, *A China Passage* (London, Deutsch, 1973) 1973)

4 See W. M. Williams, *The Country Craftsman*, Dartington Hall Studies in Rural Sociology (London, Routledge, 1958)

5 Peter Kropotkin, 'Must We Occupy Ourselves with an Examination of the Ideal of a Future System?', first published in English in P. A. Kropotkin, *Selected Writings on Anarchism and Revolution*, edited by Martin A. Miller (Cambridge, Mass. and London, M.I.T. Press, 1970)

6 Stephen Cotgrove, *Technical Education and Social Change* (London, Allen & Unwin, 1958)

7 Michael Allaby, 'Farming for a Culture', the *Guardian* (1 December 1971)

8 See Colin Ward, 'The Role of the State', in *Education Without Schools*, edited by Peter Buckman (London, Souvenir Press, 1973)

9 Ken Coates, 'Education as a Lifelong Experience', in Buckman (ed.), *ibid.*

Chapter 5

Conclusion

Readers who have had the patience to follow the facts accumulated in this book, especially those who have given them a thoughtful attention, will probably feel convinced of the immense powers over the productive forces of Nature that man has acquired within the last half a century. Comparing the achievements indicated in this book with the present state of production, some will, I hope, also ask themselves the question which will be ere long, let us hope, the main object of a scientific political economy: Are the means now in use for satisfying human needs, under the present system of permanent division of functions and production for profits, really *economical*? Do they really lead to economy in the expenditure of human forces? Or, are they not mere wasteful survivals from a past that was plunged into darkness, ignorance and oppression, and never took into consideration the economical and social value of the human being?

In the domain of agriculture it may be taken as proved that if a small part only of the time that is now given in each nation or region to field culture was given to well thought out and socially carried out permanent improvements of the soil, the duration of work which would be required afterwards to grow the yearly bread-food for an average family of five would be less than a fortnight every year; and that the work required for that purpose would not be the hard toil of the ancient slave, but work which would be agreeable to the physical forces of every healthy man and woman in the country.

It has been proved that by following the methods of intensive market-gardening – partly under glass – vegetables and fruit can be grown in such quantities that men could be provided with a rich vegetable food and a profusion of fruit, if they simply devoted to the task of growing them the hours which

N

everyone willingly devotes to work in the open air, after having spent most of his day in the factory, the mine or the study. Provided, of course, that the production of food-stuffs should not be the work of the isolated individual, but the planned-out and combined action of human groups.

It has also been proved – and those who care to verify it by themselves may easily do so by calculating the real expenditure for labour which was lately made in the building of workmen's houses by both private persons and municipalities – that under a proper combination of labour, twenty to twenty-four months of one's man work would be sufficient to secure for ever, for a family of five, an apartment or a house provided with all the comforts which modern hygiene and taste could require.

And it has been demonstrated by actual experiment that, by adopting methods of education, advocated long since and partially applied here and there, it is most easy to convey to children of an average intelligence, before they have reached the age of 14 or 15, a broad general comprehension of Nature, as well as of human societies; to familiarise their minds with sound methods of both scientific research and technical work, and to inspire their hearts with a deep feeling of human solidarity and justice; and that it is extremely easy to convey during the next four or five years a reasoned, scientific knowledge of Nature's laws, as well as a knowledge, at once reasoned and practical, of the technical methods of satisfying man's material needs. Far from being inferior to the 'specialised' young persons manufactured by our universities, the *complete* human being, trained to use his brain and his hands, excels them, on the contrary, in all respects, especially as an initiator and an inventor in both science and technics.

All this has been proved. It is an acquisition of the times we live in – an acquisition which has been won despite the innumerable obstacles always thrown in the way of every initiative mind. It has been won by the obscure tillers of the soil, from whose hands greedy states, landlords and middlemen snatch the fruit of their labour even before it is ripe; by obscure teachers who only too often fall crushed under the weight of

[194]

church, state, commercial competition, inertia of mind and prejudice.

And now, in the presence of all these conquests – what is the reality of things?

Nine-tenths of the whole population of grain-exporting countries like Russia, one-half of it in countries like France which live on home-grown food, work upon the land – most of them in the same way as the slaves of antiquity did, only to obtain a meagre crop from a soil, and with a machinery which they cannot improve, because taxation, rent and usury keep them always as near as possible to the margin of starvation. In this twentieth century, whole populations still plough with the same plough as their medieval ancestors, live in the same incertitude of the morrow, and are as carefully denied education as their ancestors; and they have, in claiming their portion of bread, to march with their children and wives against their own sons' bayonets, as their grandfathers did hundreds of years ago.

In industrially developed countries, a couple of months' work, or even much less than that, would be sufficient to produce for a family a rich and varied vegetable and animal food. But the researches of Engel (at Berlin) and his many followers tell us that the workman's family has to spend one full half of its yearly earnings – that is, to give six months of labour, and often more – to provide its food. And what food! Is not bread and dripping the staple food of more than one-half of English children?

One month of work every year would be quite sufficient to provide the worker with a healthy dwelling. But it is from 25 to 40 per cent of his yearly earnings – that is, from three to five months of his working time every year – that he has to spend in order to get a dwelling, in most cases unhealthy and far too small; and this dwelling will never be his own, even though at the age of 45 or 50 he is sure to be sent away from the factory, because the work that he used to do will by that time be accomplished by a machine and a child.

We all know that the child ought, at least, to be familiarised with the forces of Nature which some day he will have to utilise;

[195]

that he ought to be prepared to keep pace in his life with the steady progress of science and technics; that he ought to study science and learn a trade. Everyone will grant thus much; but what do we do? From the age of 10 or even 9 we send the child to push a coal-cart in a mine, or to bind, with a little monkey's agility, the two ends of threads broken in a spinning gin. From the age of 13 we compel the girl – a child yet – to work as a 'woman' at the weaving-loom, or to stew in the poisoned, over-heated air of a cotton-dressing factory, or, perhaps, to be poisoned in the death chambers of a Staffordshire pottery. As to those who have the relatively rare luck of receiving some more education, we crush their minds by useless overtime, we consciously deprive them of all possibility of themselves become producers; and under an educational system of which the motive is 'profits', and the means 'specialisation', we simply work to death the women teachers who take their educational duties in earnest. What floods of useless sufferings deluge every so-called civilised land in the world!

When we look back on ages past, and see there the same sufferings, we may say that perhaps then they were unavoidable on account of the ignorance which prevailed. But human genius, stimulated by our modern Renaissance, had already indicated new paths to follow.

For thousands of years in succession, to grow one's food was the burden, almost the curse, of mankind. But it need be so no more. If you make yourselves the soil, and partly the temperature and the moisture which each crop requires, you will see that to grow the yearly food of a family, under rational conditions of culture, requires so little labour that it might almost be done as a mere change from other pursuits. If you return to the soil, and co-operate with your neighbours instead of erecting high walls to conceal yourself from their looks; if you utilise what experiment has already taught us, and call to your aid science and technical invention, which never fail to answer to the call – look only at what they have done for warfare – you will be astonished at the facility with which you can bring a rich and varied food out of the soil. You will admire the amount of sound knowledge which your children will acquire by your side, the rapid growth of their intelligence, and the facility with which they will grasp the laws of Nature, animate and inanimate.

Have the factory and the workshop at the gates of your fields and gardens, and work in them. Not those large establishments, of course, in which huge masses of metals have to be dealt with and which are better placed at certain spots indicated by Nature, but the countless variety of workshops and factories which are required to satisfy the infinite diversity of tastes among civilised men. Not those factories in which children lose all the appearance of children in the atmosphere of an industrial hell, but those airy and hygienic, and consequently economical, factories in which human life is of more account than machinery and the making of extra profits, of which we already find a few samples here and there; factories and workshops into which men, women and children will not be driven by hunger, but will be attracted by the desire of finding an activity suited to their tastes, and where, aided by the motor and the machine, they will choose the branch of activity which best suits their inclinations.

Let those factories and workshops be erected, not for making profits by selling shoddy or useless and noxious things to enslaved Africans, but to satisfy the unsatisfied needs of millions of Europeans. And again, you will be struck to see with what facility and in how short a time your needs of dress and of thousands of articles of luxury can be satisfied, when production is carried on for satisfying real needs rather than for satisfying shareholders by high profits, or for pouring gold into the pockets of promoters and bogus directors. Very soon you will yourselves feel interested in that work, and you will have occasion to admire in your children their eager desire to become acquainted with Nature and its forces, their inquisitive inquiries as to the powers of machinery, and their rapidly developing inventive genius.

Such is the future – already possible, already realisable; such is the present – already condemned and about to disappear. And what prevents us from turning our backs to this present and from marching towards that future, or, at least, making the first steps towards it, is not the 'failure of science', but first of all our crass cupidity – the cupidity of the man who killed the hen that was laying golden eggs – and then our laziness of mind – that mental cowardice so carefully nurtured in the past.

For centuries science and so-called practical wisdom have said to man: 'It is good to be rich, to be able to satisfy, at least, your material needs; but the only means to be rich is to so train your mind and capacities as to be able to compel other men – slaves, serfs or wage-earners – to make these riches for you. You have no choice. Either you must stand in the ranks of the peasants and the artisans who, whatsoever economists and moralists may promise them in the future, are now periodically doomed to starve after each bad crop or during their strikes, and to be shot down by their own sons the moment they lose patience. Or you must train your faculties so as to be a military commander of the masses, or to be accepted as one of the wheels of the governing machinery of the state, or to become a manager of men in commerce or industry.' For many centuries there was no other choice, and men followed that advice, without finding in it happiness, either for themselves and their own children, or for those whom they pretended to preserve from worse misfortunes.

But modern knowledge has another issue to offer to thinking men. It tells them that in order to be rich they need not take the bread from the mouths of others; but that the more rational outcome would be a society in which men, with the work of their own hands and intelligence, and by the aid of the machinery already invented and to be invented, should themselves create all imaginable riches. Technics and science will not be lagging behind if production takes such a direction. Guided by observation, analysis and experiment, they will answer all possible demands. They will reduce the time which is necessary for producing wealth to any desired amount, so as to leave to everyone as much leisure as he or she may ask for. They surely cannot guarantee happiness, because happiness depends as much, or even more, upon the individual himself as upon his surroundings. But they guarantee, at least, the happiness that can be found in the full and varied exercise of

[198]

the different capacities of the human being, in work that need not be overwork, and in the consciousness that one is not endeavouring to base his own happiness upon the misery of others.

These are the horizons which the above inquiry opens to the unprejudiced mind.

Editor's Postscript

In introducing this book I described it as a great prophetic work. How can this claim be made, when Kropotkin's predictions of twentieth-century economic trends have simply not come true? Well, I did add that the book's hour has yet to come. It is a work whose real significance is for the future, which is why I have added the word *Tomorrow* to the title of this edition.

Kropotkin sought a society which combined labour-intensive agriculture and small-scale industry, both producing for local needs, in a decentralised pattern of settlement in which the division of labour had been replaced by the integration of brain-work and manual work, and he was optimistic enough to believe that trends current in his day were leading to this kind of society. His picture of the future appealed to his fellow anarchists as the kind of economic structure which would suit a worker-controlled federation of self-governing workshops and rural communes. It appealed to the ideologists of decentralist planning like Howard, Geddes and Mumford. It appealed to the advocates of small-holdings: those who wanted to see a highly productive intensive horticulture provide a good living for a new kind of sophisticated peasantry.

If we were asked today to point to actual human societies which exemplify the ideas set out by Kropotkin in this book, we would have to admit that there are only three contemporary models, each riddled by contradictions which may rule them out for the reader. The first, as I have indicated, is China. The difficulty here is not the credibility of the travellers' tales brought back by Western visitors, but the knowledge that some great shift in policy might put into reverse the trends which, at a distance, we admire. As George Orwell remarked of Stalin's Russia, it is like the family who all slept in one bed: when father turns, we all turn. Nevertheless, the stress on decentralist economic policy in China has been a consistent theme at least since 1956.

The second in Tanzania. No one who has followed the evolution of Julius Nyerere's ideas can fail to see their relevance and their resemblance to those of Kropotkin. But Nyerere's prob-

[201]

lem, like that of any political leader, is that of staying in power, and his country's ruling élite may have quite different ambitions. They know all too well how European-style development benefits the people at the top. One can only hope that Nyerere succeeds in implanting a style of thinking about economic and social priorities which will slowly permeate the African nations.

A third model is the *kibbutz*. In citing the Jewish collective settlements as an exemplification of Kropotkin's ideal commune, several qualifications have to be made. Firstly, of course, that they involve a small proportion of the population. Secondly, that the various *kibbutzim, kvutzot* and *moshavim* represent a variety of different ideologies. Thirdly, that we have to consider them without reference to the functions they have performed in the last decades in the service of Israeli nationalism and imperialism. Many of them are very much older than the state, and many of their pioneers were opposed to the idea of a State of Israel, and in fact urged their Arab neighbours to set up similar collectives. It is well over fifty years since Martin Buber warned his fellow Zionists that if the Jews in Palestine did not live *with* the Arabs as well as *next* to them, they would find themselves living in enmity to them. Buber devoted his book, *Paths in Utopia*, to a vindication of the ideas of the 'utopian' socialists, including the anarchist legacy of Proudhon, Kropotkin, and his friend Gustav Landauer, seeing their apotheosis in the *kibbutz* as 'an experiment that did not fail', and pointing to the significance of *Fields, Factories and Workshops*. In his view, Kropotkin

'makes, on purely economic and industrial-psychological grounds, a weighty contribution to the picture of a new social unit fitted to serve as a cell for the formation of a new society in the midst of the old. . . . He sketches the picture of a village based on field and factory alike, where the *same* people work in the one as in the other alternately without this in any way entailing a technological regress, rather in close association with technical developments and yet in such a way that man enters into his rights as a human being. Kropotkin knows that such an alteration cannot be 'completely carried through' in a society like ours, nevertheless he plans not merely for tomorrow but for today as well.'[1]

As a book for today with a message for tomorrow, the significance of Kropotkin's work is clear. In the last decade we have become ever more conscious that there is a crisis of the environment, a crisis of resources, consumption and population. There is no need for me to spell out details, as whole

[202]

libraries have been written on the theme, and every day's news-paper brings more evidence. The incontrovertible facts are that the world's resources are finite, that the rich nations have been consuming unrenewable resources at a rate which the planet cannot sustain, that the 'developed' economies are exploiting the resources of the 'undeveloped' economies as cheap raw materials. The implication is not only that the poor countries never hope to attain the levels of consumption taken for granted in the rich countries, but that the rich world itself cannot hope to continue on its present course.

Of all the innumerable diagnoses of this crisis of the human environment, one of the most intelligent is the British document, *A Blueprint for Survival*. When it appeared, its authors were described as pedlars of doom and gloom, which was an odd, if predictable, reaction, because in fact it was a hopeful report. For unlike many of the commentators on the ecological crisis, its authors have looked beyond the consequences of resource depletion to envisaging the kind of economic structure which they regard as indispensable for a viable future. They present a long-term time-table for change, covering the years of 1975–2075, anticipating by the middle of the next century, 'sufficient diversity of agriculture, decentralisation of industry and redistri-bution of government, together with a large proportion of people whose education is designed for life in the stable society, for the establishment of self-sufficient, self-regulating communities to be well-advanced'.[2]

There are differences between their programme and Kropotkin's, of course. Population growth is one of their nightmares, while Kropotkin dismisses the Malthusian argument. But their vision of an ecologically viable human society is essentially that set out in *Fields, Factories and Workshops*. And even forth-right opponents of the *Blueprint*, like Peter Self, urge a switch of priorities along the following lines:[3]

More Stress On	Less Stress On
Intrinsic satisfaction of work	Maximum consumption
Durable artifacts	Rapid turnover
Craft apprenticeship	Activity rates
Quality of environment	Increases in G.N.P.
Balanced community	Physical mobility
Devolution of government	(Alleged) economies of scale

These too reflect Kropotkin's programme, but, as Professor Self asks, when are such ideas to find a place in *actual* pro-grammes? All the current trends of government and industry are in the opposite direction.

One analysis of the *Blueprint* made the criticism that Kropotkin would have made, pointing out that while the document calls for a return to small communities responsible as far as possible for their own decision-making, this is likely to conflict with the need for such a drastic restructuring of social systems to be highly controlled from the centre. The *Blueprint* demands governmental action. Kropotkin, as an anarchist, hoped for a great popular movement for change. Let us give him the last word. In December 1919, at the very end of his life, in the midst of the civil war that followed the Russian Revolution, he wrote:

'Today, however, after the cruel lesson of the last war, it should be clear to every serious person and above all to every worker, that such wars, and even crueller ones still, *are inevitable so long as certain countries consider themselves destined to enrich themselves by the production of finished goods and divide the backward countries up among themeselves*, so that these countries provide the raw materials while *they accumulate wealth themselves on the basis of the labour of others*.

'More than that. We have the right to assert that the reconstruction of society on a socialist basis will be impossible so long as manufacturing industry and, in consequence, the prosperity of the workers in the factories, depend as they do today on the exploitation of the peasants of their own or other countries.

'We should not forget that at the moment it is not only the capitalists who exploit the labour of others and who are "imperialists". They are not the only ones who aspire to conquer cheap manpower to obtain raw materials in Europe, Asia, Africa and elsewhere. As the workers are beginning to take part in political power, the contagion of colonial imperialism is infecting them too. . . . It is clear that in these conditions one may still predict a series of wars for the civilised countries – wars even more bloody and even more savage – if these countries do not bring about among themselves a social revolution, and do not reconstruct their lives on a new and more social basis. All Europe and the United States, with the exception of the exploiting minority, feels this necessity.

'But it is impossible to achieve such a revolution by means of dictatorship and state power. Without a widespread reconstruction coming from below – put into practice by the workers and peasants themselves – the social revolution is condemned to bankruptcy. The Russian Revolution has confirmed this again, and we must hope that this lesson will be understood; that everywhere in Europe and America serious efforts will be made to create within the working class – peasants, workers and intellectuals – the personnel of a future revolution which will not obey orders from above but will be capable of elaborating for itself the free forms of the whole new economic life.'[4]

Editor's Notes

1 Martin Buber, *Paths in Utopia* (London, Routledge, 1949; Boston, Beacon Paperbacks, 1958)

2 Edward Goldsmith (ed.), *Blueprint for Survival* (*The Ecologist*), January 1972; (Harmondsworth, Penguin, 1972)

3 Peter Self in *The Times* (9 March 1972)

4 Peter Kropotkin, postscript to Russian edition of *Words of a Rebel* (Petrograd and Moscow, 1921); translated by Nicolas Walter in *Freedom*, Anarchist Pamphlet No. 5 (London, Freedom Press, 1970)

ABOUT FREEDOM PRESS

Kropotkin was a member of the Freedom Group which in October 1886 produced the first issue of the anarchist monthly *Freedom*. Sixty years later the editor of this volume, Colin Ward, was himself a member of the FREEDOM PRESS group, an editor of the weekly journal *Freedom* and from 1961-70 he edited one of its most prestigious publications, the monthly journal *Anarchy* of which 118 issues were published.

Since 1886 successive FREEDOM PRESS groups have produced a series of journals. The original *Freedom* was published from 1886 to 1927. Between 1927 and 1935 fifteen issues of a *Freedom Bulletin* were issued. But from 1936 with one or two very brief interruptions there has been a regular flow of journals: *Spain and the World* (fortnightly 1936-1939); *War Commentary* (monthly/fortnightly 1939-1945); *Freedom* (fortnightly/weekly/fortnightly/monthly 1945 onwards), and, when finances permitted, the publication of books and pamphlets.

FREEDOM PRESS books and pamphlets have dealt both with practical and theoretical questions of concern to anarchists and libertarian socialists. Not only did FREEDOM PRESS publish the first translations of many of the writings of Kropotkin and Malatesta but at a time when the commercial publishers saw no profit in Berkman, Bakunin or Proudhon, nor in Kronstadt, the Spanish collectives or indeed in anarchism, FREEDOM PRESS went on publishing. In the late 1940s and early '50s we published Alex Comfort's *Barbarism and Sexual Freedom* and *Delinquency*, John Hewetson's *Sexual Freedom for the Young* and *Ill-health, Poverty and the State*, and in the middle of the last 'war against fascism' FREEDOM PRESS issued John Olday's *March to Death*, a volume of telling anti-war cartoons, and Marie Louise Berneri's *Workers in Stalin's Russia* at a time when all parties from Tories to Trotskyists were united in closing their eyes and ears to the excesses of Stalinism. Some of FREEDOM PRESS's current titles will be found overleaf.

FREEDOM PRESS has an ambitious programme of publications to mark the centenary of its activities for the anarchist idea. If you are interested please send us your name and address and we will keep you informed of new publications, meetings and social events to celebrate our centenary.

FREEDOM PRESS also run a well-stocked bookshop and an efficient mail order service to all parts of the world. Write to us for more details and for a specimen copy of the 16-page journal *Freedom* at **FREEDOM PRESS in Angel Alley, 84b Whitechapel High Street, London E1 7AX.**

WHY WORK?
Arguments for the Leisure Society
210 pages   paperback   £3.00

This volume can best be summed up in the words of Lewis Mumford: "No working ideal for machine production can be based solely on the gospel of work; still less can it be a quantitative standard of consumption. If we are to achieve a purposive and cultivated use of the enormous energies so happily at our disposal, we must examine in detail the processes that lead up to the final state of leisure, free activity, creation". The contributions range from classics such as William Morris' *Useful Work versus Useless Toil* and Kropotkin's *Wage System* (in a new translation) to considerations of the problems and pleasures of work which include Camillo Berneri's *Il Lavoro Attraente* in a new translation, Tony Gibson's forceful essay on *Who Will do the Dirty Work?* and Ifan Edwards' lyrical piece on *The Art of Channelling.*

In the section on Alternatives and Futures, Denis Pym offers an original and provocative essay on *The Other Economy as a Social System*, Gaston Leval writes on *Collectives in Spain*, and S F on *The Kibbutzim in Israel*. There is also a valuable study of Leisure in America (almost a warning) and the section is rounded off with Cliff Harper's *Visions* — six double-spread drawings with a commentary by Colin Ward.

A concluding section on Production for Use versus Production for Profit consists of fifteen editorials from the anarchist journal *Freedom*. The problems dealt with are today as relevant as they were in the late '50s and early '60s when they were written as the editor points out in a long Preface to this volume, which incidentally also offers its readers W H Davies' delightful poem on *Leisure*, and a savage cartoon *Call of the Wild* by Gibbard (from *The Guardian*, 1982).

And that is not all in this 210-page book which can be purchased direct from the publishers at only £3.00, and we pay the postage as we do for all the titles listed on the next page.